Springer Undergraduate Texts in Philosophy

The Springer Undergraduate Texts in Philosophy offers a series of self-contained textbooks aimed towards the undergraduate level that covers all areas of philosophy ranging from classical philosophy to contemporary topics in the field. The texts will include teaching aids (such as exercises and summaries) and will be aimed mainly towards more advanced undergraduate students of philosophy.

The series publishes:

- All of the philosophical traditions
- Introduction books with a focus on including introduction books for specific topics such as logic, epistemology, German philosophy etc.
- Interdisciplinary introductions – where philosophy overlaps with other scientific or practical areas

This series covers textbooks for all undergraduate levels in philosophy particularly those interested in introductions to specific philosophy topics.

We aim to make a first decision within 1 month of submission. In case of a positive first decision the work will be provisionally contracted: the final decision about publication will depend upon the result of the anonymous peer review of the complete manuscript. We aim to have the complete work peer-reviewed within 3 months of submission.

Proposals should include:

- A short synopsis of the work or the introduction chapter
- The proposed Table of Contents
- CV of the lead author(s)
- List of courses for possible course adoption

The series discourages the submission of manuscripts that are below 65,000 words in length.

More information about this series at http://www.springer.com/series/13798

Andrea Iacona

LOGIC: Lecture Notes for Philosophy, Mathematics, and Computer Science

 Springer

Andrea Iacona
Center for Logic, Language and Cognition
University of Turin, Department of
Philosophy and Education
Torino, Italy

ISSN 2569-8737   ISSN 2569-8753   (electronic)
Springer Undergraduate Texts in Philosophy
ISBN 978-3-030-64810-7   ISBN 978-3-030-64811-4   (eBook)
https://doi.org/10.1007/978-3-030-64811-4

This Springer imprint is published by the registered company Springer Nature Switzerland AG
The registered company address is: Gewerbestrasse 11, 6330 Cham, Switzerland

Preface

This book is an introduction to logic. It starts from zero and covers the main topics that are usually taught in elementary and advanced logic courses. Its measured pace, its controlled level of technicality, and its constant search for clarity and precision make it particularly suited for philosophy students. But also mathematics or computer science students may appreciate its style of exposition, especially if they have some inclination for pure theoretical issues.

The book is structured as follows. Chapters 1–3 provide some preliminary clarifications and define the basic vocabulary of logic. Chapters 4–6 present a propositional language and explain its semantics. Chapters 7 and 8 set out a natural deduction system in that language. Chapters 9 and 10 outline a deductively equivalent axiomatic system and prove its consistency, soundness, and completeness. Chapters 11–13 present a predicate language and explain its semantics. Chapters 14–15 outline an axiomatic system in that language and prove its consistency, soundness, and completeness. Chapters 16–18 deal with some general results about first-order theories. Chapter 19 is devoted to Gödel's incompleteness theorems. Finally, Chapter 20 introduces the fundamentals of modal logic.

Since it is practically impossible to study this entire material within a single course, some selection of chapters must be made, depending on the kind of course and the time available. One way to divide the book, perhaps the simplest way, is to use Chapters 1–10 for an elementary course and Chapters 11–20 for an advanced course. If instead the time available is not enough to cover ten chapters, which is quite likely, one can use Chapters 1–8 for an elementary course and Chapters 9–18 for an advanced course, leaving out Chapters 19 and 20. A third option, which might be considered if one has only one course instead of two, and one wants to include both propositional and predicate logic, is to use Chapters 1–6 and 11–13. In this case, one will focus on the semantics of propositional and predicate languages, leaving out the proof theory and the metatheory.

Each chapter includes ten exercises. Some of them are relatively simple and mechanical, others require a firm grasp of the contents presented in the chapter and a bit of creativity. The reader is not expected to solve all the exercises at first glance.

But at least it is worth trying. The solutions are listed at the end of the book, so one can rely on them to measure one's understanding and learn from one's mistakes.

I drew from the following sources, which would be good for supplemental reading and are listed in the final bibliography: G. S. Boolos, J. P. Burgess, and R. Jeffrey, *Computability and Logic* (2010); H. B. Enderton, *A Mathematical Introduction to Logic* (1972); G. E. Hughes and M. J. Cresswell, *A New Introduction to Modal Logic* (1996); G. Hunter, *Metalogic* (1971); E. J. Lemmon, *Beginning Logic* (1993); M. Sainsbury, *Logical Forms* (2001); and P. Smith, *Introduction to Gödel's Theorems* (2013). Further references on specific issues are mentioned in the footnotes.

This book is based on a set of lecture notes that I have consistently used in my logic courses at the University of Turin, and that I have revised year after year. Due to innumerable corrections, adjustments, and modifications, I'm no longer in a position to tell how many versions of the text circulated among students, and I don't have a list of all those who found errors or suggested improvements. But I know for sure that I received a great deal of helpful comments from Gabriele Abate, Martina Calderisi, Daniel Crowley, Gabriele Chiriotti, Paolo Grugnetti, Martino Paschetto, Stefano Romeo, Giuliano Rosella, Cristina Sagafrena, Francesco Scarpiello, Davide Sutto, and Martina Zirattu.

Among the many intellectual debts that I have acquired in the course of writing this book, some deserve special mention. Pasquale Frascolla has been an inspiring presence ever since we started discussing about the logic exams of our doctoral students. Matteo Plebani and Eric Raidl gave me particularly extensive and extremely helpful comments, which prompted numerous substantial improvements. Finally, Diego Marconi revised the final version of the manuscript and spotted some still remaining historical inaccuracies. I am very grateful to them all for the time they spent on my work.

Torino, Italy   Andrea Iacona

Contents

1 Basic Notions 1
   1.1   What Is Logic? 1
   1.2   Arguments and Their Formulation 3
   1.3   Complex Reasoning 4
   1.4   Truth and Falsity 6
   1.5   Bivalence 8

2 Validity 11
   2.1   Some Set-Theoretical Notions 11
   2.2   True Premises 12
   2.3   Validity as Necessary Truth Preservation 13
   2.4   Other Logical Properties and Relations 15
   2.5   Important Facts About Validity 16
   2.6   Validity Is Not Everything 20

3 Formality 25
   3.1   Formal Validity 25
   3.2   Formal Invalidity 28
   3.3   Formal Language 29
   3.4   Formal System 30
   3.5   Object Language and Metalanguage 31
   3.6   Further Set-Theoretical Notions 32

4 The Symbols of Propositional Logic 35
   4.1   Sentence Letters 35
   4.2   Sentential Connectives 36
   4.3   Brackets 38
   4.4   Expressive Completeness 39
   4.5   Truth-Functionality and Substitutivity 41
   4.6   Formalization in a Propositional Language 41

5 The Language L 45
   5.1   Formation Rules 45

	5.2	Syntactic Trees	46
	5.3	Scope	47
	5.4	Interpretation	48
	5.5	Truth Tables	49
6	**Logical Consequence in L**		**53**
	6.1	Definition of Logical Consequence	53
	6.2	Other Logical Properties and Relations	54
	6.3	Important Facts About Logical Consequence	55
	6.4	Logical Consequence as a Test for Validity	56
	6.5	Effective Computability	57
7	**The System G**		**61**
	7.1	Derivation	61
	7.2	Rules for $\sim$	62
	7.3	Rules for $\supset$	64
	7.4	Rules for $\wedge$	65
	7.5	Rules for $\vee$	68
8	**Derivability in G**		**71**
	8.1	Derivability and Related Notions	71
	8.2	Important Facts About Derivability	72
	8.3	Some Tips	73
	8.4	Derived Rules	75
	8.5	Other Natural Deduction Systems	76
9	**The System L**		**79**
	9.1	Axioms and Inference Rule	79
	9.2	Deduction Theorem	81
	9.3	Explosion, Double Negation, Contraposition	83
	9.4	Substitution of Equivalents	85
	9.5	Reductio Ad Absurdum	87
	9.6	Deductive Equivalence Between $\mathbf{G}^-$ and $\mathbf{L}$	88
	9.7	Systems and Theories	89
10	**Consistency, Soundness, Completeness**		**91**
	10.1	Consistency of $\mathbf{L}$	91
	10.2	Definitions of Soundness and Completeness	92
	10.3	Soundness of $\mathbf{L}$	93
	10.4	Completeness of $\mathbf{L}$	93
	10.5	Extension to $\mathbf{G}^-$	96
11	**Quantification**		**99**
	11.1	Quantified Sentences	99
	11.2	A Brief Historical Survey	101
	11.3	Existential Import	103
	11.4	Multiple Generality	104
	11.5	Definite Descriptions	106

12 The Symbols of Predicate Logic 109
   12.1 Non-logical Expressions 109
   12.2 Logical Constants and Auxiliary Symbols 110
   12.3 Other Symbols 111
   12.4 Numerical Expressions 113
   12.5 Multiple Generality and Scope Ambiguity 114
   12.6 Existence 115

13 The Language L_q 119
   13.1 Syntax 119
   13.2 Basic Semantic Notions 121
   13.3 Satisfaction 122
   13.4 Truth 123
   13.5 Logical Consequence 126
   13.6 Undecidability 127

14 The System Q 131
   14.1 Axioms and Inference Rule 131
   14.2 Derivability in **Q** 132
   14.3 Generalization Theorem 133
   14.4 Validity and Derivability 133
   14.5 Deduction Theorem and Other Syntactic Results 134
   14.6 Alphabetic Variants 135

15 Consistency, Soundness, Completeness 139
   15.1 Consistency of **Q** 139
   15.2 Soundness of **Q** 140
   15.3 Completeness of **Q** 141
   15.4 Compactness Theorem 143
   15.5 Final Remarks 144

16 Undecidability and Related Results 147
   16.1 Undecidability of **Q** 147
   16.2 Gödel Numbering 148
   16.3 Effective Enumerability of the Theorems of **Q** 149
   16.4 A Further Corollary 149
   16.5 Recursive Axiomatization and Decidability 150

17 First-Order Logic 153
   17.1 First-Order Languages and Systems 153
   17.2 First-Order Logic with Identity 154
   17.3 First-Order Theory 155
   17.4 The Language of Basic Arithmetic 156
   17.5 Peano Arithmetic 158

18 Theories and Models 161
   18.1 Cardinality 161
   18.2 Löwenheim-Skolem Theorems 162

18.3   Isomorphism.. 164
18.4   Isomorphic Models of a Theory 166
18.5   Categoricity.. 167

19   Gödel's Incompleteness Theorems...................................... 171
19.1   Overview.. 171
19.2   The Arithmetization of Syntax 172
19.3   The Gödel Sentence... 174
19.4   First Incompleteness Theorem: Semantic Version................. 175
19.5   First Incompleteness Theorem: Syntactic Version................. 176
19.6   Second Incompleteness Theorem................................... 178

20   Rudiments of Modal Logic 181
20.1   Modal Operators.. 181
20.2   A Modal Propositional Language 182
20.3   The System **K** 184
20.4   The Systems **T**, **B**, **S4**, **S5**... 187
20.5   A Modal Predicate Language....................................... 191
20.6   Systems of Modal Predicate Logic 193
20.7   Soundness and Completeness...................................... 195

Solutions... 199

Bibliography 221

Index... 225

Chapter 1
Basic Notions

1.1 What Is Logic?

Logic has been defined in many ways in the course of its history, as different views have been held about its aim, scope, and subject matter. But if there is one thing on which most definitions agree, it is that logic deals with the principles of correct reasoning. To explain what this means, we will start with some preliminary clarifications about the terms 'reasoning', 'correct', and 'principles'.

Here is a simple example of reasoning. Imagine that a detective investigates a murder in a mansion. The suspects are the butler and the gardener. Once some clues are collected, it turns out that the butler has an airtight alibi. The detective then reasons as follows: either the butler or the gardener did it, but it can't be the butler; so it must be the gardener. In more explicit form,

(1) Either the butler or the gardener did it
(2) It's not the butler who did it
(3) The gardener did it

The horizontal line indicates that (3) is inferred from (1) and (2), that is, (1) and (2) are *premises* from which (3) is drawn as a *conclusion*. This means that the detective's reasoning can be phrased as an argument:

Definition 1.1 An *argument* consists of a set of sentences, the premises, and a sentence which is inferred from them, the conclusion.

A sentence—in the sense of 'sentence' that matters here—is a string of words that conveys a statement, so it is used to assert that things are a certain way. For example, 'Snow is white' is a sentence in this sense, while 'Leave me alone!' or 'Are you

© The Author(s), under exclusive license to Springer Nature Switzerland AG 2021
A. Iacona, *LOGIC: Lecture Notes for Philosophy, Mathematics, and Computer Science*, Springer Undergraduate Texts in Philosophy,
https://doi.org/10.1007/978-3-030-64811-4_1

there?' are not. In other words, we will restrict consideration to sentences that are usually classified as declaratives, as distinct from imperatives or interrogatives.

People commonly judge arguments as good or bad. For example, the detective's argument is intuitively good. In the situation described, it is reasonable to believe that (1) and (2) are true. Moreover, (1) and (2) warrant (3), as the following notation shows:

(1)   Either the butler or the gardener did it
(2)   It's not the butler who did it
(3)   The gardener did it   1,2

The argument below, instead, is intuitively bad:

(1)   Either the butler or the gardener did it
(2)   It's not the butler who did it
(3)   The Yeti exists

A good argument, unlike a bad argument, can justify what one thinks or says. The detective can plausibly appeal to (1) and (2) to support his claim that the gardener is the murderer. By contrast, the same premises provide no reason for believing that the Yeti exists.

When an argument is used to support a claim, as in the case of the detective, two key assumptions need be made about the argument: one is that its premises are true, the other is that the inference from its premises to its conclusion is correct, namely, that its premises warrant its conclusion. The argument is *valid* when the second condition is satisfied, otherwise it is *invalid*. The argument is *sound* when both conditions are satisfied, otherwise it is *unsound*. Intuitively, a good argument is a sound argument.

Logic focuses on validity, which is one of the two constitutive conditions of soundness. It does not deal with the other condition, the truth of the premises, because whether a sentence is true depends on how things actually are, and it is no business of the logician to tell how things actually are. Since the premises of an argument can pertain to all sorts of subjects—physics, history, biology, and so on—their truth concerns the experts in those subjects. What the logician wants to know is whether the premises of an argument, assuming that they are true, provide compelling grounds for accepting its conclusion. Thus, as far as logic is concerned, it doesn't really matter whether the premises of the detective's argument are true. The only question that matters is what follows from them, that is, what one can rightfully conclude on the assumption that they are true.

Now it remains to be said how the principles of correct reasoning are understood. The thought that underlies logic is that the validity of an argument can be explained in terms of its *form*, a structural property that characterizes a whole class of valid arguments. As we shall see, the intuitive difference between the two arguments above can be explained in terms of their form: while the first instantiates a valid pattern of inference, the same does not hold for the second.

This is the kind of explanation that characterizes logic as a theory. Through the study of argument forms, which are expressed by using appropriate symbols, logicians describe wide classes of valid arguments in a rigorous and systematic way. So, the principles of correct reasoning they investigate are formal principles, that is, principles that concern argument forms. The next two chapters provide detailed explanations about validity and its relation to form. The rest of this chapter, instead, offers some further clarifications about arguments and sentences.

1.2   Arguments and Their Formulation

An argument is properly formulated when it is phrased in the way illustrated above, that is, as a vertical sequence of sentences whose last item is the conclusion. However, this is not the way in which arguments are phrased when they are actually used. Normally, what the proponent of an argument utters is a discourse—call it a *text*—from which one can "extract" a properly formulated argument. The conclusion of the argument expresses the claim made in the text, and its premises state the reasons offered in support of that claim. Typically, the inference from the premises to the conclusion is indicated by words such as 'so', 'hence', or 'therefore'.

The proper formulation of an argument is the result of an analysis that may be more or less demanding for a variety of reasons. In the first place, a text often leaves room for implicit material. Suppose that the detective utters the following words:

It's not the butler. So it's the gardener.

In this case, the argument stated in Sect. 1.1 does not match exactly the detective's words, for it includes a premise that the detective does not utter, namely (1). Nonetheless, that argument can plausibly be ascribed to the detective, on the assumption that the detective takes (1) for granted. That is, (1) features as an implicit premise.

In the second place, a text may contain expressions that are irrelevant from the logical point of view. This is to say that if the text did not contain those expressions, the reasoning conveyed would be essentially the same. Of course, 'essentially' is not a precise term. But in many cases it is evident that certain expressions play no substantial logical role. Consider the following text:

In fact, it's not the butler who did it. So we can conclude that it is the gardener.

In this case the expressions 'In fact' and 'we can conclude that' are dispensable, for the reasoning is exactly the same as in the previous text. So the argument, once properly formulated, will not include these expressions.

In the third place, a text may contain obscure expressions which prevent it from being immediately understandable. Consider the following text:

The number of the suspects is the number that the Pythagoreans regarded as the dyad, symbol of otherness. If it's not the butler who did it, then we must subtract 1 from that number and say that it is the gardener.

The complex expression 'The number that etc.' refers to the number 2, so the whole sentence can be replaced by 'There are two suspects: the butler and the gardener'. In the proper formulation of an argument, obscure expressions should be replaced with more intelligible expressions, when this is possible.

1.3   Complex Reasoning

The examples of reasoning considered so far are simple, in that each of them boils down to a single argument. A complex reasoning, instead, is a structured set of arguments. There are different ways in which two or more arguments can be combined. One is *chaining*: two arguments are chained when the same sentence occurs both as the conclusion of one of them and as a premise of the other. Suppose that the detective, after concluding that the gardener is the murderer on the basis of the argument stated in Sect. 1.1, uses this conclusion to obtain a further conclusion:

(1)   If the gardener did it, the driver is innocent
(2)   The gardener did it
(3)   The driver is innocent

In this case the two arguments are chained, because (2) occurs in the former as conclusion and in the latter as premise. The whole reasoning can be stated as follows:

(1)   Either the butler or the gardener did it
(2)   It's not the butler who did it
(3)   The gardener did it   1,2
(4)   If the gardener did it, the driver is innocent
(5)   The driver is innocent   3,4

The numbers on the right display the two inferential steps involved in this reasoning. When one reasons by chaining, one proceeds linearly through a series of arguments each of which serves to justify the following, until one gets to a final conclusion.

Other kinds of complex reasoning are those in which some premises are entertained only hypothetically, in order to show what consequences can be drawn from them. The reasoning known as *reductio ad absurdum* belongs to this category, as it occurs when a hypothesis that is contrary to the conclusion to be proved is reduced to absurdity. For example, the detective might rule out that the butler is the murderer by reasoning as follows. Suppose that the butler did it. Then, he must have been in the mansion at 8 pm, the time of the murder. But a recorded phone call proves that he was at home at 8 pm, hence that he was not in the mansion at that time. So, the hypothesis that the butler did it, together with other assumptions, leads to the absurd conclusion that he was and he was not in the mansion at 8 pm. The reasoning can be stated as follows:

(1) The butler did it
(2) If he did it, he was in the mansion at 8 pm
(3) He was in the mansion at 8 pm   1,2
(4) The butler made a phone call
(5) If he made it, he was not in the mansion at 8 pm
(6) He was not in the mansion at 8 pm   4,5
(7) It's not the butler who did it   1,3,6

The first three lines show that (1), together with (2), yields (3). The next three lines show that (4) and (5) yield (6). This means that, as long as (2), (4), and (5) are granted, if one accepts (1), one gets (3) and (6). Since it is impossible for the butler to be and not to be in the mansion at 8 pm, this justifies the rejection of (1), provided that (2), (4), and (5) hold.

A paradigmatic example of *reductio ad absurdum* is the reasoning employed by Euclid to prove that there are infinitely many prime numbers. A prime number, or prime, is a natural number greater than 1 that can be divided only by 1 or by itself. The natural numbers are $0, 1, 2, 3 \ldots$. Suppose that there are only finitely many primes, that is, that the primes are exactly $p_1, \ldots, p_n$ for some n. Now take the number m such that $m = (p_1 \times \cdots \times p_n) + 1$. Since m differs from $p_1, \ldots, p_n$, by hypothesis it is not prime, so it must be divisible by some p_i, where $1 \leq i \leq n$. This follows from the *fundamental theorem of arithmetic*, according to which every integer greater than 1 is either a prime or can be represented as a unique product of primes, where 'unique' means that there is only one set of primes that works. If one divides m by some p_i, however, one will get a remainder 1. So, the supposition that there are only finitely many primes leads to an absurdity. The number of primes must be infinite.[1]

As these two examples show, a *reductio ad absurdum* can take two distinct forms: one is negative, the other is positive. In the first case one derives an absurdity from a given sentence in order to justify the negation of that sentence: from the absurd consequences of the hypothesis that the butler is the murderer, the detective concludes that the butler is not the murderer. In the second case one derives an absurdity from the negation of a given sentence in order to justify the sentence itself: from the absurd consequences of the hypothesis that the number of primes is not infinite, Euclid concludes that there are infinitely many primes.

---

[1] Euclid (c.325–c.365 BC), the most prominent mathematician of antiquity, is best known for his treatise on geometry, the *Elements*. The proof that there are infinitely many primes is there, book IX, proposition 20.

Since a complex reasoning results from the combination of two or more arguments, to analyze a text which contains a complex reasoning is to make fully explicit the arguments that constitute the reasoning. One way to do that is to mark each inferential step in the way illustrated above, that is, by using numbers that refer to the sentences from which a given sentence is obtained.

1.4 Truth and Falsity

When one utters a sentence, one asserts that things are a certain way. The sentence is true if things are actually that way, false otherwise. Truth and falsity are distinct *truth values* that a sentence can have. For example, 'Snow is white' is true, since snow is white. Instead, 'The earth is a star' is false, since the earth is not a star. These two sentences have different truth values.

The notion of truth value was explicitly introduced into logic by Gottlob Frege. In his seminal article *Über Sinn und Bedeutung* (1892), Frege draws a distinction between the sense ('Sinn') of a sentence and its reference ('Bedeutung'). Intuitively, the sense of a sentence is its meaning, that is, what one grasps when one understands the sentence. This sense determines a reference, which Frege identifies with the sentence's truth value.[2]

One coherent way to develop Frege's distinction is to equate the sense of a sentence with its *truth conditions*, that is, the conditions under which the sentence is true. According to a widely held hypothesis, originally advanced by Ludwig Wittgenstein in his *Tractatus Logico-Philosophicus* (1921), to understand a sentence is to know its truth conditions. For example, to grasp the meaning of 'Snow is white' is to know that 'Snow is white' is true if and only if a certain state of affairs obtains, namely, snow being white. The truth value of 'Snow is white'—the fact that it is true—depends on its truth conditions and on the obtaining of that state of affairs.[3]

The difference between truth values and truth conditions is easy to grasp. If two sentences have the same truth conditions, then they have the same truth value, given the way things are. For example, 'Either the butler or the gardener did it' and 'Either the gardener or the butler did it' have the same truth conditions. So they must have

---

[2]Frege [16]. Friedrich Ludwig Gottlob Frege (1848–1925) was a German logician, mathematician, and philosopher who studied and taught at the University of Jena. He was primarily interested in understanding the nature of mathematical truths and the means whereby they are ultimately justified. With extreme clarity, rigour, and technical brilliance, he articulated some fundamental ideas that have made possible the developement of modern logic and analytic philosophy.

[3]Wittgenstein [68], 4.431, p. 95. Ludwig Josef Johann Wittgenstein (1889–1951), one of the most influential thinkers of the twentieth century, was an Austrian philosopher who taught at the University of Cambridge and was primarily interested in logic and the philosophy of language. His works have inspired a vast secondary literature and have done much to shape subsequent developments in philosophy. In particular, they originated logical positivism and the philosophy of ordinary language.

the same truth value. But having the same truth value does not entail having the same truth conditions. For example, 'Snow is white' and 'The earth is a planet' are both true, yet they have different truth conditions.

Another way to phrase this distinction is to say that sentences have *intension* and *extension*, where the latter depends on the former and on the way things are. The notions of intension and extension apply to various kinds of linguistic expressions, including singular terms, such as 'the earth', or predicates, such as 'planet'. The intension of an expression is its sense or meaning, that is, what one grasps when one understands the expression. Instead, the extension of an expression, which is determined by its intension, is its reference or denotation, that is, the semantic property that accounts for the relation between the expression and the extra-linguistic reality. Thus, the extension of a singular term is the object it denotes, and the extension of a predicate is the set of objects to which it applies. Following the line of thought initiated by Frege and developed by Wittgenstein, it is now relatively common to identify the intension of a sentence with its truth conditions and its extension with its truth value.

Note that this way of talking does not imply that, for every sentence, there is a unique intension that is "the" intension of the sentence. Different truth conditions can be associated to the same sentence, for at least two reasons. First, a sentence may be *ambiguous*, that is, it may have more than one meaning. For example, 'Alf goes to the bank' is ambiguous because it can mean either that Alf goes to the edge of a river or that Alf goes to a financial institution. Similarly, 'Visiting relatives can be boring' is ambiguous because it can mean either that it can be boring to visit relatives or that it can be boring to receive their visits. In the first case the ambiguity is "lexical", as it depends on the ambiguity of a single word, while in the second it is "structural", as it is explainable in terms of distinct syntactic structures.

Second, a sentence may contain *context sensitive* expressions, that is, expressions whose content varies as a function of the context. A plain example is the pronoun 'I'. If 'I' is used by Alf, it refers to Alf, while if it is used by Betty, it refers to Betty. Thus, if Alf says 'I like ice cream', he asserts that Alf likes ice cream, while if Betty says 'I like ice cream', she asserts that Betty likes ice cream. Assuming that a context is a set of circumstances which includes a speaker, this is to say that 'I like ice cream' has different truth conditions in different contexts. Similar considerations hold for 'you', 'now', 'here', and many other kinds of expressions.

Since natural language is affected by ambiguity and context sensitivity, it cannot be taken for granted that every sentence has a unique intension. The same sentence may be understood in different ways on different occasions. So its truth conditions—and consequently its truth value—may vary depending on how it is understood.

1.5 Bivalence

But is it right to assume that every intension determines an extension? In general, it is not. For example, it is entirely plausible to say that a meaningful singular term, such as 'Sherlock Holmes' lacks denotation, or that a meaningful predicate, such as 'unicorn', applies to nothing. Therefore, one may wonder whether it should be assumed that every sentence, once its ambiguity or context sensitivity is resolved, is either true or false.

This question has been widely discussed in the history of logic, and is still a source of constant controversy. Classical logic, the theory that is most widely adopted and is usually taught in logic courses, rests on *Bivalence*, the principle according to which truth and falsity are mutually exclusive and jointly exhaustive values. Bivalence is closely related to a distinct principle that Aristotle regarded as indubitable, *Excluded Middle*: either things are a certain way or they are not that way. To see the connection between these two principles it suffices to bear in mind what has been said about truth conditions. If one thinks that either snow is white or snow is not white, then, as long as one grants that 'Snow is white' is true if snow is white and that 'Snow is white' is false if snow is not white, one must accept that either 'Snow is white' is true or it is false, or so is reasonable to expect.[4]

However, Bivalence is far from being universally accepted, and it is often perceived as more problematic than Excluded Middle. At least three major objections have been raised against Bivalence. The first concerns *future contingents*, that is, sentences about future events that can occur or not occur, such as 'It will rain tomorrow'. According to a line of argument that goes back to Aristotle himself, future contingents are neither true nor false, because the supposition that they are either true or false implies fatalism. If 'It will rain tomorrow' were true, then it would be settled today that it will rain tomorrow, so the rain would be necessary. Similarly, if it were false, it would be settled today that it will not rain tomorrow, so the rain would be impossible. Since the rain is contingent, that is, neither necessary nor impossible, this shows that 'It will rain tomorrow' is neither true nor false.[5]

The second objection concerns *vagueness*, a feature of natural language that is distinct both from ambiguity and from context sensitivity. Vague expressions are expressions that lack definite extensions. For example, the predicate 'bald' is vague. This predicate definitely applies to a man with no hair at all, and it definitely does not apply to a man with a huge amount of hairs. But there are men with a number of

---

[4]Aristotle (c.384–c.322 BC), one of the greatest philosophers of all time, is widely recognized as the founder of logic. When his works were collected by his pupils after his death, a number of his treatises were grouped together, and the collection came to be called *Organon*, or instrument of science. The term 'logic' was introduced about 500 years later, but the scope of the study denoted by this term was determined by the contents of the *Organon*. Aristotle stated Excluded Middle in *Metaphysics*, Γ, 7, 1011^b 23–24.

[5]The original formulation of Aristotle's argument is in *De interpretatione* IX, 18b23 ff. For an introduction to the contemporary debate on future contingents see Iacona [31].

hairs such that it is unclear whether 'bald' applies to them. If Alf has such a number, then 'Alf is bald' is neither definitely true nor definitely false. More generally, vague expressions admit borderline cases, that is, cases in which they neither definitely apply nor definitely do not apply. So the sentences in which they occur may be neither definitely true nor definitely false.[6]

The third objection comes from *antirealism*, the conception of truth that rejects the commonsense idea that truth is correspondence with reality. Antirealism is often associated with intuitionism, the view according to which the only intelligible way to make sense of the truth conditions of mathematical sentences is to understand them as proof conditions, where a proof is a mental construction of a certain kind. This view implies that some mathematical sentences are neither true nor false. Their status is currently undecided. Consider Goldbach's conjecture that every even number (other than two) is the sum of two primes. There is presently no proof of this conjecture, nor is there a proof of its negation. So, for an intuitionist there is no principled reason for asserting that Goldbach's conjecture is either true or false.[7]

The three objections considered, just as many others, arouse thorny philosophical questions that are far from being settled. But we can't even begin to discuss these questions here. We will have to follow standard practice and assume Bivalence. This book focuses on classical logic, so any theory that implies rejection of Bivalence falls outside its scope.

Exercises

1.1 What is the conclusion of this argument?

The butler is not the murderer, he was at home at 8 pm.

1.2 Are there arguments that nobody has ever uttered or thought?

1.3 Provide a proper formulation of the following argument:

If I'm innocent, I will appear before the judges. But I will appear before the judges. So, I'm innocent.

1.4 Provide a proper formulation of the following argument:

If I appear before the judges, I'm guilty. But I will not appear before the judges. So I'm not guilty.

1.5 Find the implicit premise:

You don't love me! If you did, you would have come to my aunt's dinner.

---

[6]The reflection on vagueness started with Eubulides of Miletus (fourth century BC), a Greek philosopher known as the inventor of the Sorites paradox. Williamson [66] provides a detailed historical survey and discusses the main contemporary views of vagueness.

[7]This line of thought was initiated by Luitzen Egbertus Jan Brouwer (1881–1966), a Duch mathematician who worked in topology, set theory, and measure theory. De Swart [7], pp. 379–426, articulates the intuitionist position and outlines its logic.

1.6 Find the implicit conclusion:

> If he is a surfer, I'm Napoleon.

1.7 According to a legend that circulated in ancient Greece, Córax of Syracuse taught his pupil Tisias the art of rethoric, but then Tisias refused to pay him. Tisias defended himself by saying that Córax had promised to teach him to persuade anyone of anything. So, either Córax kept his promise, and admitted that Tisias was able to persuade him to renounce his claim, or he didn't keep his promise, and Tisias did not have to pay him. What is exactly Tisias' argument?

1.8 Can an argument have just one premise?

1.9 How many arguments do you see in this quote from David Hume?

> Nothing is demonstrable unless its contrary implies a contradiction. Nothing that is distinctly conceivable implies a contradiction. Whatever we conceive as existent, we can also conceive as non-existent. So there is no being whose non-existence implies a contradiction. So there is no being whose existence is demonstrable.[8]

1.10 Explain why each of these two sentences is plausibly true in one sense but false in another sense:

(a) The end of a thing is its perfection
(b) Death is the end of life

---

[8]Hume, [28], D 9.5, KS 189.

Chapter 2
Validity

2.1 Some Set-Theoretical Notions

In order to elucidate the understanding of validity that underlies logic, it is useful to introduce some symbols that belong to the vocabulary of set theory. A *set* is a collection of things, called its *elements*. We will write $a \in A$ to say that a is an element of A, and $a \notin A$ to say that a is not an element of A. The main thing to bear in mind about sets is that their identity is determined by their elements. If A and B have the same elements, then $A = B$. The converse also holds: if $A = B$, then A and B have the same elements, for identical objects cannot have different properties.

The curly brackets are used to refer to sets by listing their elements. For example, $\{1, 2\}$ is the set whose elements are the numbers 1 and 2. Note that, when curly brackets are used, it doesn't really matter how the elements of a set are listed, or how many times they occur in the list. For example, it makes no difference whether we write $\{1, 2\}$, $\{2, 1\}$, or $\{1, 2, 2\}$: the set denoted is the same.

The symbol $\subseteq$ expresses the *subset* relation. A is a subset of B, that is, $A \subseteq B$, if and only if every element of A is an element of B. This means that nothing belongs to A without belonging to B. For example, $\{1\} \subseteq \{1, 2\}$. Note that $A \subseteq A$, and that if $A \subseteq B$ and $B \subseteq A$, then $A = B$. Another way to say that A is a subset of B is to say that B is a *superset* of A.

The symbol $\cup$ indicates the *union* of two sets. The union of A and B, that is, $A \cup B$, is the set that contains all the elements of A and all the elements of B. For example, $\{1, 2\} \cup \{2, 3\} = \{1, 2, 3\}$. Note that $A \cup A = A$ and $A \subseteq (A \cup B)$.

The symbol $\emptyset$ denotes *the empty set*, the set that has no elements. It is easy to see that $\emptyset \subseteq A$ for any A: since nothing belongs to $\emptyset$, nothing belongs to $\emptyset$ without belonging to A. This is why the empty set is unique, that is, there are no distinct empty sets. If A and B are both empty, then each of them is a subset of any set. It follows that $A \subseteq B$ and $B \subseteq A$, so that $A = B$.

© The Author(s), under exclusive license to Springer Nature Switzerland AG 2021
A. Iacona, *LOGIC: Lecture Notes for Philosophy, Mathematics, and Computer Science*, Springer Undergraduate Texts in Philosophy,
https://doi.org/10.1007/978-3-030-64811-4_2

As explained above, the identity of a set does not imply an order among its elements. However, there are cases in which it is useful to talk about ordered sets of objects. The simplest case is that in which one wants to talk about two objects such that one of them is the first and the other is the second: an *ordered pair*. Given two objects x and y, the notation $\langle x, y \rangle$ indicates the ordered pair formed by x and y. The identity condition for ordered pairs is the following: $\langle x, y \rangle = \langle u, v \rangle$ if and only if $x = u$ and $y = v$. Thus, $\langle 1, 2 \rangle = \langle 1, 2 \rangle$, but $\langle 1, 2 \rangle \neq \langle 2, 1 \rangle$. Similarly, one can talk about ordered triples, ordered quadruples, and so on. In general, an *n-tuple* is constituted by n objects ordered in a certain way.

A *binary relation* is a set of ordered pairs. Given a binary relation R, the *domain* of R is the set of all x such that $\langle x, y \rangle \in R$ for some y, and the *range* of R is the set of all y such that $\langle x, y \rangle \in R$ for some x. For example, the less-than relation is the set of ordered pairs of numbers $\langle x, y \rangle$ such that $x < y$, like $\langle 0, 1 \rangle$, $\langle 1, 3 \rangle$, $\langle 2, 4 \rangle$, and so on. Similarly, the less-than-or-equal relation is the set of ordered pairs of numbers $\langle x, y \rangle$ such that $x \leq y$, like $\langle 0, 0 \rangle$, $\langle 0, 1 \rangle$, $\langle 1, 3 \rangle$, and so on. Another example is the identity relation. This relation is the set of ordered pairs of objects $\langle x, y \rangle$ such that $x = y$, that is, $\langle 0, 0 \rangle$, $\langle 1, 1 \rangle$, $\langle 2, 2 \rangle$, and so on. Beside binary relations, we can talk of ternary relations, quaternary relations, and so on. In general, an *n-ary relation* is a set of n-tuples, and it is assumed that when $n = 1$ the relation is simply a set. From now on, 'relation' will be used as a synonym for 'binary relation', unless otherwise specified.

Some of the properties that a relation R may have deserve attention. First, R is *reflexive* if and only if, for every x, $\langle x, x \rangle \in R$. For example, $=$ and $\leq$ are reflexive, whereas $<$ is not reflexive. Second, R is *symmetric* if and only if, for every x and y, if $\langle x, y \rangle \in R$ then $\langle y, x \rangle \in R$. For example, $=$ is symmetric, whereas $<$ and $\leq$ are not symmetric. Third, R is *transitive* if and only if, for every x, y, and z, if $\langle x, y \rangle \in R$ and $\langle y, z \rangle \in R$ then $\langle x, z \rangle \in R$. For example, the three relations considered are all transitive. When a relation is reflexive, symmetric, and transitive, it is an *equivalence relation*.

2.2 True Premises

Arguments may be described as ordered pairs of sets of premises and conclusions: an argument is an ordered pair $\langle \Gamma, \alpha \rangle$, where Γ is a set of sentences and α is a sentence. To simplify the notation, we will write Γ/α instead of $\langle \Gamma, \alpha \rangle$. Moreover, we will assume that Γ can contain any number of sentences, including zero sentences. An argument with zero premises is an argument in which the conclusion is inferred from nothing, for it is taken to justify itself. Self-evident truths, if there are such truths, can be treated as conclusions of this kind.

As explained in Sect. 1.1, there are two distinct properties that an argument Γ/α can have: being valid and having true premises. The question whether Γ/α is valid is independent of the question whether its premises are true. The truth of the premises of Γ/α is neither necessary nor sufficient for its validity. That is, Γ/α can be valid even if some of (or all) the sentences in Γ are false, and it can be invalid even if the sentences in Γ are all true.

The following example shows that the truth of the premises of an argument is not necessary for its validity:

(1)   Either the earth is a star or it is a planet

(2)   The earth is not a planet

(3)   The earth is a star

This argument has a false premise, namely, (2). But the inference from (1) and (2) to (3) is compelling. Even though (3) is false, if (1) and (2) were both true, we would be entitled to conclude that (3) is true.

The following example, instead, shows that the truth of the premises of an argument is not sufficient for its validity:

(1)   Either the earth is a star or it is a planet

(2)   The earth is not a star

(3)   The Yeti exists

Although (1) and (2) are true, the inference from (1) and (2) to (3) is patently unjustified.

More generally, four cases are possible: an argument can be valid and have true premises, it can be valid and have (some) false premises, it can be invalid and have true premises, or it can be invalid and have (some) false premises. Since logic deals with validity, the difference between the first and the second case, or between the third and the fourth case, does not really matter here. What matters is how the first two cases differ from the other two. From now on we will focus on the distinction between correct and incorrect inferences.

2.3   Validity as Necessary Truth Preservation

What is a correct inference? This question admits at least two distinct answers. In one sense—the *deductive* sense—the inference from Γ to α is correct when the truth of Γ fully guarantees the truth of α, in that it rules out the possibility that α is false. This is to say that Γ provides a conclusive reason, or a non-defeasible reason, for accepting α. In the other sense—the *inductive* sense—the inference from Γ to α is correct when the truth of Γ guarantees to some extent, even if not fully, the truth of α. This is to say that Γ provides a non-conclusive reason, or a defeasible reason, for accepting α. For example, the inference in the first of the two arguments above is correct in the deductive sense, while the following is correct in the inductive sense:

(1)   Every cat I know loves milk

(2)   Greg is a cat

(3)   Greg loves milk

The truth of (1) and (2) makes improbable that (3) is false, that is, it makes the probability of (3) higher than the probability of its negation. Yet it does not rule out the possibility that (3) is false.

The notion of correctness that matters here is the deductive notion. Logic is mainly concerned with validity understood as necessary truth preservation: if the premises are true, the conclusion must be true as well. Necessary truth preservation has always been regarded as a paradigm of validity. Here is a famous quote from Aristotle:

> Now a reasoning is an argument in which, certain things being laid down, something other than these necessarily comes about through them.[1]

According to a widely shared reading of this passage, the distinctive feature of correct reasoning is that it never takes us from truth to falsity: if the things "being laid down" are true, then the thing "other than these" must also be true. This is the idea expressed by the definition of validity that we will adopt:

Definition 2.1 An argument Γ/α is *valid* if and only if it is impossible that the sentences in Γ are true and α is false.

An equivalent formulation is the following: Γ/α is valid if and only if, necessarily, if the sentences in Γ are true, then α is true. This formulation is equivalent because possibility and necessity are interdefinable: it is possible that things are a certain way if and only if it is not necessary that things are not that way, and it is necessary that things are a certain way if and only if it is not possible that things are not that way.

Since validity is defined in terms of possibility, or equivalently in terms of necessity, it is natural to wonder what need be assumed about these notions. In ordinary talk, 'possible' and 'necessary' admit different readings, and the same goes for other modal expressions, such as 'can' or 'must'. This has led philosophers to distinguish different kinds of modality. However, we will not dwell on such distinctions. All that we need to assume is that some intelligible notion of possibility is suitably unrestricted, namely, not constrained by what we currently know about the physical world or what our best scientific theories predict. For example, even though it makes sense to say that nothing can move faster than light, given that the laws of nature rule out superluminal motion, this is not the sense of 'possible' that matters to logic. In the sense of 'possible' that matters to logic, superluminal motion is possible, because the laws of nature are not inherently necessary. The same goes for any hypothesis that is compatible with the kind of general truths that qualify as logical principles.

---

[1] Aristotle, *Topics* 100a25.

So, Definition 2.1 is to be read as follows: Γ/α is valid just in case it is not possible even in the most generously inclusive sense—it is not even coherently conceivable—that the sentences in Γ are true and α is false. Equivalently, Γ/α is valid just in case every coherently conceivable situation in which the sentences in Γ are true is a situation in which α is also true.

2.4   Other Logical Properties and Relations

The same notion of possibility that occurs in Definition 2.1 is employed to define other fundamental logical properties and relations. This section adds four definitions to our repertory.

Definition 2.2 A set of sentences Γ *entails* a sentence α if and only if it is impossible that the sentences in Γ are true and α is false.

When Γ contain a single sentence β, that is, when $\Gamma = \{\beta\}$, we simply say that β entails α. As it turns out from Definitions 2.1 and 2.2, validity and entailment are interdefinable: Γ/α is valid if and only if Γ entails α.

Definition 2.3 A set of sentences Γ is *consistent* if and only if it is possible that all the sentences in Γ are true.

Here, again, Γ can contain any number of sentences. We stipulate that Γ is consistent when $\Gamma = \emptyset$, for in that case Γ does not contain sentences whose truth is impossible. A set of sentences that is not consistent is *inconsistent*. For example, the set formed by 'It is cold' and 'It is raining' is consistent, for it is possible that it is cold and raining. Instead, the set formed by 'It is raining' and 'It is not raining' is inconsistent. The second sentence is the negation of the first, so it cannot be true if the first is true. From now on we will represent negation by using the symbol $\sim$, following a convention that goes back to Giuseppe Peano, and we will assume that $\sim\alpha$ is false if α is true, just as $\sim\alpha$ is true if α is false.[2]

Definition 2.4 Two sentences α and β are *equivalent* if and only if it is impossible that one of them is true and the other is false.

To say that two sentences are equivalent is to say that they entail each other. For example, 'It is not the case that it is not raining' is equivalent to 'It is raining'. In general, according to the principle of *Double Negation*, first elucidated by the Stoics, the double negation of a sentence is equivalent to the sentence itself. Since $\sim\alpha$ is

---

[2]Giuseppe Peano (1858–1932) was an Italian mathematician who studied and taught at the University of Turin. He aimed at developing mathematics in its entirety from a set of fundamental postulates, using new symbols and a simplified language of his own invention called *Latino sine flexione*. The symbol $\sim$ occurs in Peano [48].

false if and only if α is true, and $\sim\sim\alpha$ is true if and only if $\sim\alpha$ is false, $\sim\sim\alpha$ is true if and only if α is true.[3]

Definition 2.5 Two sentences α and β are *contradictory* if and only if it is impossible that they are both true or both false.

To say that two sentences are contradictory is to say that each of them entails the negation of the other. For example, 'It is raining' and 'It is not raining' are contradictory: if one of them is true, the other must be false. According to the principle of *Non-Contradiction*, originally formulated by Aristotle, two contradictory sentences form an inconsistent set, so it is correct to deny that both of them hold. Thus, for example, it is correct to say 'It is not the case that it is raining and not raining'.[4]

As the examples in Sect. 1.3 show, the absurdity involved in a *reductio ad absurdum* is a contradiction: to reduce a hypothesis to absurdity is to show that it entails a contradiction. This is why the principle that underlies a *reductio* may be called *Proof by Contradiction*: if a sentence α, together with other assumptions, entails two contradictory sentences, then α can be rejected on the basis of those assumptions. This principle directly justifies the first of the two forms of *reductio* considered in Sect. 1.3, that in which one assumes α in order to prove $\sim\alpha$. To justify the second, that in which one assumes $\sim\alpha$ in order to prove α, it suffices to add Double Negation. For if one starts with $\sim\alpha$ and obtains $\sim\sim\alpha$ through a reasoning of the first kind, then one can get α by Double Negation.[5]

Note that, although any set of sentences which includes a contradiction is inconsistent, the converse does not hold. A set of sentences can be inconsistent even if it does not contain a contradiction. For example, the set formed by 'Alf is less than 40 years old' and 'Alf is more than 40 years old' is inconsistent. But these two sentences are not contradictory, for they can both be false: it can be the case that Alf is just 40 years old.

2.5   Important Facts About Validity

This section spells out some important facts about validity that follow from Definition 2.1. Since validity and entailment are interdefinable, these facts can be phrased as properties of entailment. From now on we will use the symbol $\square$, aligned on the right, to mark the end of a proof.

---

[3] Our knowledge of Stoic logic, including the acceptance of Double Negation, is based on indirect sources, see Kneale and Kneale [33], p. 147.

[4] Aristotle *Metaphysics* IV, Γ, 3, 1005^b 19–23. For Aristotle, first philosophy, or metaphysics, deals with first principles, of which Non-Contradiction is the firmest: without this principle we could not know anything that we do know.

[5] The Stoics recognized the cogency of Proof by Contradiction, which was employed by the Eleatics and the Megarians in some arguments that they held in high esteem, see Kneale and Kneale [33], p. 172.

Let us start with three constitutive properties of entailment. The first is *Reflexivity*:

Theorem 2.1 α *entails* α

Proof Trivially, it cannot be the case that α is both true and false.   □

The second is *Monotonicity*, understood as follows:

Theorem 2.2 *If* Γ *entails* α, *and* $\Gamma \subseteq \Delta$, *then* Δ *entails* α.

Proof Assume that Γ entails α and that $\Gamma \subseteq \Delta$. Now suppose that all the sentences in Δ are true. Since $\Gamma \subseteq \Delta$, this implies that all the sentences in Γ are true. It follows that α is true, given that Γ entails α.   □

Theorem 2.2 says that no addition of premises to a valid argument can affect its validity. Monotonicity characterizes validity as distinct from any inductive property of the sort considered in Sect. 2.3. While validity is monotonic, such a property would be non-monotonic. For example, assuming that the argument about the cat Greg has a certain inductive strength, if one adds 'Greg is allergic to lactose' as a premise, one gets an inductively weaker argument.

Note that Reflexivity and Monotonicity imply that any argument whose premises include the conclusion is valid. Suppose that $\alpha \in \Gamma$. By Theorem 2.1, α entails α. Since $\{\alpha\} \subseteq \Gamma$, by Theorem 2.2 it follows that Γ entails α.

Third, entailment satisfies a condition called *Cut*:

Theorem 2.3 *If* Γ *entails* α, *and* $\Delta \cup \{\alpha\}$ *entails* β, *then* $\Gamma \cup \Delta$ *entails* β.

Proof Assume that Γ entails α and that $\Delta \cup \{\alpha\}$ entails β. Now suppose that the sentences in $\Gamma \cup \Delta$ are true. From the first assumption we get that α is true. So, the sentences in $\Delta \cup \{\alpha\}$ are true. From the second assumption it follows that β is true.   □

Theorem 2.3 says that if two valid arguments are chained, then a third argument formed by the premises of the first two and the conclusion of the second is valid. This guarantees that, if a complex reasoning is formed by a set of chained arguments and each of the arguments in the set is valid, the whole reasoning is valid as well.

Note that Cut implies transitivity, that is, if γ entails α, and α entails β, then γ entails β. To see this it suffices to take Theorem 2.3 and suppose that $\Gamma = \{\gamma\}$ and $\Delta = \emptyset$. So entailment is both reflexive and transitive, although it is clearly not symmetric: it can be the case that α entails β but β does not entail α. For example, 'The earth is a planet' entails 'Either the earth is a star or it is a planet', but not the other way round.

A fourth property of entailment is Proof by Contradiction:

Theorem 2.4 *If* $\Gamma \cup \{\alpha\}$ *entails* β *and* $\sim\beta$, *then* Γ *entails* $\sim\alpha$.

Proof Assume that $\Gamma \cup \{\alpha\}$ entails β and $\sim\beta$. If the sentences in $\Gamma \cup \{\alpha\}$ were all true, β and $\sim\beta$ would both be true. But β and $\sim\beta$ cannot be true together. So, $\Gamma \cup \{\alpha\}$ is inconsistent. This is to say that it is impossible that the sentences in Γ are true and α is true: if the sentences in Γ are true, α must be false. Equivalently, if the sentences in Γ are true, $\sim\alpha$ must be true.   □

A fifth property concerns consistency:

Theorem 2.5 Γ *entails* $\sim\alpha$ *if and only if* $\Gamma \cup \{\alpha\}$ *is inconsistent.*

Proof Assume that Γ entails $\sim\alpha$. This means that, necessarily, if the sentences in Γ are true, $\sim\alpha$ is true, and consequently α is false. Therefore, $\Gamma \cup \{\alpha\}$ is inconsistent. Now assume that $\Gamma \cup \{\alpha\}$ is inconsistent. Then Γ entails $\sim\alpha$ for the reason stated in the proof of Theorem 2.4, that is, if it is impossible that the sentences in Γ are true and α is true, it is impossible that the sentences in Γ are true and $\sim\alpha$ is false.   □

A direct corollary of Theorem 2.5 is that, for any inconsistent set of sentences Δ, there is a set of sentences Γ and a sentence α such that $\Delta = \Gamma \cup \{\alpha\}$ and Γ entails $\sim\alpha$. This holds because if Δ is inconsistent, by definition it is not empty. So, it contains at least one sentence α such that $\Delta = \Gamma \cup \{\alpha\}$ for some Γ. Note that it is not necessary that Δ contains more than one sentence, for it can happen that $\Gamma = \emptyset$ and $\Delta = \{\alpha\}$.

Finally, two facts about entailment that deserve attention may be described as cases of vacuous necessary truth preservation. One is the following:

Theorem 2.6 *If* Γ *is inconsistent, then* Γ *entails* α, *for any* α.

Proof Assume that Γ is inconsistent. Then it is impossible that the sentences in Γ are true. So, for any α, it is impossible that the sentences in Γ are true and α is false.   □

Here the condition required by Definition 2.1 is vacuously satisfied: the argument is valid simply because it is impossible that its premises are true, independently of what its conclusion says. Theorem 2.6 warrants the principle of *Explosion*, traditionally known as *Pseudo Scotus*, according to which anything follows from a contradiction.[6]

The other case is the following:

Theorem 2.7 *If* α *is necessarily true, then* Γ *entails* α, *for any* Γ.

Proof Assume that α is necessarily true. Then, for any Γ, it is impossible that the sentences in Γ are true and α is false.   □

Here, again, the condition required by Definition 2.1 is vacuously satisfied: the argument is valid simply because it is impossible that its conclusion is false, independently of what its premises say. Note that α is entailed by any Γ just in case it is entailed by $\emptyset$. On the one hand, if α is entailed by any Γ, then it is entailed by $\emptyset$, because $\emptyset$ is one possible Γ. On the other, if α is entailed by $\emptyset$, then it is entailed by any Γ in virtue of Monotonicity (Theorem 2.2), given that $\emptyset \subseteq \Gamma$.

---

[6]The name 'Pseudo Scotus' refers to the unknown author of a book called *In Universam Logicam Quaestiones*, formerly attributed to John Duns Scotus (1265–1308). In that book, the principle was formulated and proved, in the context of a vast and original discussion of consequence relations.

One might find Theorems 2.6 and 2.7 hard to accept, and this might lead one to doubt the credibility of Definition 2.1. By Theorem 2.6, the following argument is valid:

(1) It is raining
(2) It is not raining
(3) The Yeti exists

By Theorem 2.7, the following argument is valid:

(1) The Yeti exists
(2) $2 + 2 = 4$

However, it is important to understand that Theorems 2.6 and 2.7 can be justified on the basis of independently grounded assumptions. To prove Theorem 2.6, assume that Γ is inconsistent. By the corollary of Theorem 2.5 outlined above, Γ includes a subset Δ and a sentence α such that Δ entails $\sim\alpha$. Since $\alpha \in \Gamma$, Γ entails α. By Monotonicity (Theorem 2.2), Γ entails $\sim\alpha$. So, Γ entails α and $\sim\alpha$. By Monotonicity (Theorem 2.2), again, for any β, $\Gamma \cup \{\sim\beta\}$ entails α and $\sim\alpha$. From this and Theorem 2.4 it follows that Γ entails $\sim\sim\beta$, so by Double Negation Γ entails β. Since β is arbitrary, Γ entails any sentence.

To prove Theorem 2.7 it suffices to use Theorem 2.6, Double Negation, and *Contraposition*, the principle according to which, if α entails β, then $\sim\beta$ entails $\sim\alpha$. Suppose that α is necessarily true. Then $\sim\alpha$ is necessarily false. So, $\{\sim\alpha\}$ is inconsistent. By Theorem 2.6 it follows that, for any $\sim\beta$, $\{\sim\alpha\}$ entails $\sim\beta$, hence $\sim\alpha$ entails $\sim\beta$. By Contraposition, $\sim\sim\beta$ entails $\sim\sim\alpha$. Since by Double Negation $\sim\sim\beta$ is equivalent to β and $\sim\sim\alpha$ is equivalent to α, β entails α. By Monotonicity (Theorem 2.2), any superset of $\{\beta\}$ entails α. Since β is arbitrary, any Γ entails α.

The considerations just provided suggest that, if one accepts Theorems 2.1–2.5, which do not strike as counterintuitive, one must also accept Theorems 2.6 and 2.7, provided that one grants Double Negation and Contraposition. Conversely, if one wants to question the definition of validity as necessary truth preservation on the basis of examples such as those considered, one must be willing to give up other principles as well.[7]

Independently of such considerations, note that, despite the impression of oddness that the two arguments above may transmit, Theorems 2.6 and 2.7 are largely innocuous, in that they do not affect the judgements that we may give in the circumstances in which we usually assess arguments. The first argument is valid by Theorem 2.6. However, since its premises are contradictory, it cannot in principle be recognized as sound. The second argument is somehow analogous, for its validity

---

[7]Anderson and Belnap [1] is among the most important works which suggest a revision of the classical definition of validity.

can only be recognized if the necessary truth of its conclusion is acknowledged. Normally, the cases in which an argument is used are cases in which the conclusion of the argument expresses a controversial claim, that is, a claim whose truth cannot be taken for granted. But in such a case the argument could not be judged as valid.

2.6 Validity Is Not Everything

Before explaining how validity is treated at the formal level, it may be useful to dwell on three cases of faulty reasoning that are traditionally classified as *fallacies*, that is, as bad arguments that may easily be mistaken for good arguments. The interesting fact about these cases is that, in each of them, it does not suffice to appeal to Definition 2.1 to explain what is wrong with the argument. This shows that the criterion of validity is nothing but one dimension along which we can assess arguments.[8]

The first case is the *fallacy of equivocation*. An expression is used equivocally when its intended meaning changes surreptitiously within a context. The fallacy of equivocation hinges on such a shift of meaning. Here is an example:

(1)   The end of a thing is its perfection
(2)   Death is the end of life
(3)   Death is the perfection of life

This argument involves a confusion between two readings of 'end'. One is suggested by (1), which seems to say that the goal of a thing is its perfection, the other is suggested by (2), which seems to say that death is the last event of life (see Exercise 1.10). If 'end$_1$' stands for 'end' read as 'goal', while 'end$_2$' stands for 'end' read as 'last event', the reading of the argument that makes (1) and (2) plausible is that according to which (1) means that the end$_1$ of a thing is its perfection, while (2) means that death is the end$_2$ of life. On this reading, the argument is invalid: (3) can be false even if (1) and (2) are true.

What makes the argument deceiving is that one may be inclined to read 'end' univocally, and thus fail to see its invalidity. That is, one may be inclined to read (1) and (2) either as if they both concerned end$_1$ or as if they both concerned end$_2$. This inclination is due to the fact that people usually take univocality for granted. For example, if one asks whether 'Visiting relatives can be boring' and 'Visiting relatives can be tiresome' are both true, either one wants to know whether it can be boring and tiresome to visit relatives, or one wants to know whether relatives' visits can be boring and tiresome. What one does *not* want to know is whether it can be boring to visit relatives but tiresome to receive their visits. Similarly, when an

---

[8]The term 'fallacy' derives from the Latin 'fallacia', which means 'deception'.

argument is under examination, it is quite natural to restrict consideration to univocal readings. The argument above seems valid because it is valid on such readings.

The other two cases of faulty reasoning are mistakes that involve some sort of inappropriateness to the dialectic context in which the argument is used. When one offers an argument, typically it is because one intends to justify a claim that one cannot take for granted. In order to fulfill this task, the argument must satisfy at least two minimal constraints: its conclusion must express the claim that is in need of justification, and its premises must in principle be acceptable for those who might initially doubt its conclusion. However, there are cases in which one of these constraints is violated. When this happens, the argument proposed is unsuited to prove what one wants to prove, even though it may be valid.

The fallacy known as *ignoratio elenchi* is the mistake that one commits when one proposes an argument whose conclusion does not express the thesis in need of justification but some other thesis that is easier to establish. The Latin expression literally means 'ignoring the refutation', because in antiquity it was used to describe cases in which one thinks that one has refuted something while in reality one has not. In fact this is a fallacy that typically occurs in refutations, where it takes the form of the "straw man": a debater misrepresents an opponent's position to make the opponent's claims or arguments appear easily defeated. For example, in Plato's *Republic*, Socrates uses the following argument against Thrasymachus:

> You say that the just is the advantage of the stronger. What do you mean by that, Thrasymachus? You surely don't assert such a thing as this: if Polydamas, the pancratiast, is stronger than we are and beef is advantageous for his body, then this food is advantageous and just for us who are weaker than he is".[9]

When Thrasymachus claims that the just is the advantage of the stronger, he intends to use 'strong' in the sense of 'politically powerful'. But Socrates offers a blatantly captious reading of that claim, as he construes 'strong' as 'able to perform physically demanding tasks'. His argument is the following:

(1)   The just is the advantage of the stronger
(2)   Polydamas is the stronger
_____
(3)   The just is the advantage of Polydamas

From (3) Socrates obtains the ridiculous consequence that the just is eating beef. If 'strong$_1$' stands for 'politically strong', and 'strong$_2$' stands for 'physically strong', the flaw in this argument lies in the fact that (1) is used as if it meant that the just is the advantage of the stronger$_2$. Even assuming that (3) is unacceptable and that it follows from (1) and (2), the argument provides no reason to deny (1) as understood by Thrasymachus, namely, that the just is the advantage of the stronger$_1$.[10]

---

[9]Plato, [50], 338 c–d.

[10]The original meaning of the term 'ignoratio elenchi' goes back to Aristotle, *Sophistici Elenchi* 167a 21.

The fallacy known as *petitio principii*, or begging the question, is a mistake that one commits when one proposes an argument whose premises cannot be accepted by someone who does not already accept its conclusion. The Latin expression literally means 'asking what is at the beginning', because in antiquity it was used to define the mistake made by one of the two contenders in a dispute when he or she expects that the other contender grants the initial point of the dispute, that is, the controversial claim. In other words, to beg the question is to assume what is to be proved.[11]

The paradigmatic examples of *petitio principii* are arguments that include the conclusion among the premises, or in which one of the premises directly entails the conclusion, as in the following example:

(1)   The Yeti's footprints have been seen in the Himalayas
(2)   The Yeti exists

Clearly, if one uses this argument to prove (2), one assumes what is to be proved. An argument in which the conclusion occurs as a premise, or in which one of the premises directly entails the conclusion, is valid. So there is nothing wrong in the inference from the premises to the conclusion. The fallacy lies in the fact that the argument is presented as a justification of its conclusion, where it cannot be recognized as such. In any context in which the conclusion is not granted, the argument cannot be accepted as sound.

Exercises

2.1 Is the following argument valid?

Either the Yeti exists or the earth is a planet. The earth is not a planet. Therefore, the Yeti exists.

2.2 Is the argument of Exercise 2.1 sound?

2.3 Consider Tisias' argument (Exercise 1.6). Is it valid?

2.4 Is the set formed by the following sentences consistent?

(a) Snow is white
(b) Grass is green
(c) Either God exists or snow is not white

2.5 Can a set formed by a single sentence be inconsistent?

---

[11] Again, the original meaning of the expression goes back to Aristotle, *Topics*, VIII, 13, 162b 31.

2.6 Which of the following two sentences entails the other?

(a) Alf is bald
(b) Either Alf is bald or Alf is not bald

2.7 Are the following sentences equivalent?

(a) Alf is a bachelor
(b) Alf is an adult unmarried man

2.8 The corollary of Theorem 2.5 considered in Sect. 2.5 says that, for any inconsistent set of sentences Δ, there is a set of sentences Γ and a sentence α such that $\Delta = \Gamma \cup \{\alpha\}$ and Γ entails $\sim\alpha$. Why does this hold even when $\Gamma = \emptyset$ and $\Delta = \{\alpha\}$?

2.9 Explain how Socrates' attack to Thrasymachus can be reconstructed as a fallacy of equivocation.

2.10 There is a fallacy in the following text. Reconstruct the argument and explain the fallacy.

A student of mine told me that I am her favourite professor, and I know that she is telling the truth, because no student would lie to her favourite professor.

Chapter 3
Formality

3.1 Formal Validity

As anticipated in Sect. 1.1, the validity of an argument can be explained in terms of its form. To illustrate the idea of formal explanation, consider the following argument:

(1) If it's not the butler who did it, it is the gardener
(2) It's not the butler who did it
(3) It is the gardener

(1) is a complex sentence formed by two sentences, (2) and (3). More precisely, (1) is a *conditional* in which (2) occurs as *antecedent* and (3) occurs as *consequent*. If a conditional is true, and its antecedent is true, its consequent must be true as well. This is why the argument is valid.

The explanation just outlined is formal in the sense that it does not appeal to the specific content of (1)–(3). As far as the validity of the argument above is concerned, it does not really matter that (1)–(3) concern a murder. The same explanation applies equally well to the following argument:

(1) If the earth is a planet, it is spherical
(2) The earth is a planet
(3) The earth is spherical

A. Iacona, *LOGIC: Lecture Notes for Philosophy, Mathematics, and Computer Science*, Springer Undergraduate Texts in Philosophy,
https://doi.org/10.1007/978-3-030-64811-4_3

Here, again, (1) is a conditional in which (2) occurs as antecedent and (3) occurs as consequent. The form instantiated by these two arguments is called *Modus Ponens*.[1]

From now on we will assume that the symbol $\supset$ stands for 'if'. This symbol was first adopted by Bertrand Russell and Alfred North Whitehead in *Principia Mathematica* (1910–1913), a monumental treatise which had an enormous influence on the development of logic and the philosophy of mathematics. On the assumption that $\supset$ stands for 'if', the form instantiated by the two arguments above can be represented as $\alpha \supset \beta, \alpha/\beta$.[2]

Another example of structural similarity between valid arguments is the following:

(1) If the driver did it, the gardener is innocent

(2) The gardener is not innocent

(3) The driver didn't do it

(1) If the earth is pizza-shaped, it is flat

(2) The earth is not flat

(3) The earth is not pizza-shaped

The form instantiated by these two arguments can be represented as $\alpha \supset \beta, \sim\beta/\sim\alpha$. If $\alpha \supset \beta$ is true, it is not the case that α is true and β is false. So, if β is false, α must be false as well. This form is called *Modus Tollens*.[3]

To fully grasp the two schemas considered it is essential to realize that they include two kinds of expressions. The letters α and β stand for arbitrary sentences, so they can be interpreted in many different ways. For example, α can be replaced by 'The driver did it', 'The earth is pizza-shaped', and so on. To use an analogy, the role of the letters α and β is the same as the role that the letter n plays in the schema $n + 1 = n + 2 - 1$. To assert this schema is to say that the equality holds no matter how we replace n, that is, for any substitution of n with a numeral. The symbols $\sim$ and $\supset$, instead, are *logical constants*, in that they have a fixed meaning: $\sim$ and $\supset$ mean respectively 'not' and 'if' independently of the choice of α or β, just like $+$

---

[1]This form was originally identified by the Stoics, see Kneale and Kneale [33], p. 163. The term 'modus ponens' is an abbreviation of 'modus ponendo ponens' (roughly 'mode that affirms by affirming'), which was introduced in the middle ages.

[2]Russell and Whitehead [57]. Bertrand Arthur William Russell (1872–1970) was a British logician, philosopher, and essayist who spent most of his academic career at the University of Cambridge. His scientific production covers an incredibly broad range of topics, although he is mainly known for his important contributions to logic, epistemology, and the philosophy of language. Alfred North Whitehead (1861–1947) was a British logician and philosopher best known for his work in mathematics and in metaphysics. He was Russell's teacher in Cambridge, and worked with him for many years.

[3]Again, its identification goes back to the Stoics, see Kneale and Kneale [33], p. 163. The term 'modus tollens' is an abbreviation of 'modus tollendo tollens' (roughly 'mode that denies by denying'), which was introduced in the middle ages.

and $-$ indicate addition and subtraction independently of the choice of n. Logical constants play a key role in the individuation of argument forms, as the example of Modus Ponens and Modus Tollens shows.

A *valid form* is an argument form whose instances are all valid arguments. Formal validity is defined accordingly:

Definition 3.1 An argument Γ/α is *formally valid* if and only if it instantiates a valid form.

For example, the four arguments above are formally valid, because Modus Ponens and Modus Tollens are valid forms. More generally, every formally valid argument is valid by definition.

This is not to say that every valid argument is formally valid. Definition 3.1 leaves room for the possibility that some valid arguments are not formally valid. For example, the following argument is valid, for nothing can be blue and yellow at the same time:

(1)   The table is blue

(2)   The table is not yellow

But it does not instantiate a valid form, at least not according to the selection of logical constants that is normally employed to describe forms such as Modus Ponens and Modus Tollens. Obviously, this argument can be transformed into a formally valid argument by adding a premise:

(1)   If the table is blue, it is not yellow

(2)   The table is blue

(3)   The table is not yellow

Whenever the first argument can be ascribed to a person, the second argument can equally be ascribed to that person, for (1) is plausibly understood as an implicit premise, as explained in Sect. 1.2. But this does not make the first argument formally valid. Peter Abelard and other medieval logicians used to distinguish formally valid arguments from those which are valid in virtue of their content, and this distinction is perfectly consistent with Definition 3.1.[4]

---

[4]Peter Abelard (1079–1142), a brilliant, innovative, and controversial French philosopher, was perhaps the greatest logician of the middle ages. He called "perfect" an argument that is valid in virtue of its form, and "imperfect" an argument whose validity depends on content. Pseudo-Scotus then called *consequentia materialis* an argument of the latter kind, see Kneale and Kneale [33], p. 279.

3.2   Formal Invalidity

An argument Γ/α is *formally invalid* if it does not instantiate a valid form. For example, an invalid inference pattern that is traditionally classified as a fallacy is *affirming the consequent*. Consider the following arguments:

(1)   If the earth is a planet, it is spherical
(2)   The earth is spherical
(3)   The earth is a planet

(1)   If the table is blue, it is not yellow
(2)   The table is not yellow
(3)   The table is blue

These two arguments are both invalid, for in both cases it is possible that the premises are true and the conclusion is false: the earth could be a spherical fake planet created by spiteful aliens, and the table could be green. Both arguments have the form $\alpha \supset \beta, \beta/\alpha$, and the reason why they are invalid is the same: it is possible that a conditional and its consequent are true while its antecedent is false. So, it is generally wrong to infer α from $\alpha \supset \beta$ and β. An argument of this form may seem valid because it resembles an argument of the form Modus Ponens.

Another invalid inference pattern that is traditionally classified as a fallacy is *denying the antecedent*. Consider the following arguments:

(1)   If the earth is pizza-shaped, it is flat
(2)   The earth is not pizza-shaped
(3)   The earth is not flat

(1)   If the earth is flat, some planets are flat
(2)   The earth is not flat
(3)   It is not the case that some planets are flat

These two arguments are both invalid, for in both cases it is possible that the premises are true and the conclusion is false: the earth could be flat without being pizza-shaped, and there could be a flat planet other than the earth. Both arguments have the form $\alpha \supset \beta, \sim\alpha/\sim\beta$, and the reason why they are invalid is the same: it is possible that a conditional and the negation of its antecedent are true but the negation of its consequent is false. So, it is generally wrong to infer $\sim\beta$ from $\alpha \supset \beta$ and $\sim\alpha$. An argument of this form may seem valid because it resembles an argument of the form Modus Tollens.

Note, however, that there is a crucial difference between formal validity and formal invalidity. If an argument instantiates a valid form, then it is unmistakably valid: formal validity entails validity. By contrast, the fact that an argument instantiates an invalid form does not guarantee its invalidity: formal invalidity does not entail invalidity. For example, the following argument is valid, even though it has the form $\alpha \supset \beta, \beta / \alpha$:

(1) If something is a planet, the earth is a planet

(2) The earth is a planet

(3) Something is a planet

If (2) is true, then (3) must be true, independently of whether (1) is true. This asymmetry between formal validity and formal invalidity is due to the fact that an invalid form can be instantiated by valid arguments whose validity does not depend on structural properties that are expressible by the logical constants employed to represent that form. The relation of entailment between (2) and (3) depends on properties of (2) and (3) that are not expressible by logical constants such as $\sim$ or $\supset$. So, although the invalid forms just considered are generally instantiated by invalid arguments, which makes them useful to detect cases of invalidity, they can be instantiated by valid arguments.

3.3 Formal Language

The sentences that constitute an argument are strings of words that belong to a natural language, such as English, Italian, or Spanish. A natural language is so called because it has evolved naturally through the linguistic practices of a community of speakers. As a result of such practices, each natural language has its own syntactic and semantic properties, which make it unique.

Logic, however, is primarily interested in *logical form*, a structural property of sentences that is largely independent of the specific features of the natural language to which they belong. As we saw in Sects. 3.1 and 3.2, the validity of an argument is explained in terms of a structural description of its premises and conclusion that requires a high level of abstraction. In order to provide such a description, logicians employ artificial languages designed just for this purpose, namely, *formal languages*. Unlike natural languages, formal languages are defined by stipulation. Their syntactic and semantic properties derive from a set of constitutive rules that are made explicit from the very beginning.[5]

The first formal language properly understood was outlined by Frege in his seminal work *Begriffsschrift* (1879), although the very idea of a formal language goes back at least to Leibniz, who imagined a language for pure thought called *characteristica universalis*.[6] The title of Frege's book, which draws inspiration from

---

[5]Iacona [30], 1–38, spells out the idea of logical form and its history.

[6]Frege [14]. Gottfried Wilhelm Leibniz (1646–1716), one of the great thinkers of the seventeenth and eighteenth centuries, was a German philosopher and mathematician. He studied in Leipzig and

Leibniz, literally means "concept-script", and is usually translated as "ideography". This book sets out in a rigorous way the syntax and the semantics of an artificial language that is intended to formally represent what in natural language is essential to reasoning, that is, what Frege called "conceptual content". The conceptual content of a sentence is roughly what matters for its truth or falsity, and thus for the validity of the arguments in which it may occur.

After Frege, it became standard to define a formal language by means of two kinds of stipulation. One lays down the *syntax* of the language: it fixes an *alphabet*, that is, a list of symbols that includes logical constants and non-logical expressions, and a set of *formation rules* that determine which sequences of symbols of the alphabet are *formulas*. The other lays down the *semantics* of the language: it specifies a set of interpretations, each of which may be regarded as an assignment of extensions to the expressions of the language, where 'extension' is understood in the way explained in Sect. 1.4.

A formal language enables us to represent the structural properties of an argument through a *formalization* of the argument, that is, an assignment of formulas to the sentences which constitute the argument. To formalize an argument Γ/α is to represent it as Δ/β, where Δ is a set of formulas and β is a formula. That is, Δ/β is a representation of the argument in which each formula displays the logical form of the corresponding sentence. Once Γ/α is so represented, its validity can be assessed on the basis of the validity of Δ/β.

3.4 Formal System

There are essentially two ways to characterize a set of valid forms expressible in a formal language. One method is semantic, in that it hinges on a relation between sets of formulas and formulas which is defined in terms of the interpretations of the language. The other is syntactic, in that it hinges on a relation between sets of formulas and formulas which is defined within a *formal system* obtained by adding a deductive apparatus to the language.

The most traditional way to define a formal system is to stipulate that certain formulas are *axioms*, and specify a set of *inference rules* which enable one to obtain other formulas from the axioms. According to a model of scientific rigour that goes back to antiquity, and that is paradigmatically exemplified by Euclidean geometry, science proceeds by progressively deducing truths from a set of first principles that are fixed at the beginning as self-evident. The term 'axiom', which derives from a Greek word that means 'that which is thought worthy', refers to such principles. Frege followed this model in his *Begriffsschrift*, that is, he defined an *axiomatic system*. The same did Russell and Whitehead in their *Principia Mathematica*, whose

then travelled a lot around Europe. His writings, collected in Leibniz [36], contain many innovative ideas and deep insights into logic, mathematics, and metaphysics.

ultimate aim was to show that the truths of arithmetic can be deduced by a restricted set of logical axioms and definitions. This model was also essential to the program pursued by David Hilbert, who contributed substantially to the establishment of the formalistic foundations of mathematics.[7]

A different kind of formal systems are *natural deduction systems*, which are constituted only by inference rules, without axioms. The first systems of this kind were independently developed by Gerhard Gentzen and Stanisław Jaśkowski as an alternative to axiomatic systems. Gentzen and Jaśkowski intended to provide a formal justification of the proof methods actually employed in deductive practice by relying on simple inference rules that could be regarded as intuitively obvious.[8]

From now on 'language' will be used as a synonym for 'formal language', and 'system' will be used as a synonym for 'formal system'. If L is a language and S is a system obtained by defining a deductive apparatus for L, one can say that S is a system *in* L, and one can call *formulas of* S the formulas of L.

3.5 Object Language and Metalanguage

When a language L is described within a theory, it is described by means of a language other than L. So it is important to understand the distinction between L, the *object language*, and the language in which the theory is phrased, the *metalanguage*. In our case the metalanguage will be a suitably modified version of English. The qualification 'suitably modified' indicates that some abbreviations and some additional symbols will be used in combination with standard English expressions.

As far as abbreviations are concerned, one convention that will be adopted is to write 'iff' instead of 'if and only if' in definitions, theorems, and proofs. Another convention is to write 'for every x, y' instead of 'for every x and every y', 'for every x, y, z' instead of 'for every x and every y and every z', and so on. A third convention concerns quotation marks. Since the metalanguage is employed to describe the object language, the expressions of the object language appear in the

---

[7]David Hilbert (1862–1943) was a German mathematician who worked at the universities of Könisberg and Göttingen. His foundational program was based on a conception of mathematical proof which allowed for the use of non-contentual, and more specifically symbolic methods. By this is meant formal reasoning which makes no use of interpretations (or contents) of the expressions used in the reasoning.

[8]Gehrard Karl Erich Gentzen (1909–1945) was a German logician and mathematician who made major contributions to proof theory and the foundation of mathematics. His seminal work on natural deduction is Gentzen [18]. Stanisław Jaśkowski (1906–1965) was a Polish logician who worked mainly on proof theory and formal semantics. He presented his ideas about natural deduction in 1927 at the First Polish Mathematical Congress in Lvov, but developed them only later, in Jaśkowski [32], due to illness and family problems. After that, however, he had more luck than Gentzen (and more time to devote to natural deduction), because Gentzen died of starvation in a Soviet prison camp in 1945.

metalanguage, where they are not used but mentioned. The distinction between *use* and *mention* can be illustrated by means of an example. The word 'cat' is used in 'There is a cat on the mat', while it is mentioned in 'The word 'cat' has five letters'. The quotation marks which occur in the second sentence, together with the word they enclose, form a term that refers to the word itself. However, there are cases in which quotation marks can be omitted, such as the following:

+ is the symbol for addition

In other words, the sentence above can be used as an abbreviation of

'+' is the symbol for addition

This is the convention that we will adopt: every symbol of the object language can be used as an abbreviation of a term that refers to the symbol itself.

As far as the additional symbols are concerned, we will keep using lowercase greek letters $\alpha, \beta, \gamma \ldots$ to refer to arbitrary sentences or formulas, and uppercase greek letters $\Gamma, \Delta, \Sigma \ldots$ to refer to arbitrary sets of sentences or formulas. The symbols $<, >, \leq, \geq, =, \neq$ will be used with their standard mathematical meaning. Moreover, $=$ and $\neq$ will be employed in a broader sense, to indicate identity and difference between objects of any kind.

3.6 Further Set-Theoretical Notions

The remaining symbols of our metalanguage belong to the vocabulary of set theory. We have already met the symbols $\in, \notin, \subseteq, \cup, \{,\}, \langle,\rangle$. This section introduces further set-theoretical notions that will be employed in the following chapters.

As we saw in Sect. 2.1, a relation is a set of ordered pairs, so it is characterized by a domain and a range. A *function* F is a special kind of relation, that is, a relation such that for each x in the domain of F, there is only one y such that $\langle x, y \rangle \in F$. This unique y is said to be the *value* of F for x—indicated as $F(x)$—and x is said to be the *argument*. The range of F is the set of objects that are values of F for some argument. Take for example the function that assigns to each number its successor:

$$S(x) = x + 1$$

Here S denotes the successor function, so $S(x)$ denotes the successor of x, that is, the value of S for x.

We say that F *maps A into B* to mean that F is a function whose domain is A and whose range is a subset of B. We say that F *maps A onto B* if in addition the range of F is B itself. In this case F is also called a "surjective function" or simply a "surjection". We say that F is *one-to-one* if and only if, for each y in the range of F, there is only one x such that $\langle x, y \rangle \in F$. In this case F is also called an "injective function" or simply an "injection". We say that F is a *one-to-one correspondence* between A and B if and only if F maps A onto B and is one-to-one. In other words, for each element of A, there is a unique element of B assigned by F, and the other way round. In this case F is also called a "bijective function" or simply a "bijection".

A function can have one or more arguments. For example, the successor function has one argument. Instead, the addition function has two arguments:

$$A(x, y) = x + y$$

Here A indicates the addition function. This function takes ordered pairs of numbers as arguments and gives single numbers as values. For example, $A(1, 1) = 2$, $A(1, 2) = 3$, and so on. In general, an *n-ary* function that maps A into B assigns elements of B to n-tuples of elements of A. Since the set of all n-tuples of elements of A is indicated as A^n, this means that the function assigns elements of B to elements of A^n. The case in which $n = 1$ is that in which the function has a single argument, so $A^n = A$.

An *n-ary operation* on A is a function mapping A^n into A. Let $\mathbb{N}$ be the set of natural numbers, that is, $\mathbb{N} = \{0, 1, 2, 3 \dots \}$. Addition is a binary operation on $\mathbb{N}$, in that it is a function that assigns elements of $\mathbb{N}$ to ordered pairs of elements of $\mathbb{N}$. The ordered pairs that belong to the function are $\langle \langle 1, 2 \rangle, 3 \rangle$, $\langle \langle 2, 2 \rangle, 4 \rangle$, and so on.

A set A is *finite* if and only if, for some n, A contains exactly n elements. In other words, A is finite if and only if, for some n, there is a one-to-one function mapping A onto $\{0, 1, 2 \dots, n - 1\}$. If there is no such n, A is *infinite*. Recall that, in Euclid's proof (Sect. 1.3), the conclusion that there are infinitely many primes is obtained by reducing to the absurdity the hypothesis that there are n primes for some n.

A set A is *countable* if and only if there is a one-to-one function mapping A into $\mathbb{N}$, that is, A has either finitely many elements or as many elements as the natural numbers. If there is a one-to-one function mapping A onto $\mathbb{N}$, then A is *denumerable*. In other words, A is denumerable when it has as many elements as the natural numbers. Thus, a countable set is either finite or denumerable. For example, the set of primes is countable because it is denumerable. Instead, the set of real numbers, $\mathbb{R}$, is infinite but not denumerable. This set includes the rational numbers, which can be expressed by fractions, and the irrational numbers.

A *sequence* of elements of A is an ordered subset of A. A finite sequence of elements of A is an n-tuple of elements of A, so it is definable as a function that maps $\{1, \dots, n\}$ into A for some n. Similarly, an infinite sequence of elements of A is definable as a function that maps some infinite set into A, and a countable sequence of elements of A is defined as a function that maps some countable set into A. When there is a function that maps some countable set onto A, we have an *enumeration* of A. In other words, an enumeration of A is a countable sequence such that every element of A occurs in the sequence.

Exercises

3.1 Find the fallacy in the arguments of Exercises 1.3 and 1.4.

3.2 Which of these forms are valid?

(a) $\alpha / {\sim}\alpha$
(b) $\alpha / {\sim}{\sim}\alpha$
(c) $\alpha, \beta / \beta$

3.3 Is there a difference between $\{1, 2, 3\}$ and $\{\{1\}, 2, 3\}$?

3.4 Are there subsets of Ø?

3.5 Are there subsets of Ø other than Ø itself?

3.6 Complete the equality on the right:

(a) $\{1, 2, 3\} \cup \emptyset =$
(b) $\{1, 2, 3\} \cup \{1, 2\} =$
(c) $\{1, 2, 3\} \cup \{\{1\}, 2, 3\} =$

3.7 Which of the following relations are functions?

(a) the set of ordered pairs $\langle x, y \rangle$ such that y is brother or sister of x
(b) the set of ordered pairs $\langle x, y \rangle$ such that y is biological mother of x
(c) the set of ordered pairs $\langle x, y \rangle$ such that y is bigger than x

3.8 Which of the functions listed in the previous exercise are one-to-one?

3.9 If A and B are both denumerable, is $A \cup B$ denumerable?

3.10 If A is a denumerable and B is countable, is $A \cup B$ denumerable?

Chapter 4
The Symbols of Propositional Logic

4.1 Sentence Letters

This chapter introduces a propositional language called L. The alphabet of L is constituted by three categories of symbols:

$p, q, r \ldots$
$\sim, \supset, \wedge, \vee$
$(,)$

The symbols $p, q, r \ldots$ are *sentence letters*, non-logical expressions that stand for arbitrary sentences. For example, p can be used to represent 'It is raining', 'It is snowing', 'It is cold', and so on. The set of sentence letters is denumerable.

The sentence letters are *atomic formulas* in the sense that they are the simplest formulas of L, the smallest sequences of symbols that qualify as well formed expressions. Accordingly, they are used to represent simple sentences, that is, sentences which do not contain other sentences.

A sentence letter can be true or false, just as the sentences it represents. Following a convention introduced by George Boole in his *Mathematical Analysis of Logic* (1847), we assume that 1 and 0 indicate truth and falsity respectively, so that each sentence letter can take 1 or 0 as value. The rationale is that the value of the letter is 1 when the letter represents a true sentence, while it is 0 when it represents a false sentence.[1]

---

[1] Boole [3]. George Boole (1815–1864) was a British self-taught mathematician who worked for many years as a teacher in village schools and finally became professor at Queen's University, Cork. His novel ideas on symbolic reasoning, which contributed to the development of modern formal methods, derive from his attempt to express logical relations in algebraic terms.

© The Author(s), under exclusive license to Springer Nature Switzerland AG 2021
A. Iacona, *LOGIC: Lecture Notes for Philosophy, Mathematics, and Computer Science*, Springer Undergraduate Texts in Philosophy,
https://doi.org/10.1007/978-3-030-64811-4_4

4.2   Sentential Connectives

The *sentential connectives* $\sim$, $\supset$, $\wedge$, $\vee$ are the logical constants of L. Let us start with $\sim$. We have seen that a negation is a complex sentence formed by adding 'not' or a semantically equivalent expression to a sentence. For example, 'It is not raining' is the negation of 'It is raining'. Accordingly, a formula in which $\sim$ is combined with a simpler formula represents a negation. If p stands for 'It is raining', $\sim p$ stands for 'It is not raining'. From the semantic point of view, the rule for negation is very simple: the value of $\sim p$ is opposite to the value of p, that is, it is 1 if the value of p is 0, and 0 if the value of p is 1.

Now consider $\supset$. We have seen that a conditional is a complex sentence formed by combining two sentences—antecedent and consequent—by means of 'if' or a semantically equivalent expression. For example, 'If it is snowing, it is cold' is represented as $p \supset q$. According to the interpretation of 'if' adopted here, known as *material* interpretation, $p \supset q$ is true if it is not the case that p is true and q is false. So the value of $p \supset q$ is 0 when the value of p is 1 and the value of q is 0, while it is 1 in the other cases. This is one way of understanding a conditional, although it is not the only way.[2]

The symbol $\wedge$ represents *conjunction*. A conjunction is a complex sentence formed by two sentences, or *conjuncts*, by means of 'and' or a semantically equivalent expression. For example, 'It is cold and it is raining' is represented as $p \wedge q$. To assert a conjunction is to assert each of its conjuncts. So the value of $p \wedge q$ is 1 when the value of both p and q is 1, otherwise it is 0.[3]

Finally, $\vee$ is the symbol of *disjunction*. A disjunction is a complex sentence formed by two sentences, or *disjuncts*, by means of 'or' or a semantically equivalent expression. For example, 'Either it is cold or it is raining' is represented as $p \vee q$. When one asserts a disjunction, one does not assert each of its disjuncts, or one of them in particular. Rather, to assert a disjunction is to rule out that its disjuncts are both false. So, the value of $p \vee q$ is 1 when at least one of the two disjuncts has value 1, otherwise it is 0.[4]

As it emerges from what has been said so far, the truth value of a formula constructed in one of the four ways considered is determined by the truth values of its constituents. Assuming that a *truth function* is an n-ary operation on $\{1, 0\}$, that is, a function that associates elements of $\{1, 0\}$ to n-tuples of elements of $\{1, 0\}$,

---

[2] The material interpretation goes back to Philo of Megara (c.400s BC), a Stoic logician of whom we know very little, although we know that other Stoic logicians, most notably Chrysippus (c.279-c.206), did not share his view, see Kneale and Kneale [33], pp. 128–138. The label 'material', initially employed in the middle ages in connection with consequence relations, was adopted by Russell, who called 'material implication' the conditional so understood. Edgington [9] illustrates the main problems that arise in connection with the material interpretation and outlines some alternative interpretations.

[3] The symbol $\wedge$ was first adopted in Heyting [24].

[4] The symbol $\vee$, like $\sim$ and $\supset$, belongs to the Peano-Russell notation.

this is to say that every such formula realizes a truth function. In particular, the truth functions expressed by these connectives associate elements of $\{1, 0\}$ either to elements of $\{1, 0\}$ or to ordered pairs of elements of $\{1, 0\}$:

$\sim$ $\langle 1, 0 \rangle$
          $\langle 0, 1 \rangle$

$\supset$ $\langle \langle 1, 1 \rangle, 1 \rangle$
          $\langle \langle 1, 0 \rangle, 0 \rangle$
          $\langle \langle 0, 1 \rangle, 1 \rangle$
          $\langle \langle 0, 0 \rangle, 1 \rangle$

$\wedge$ $\langle \langle 1, 1 \rangle, 1 \rangle$
          $\langle \langle 1, 0 \rangle, 0 \rangle$
          $\langle \langle 0, 1 \rangle, 0 \rangle$
          $\langle \langle 0, 0 \rangle, 0 \rangle$

$\vee$ $\langle \langle 1, 1 \rangle, 1 \rangle$
          $\langle \langle 1, 0 \rangle, 1 \rangle$
          $\langle \langle 0, 1 \rangle, 1 \rangle$
          $\langle \langle 0, 0 \rangle, 0 \rangle$

The connectives $\sim$, $\supset$, $\wedge$, $\vee$ are called *truth-functional* for this reason, and the same goes for the expressions 'not', 'if', 'and', 'or', as long as they are construed in the way explained. The idea of truth-functionality, which has emerged on several occasions in the history of logic, was properly spelled out by Wittgenstein in his *Tractatus Logico-Philosophicus.*[5]

A final note. We have seen that, when sentences containing 'not', 'if', 'and', 'or' are represented by formulas containing $\sim$, $\supset$, $\wedge$, $\vee$, it is assumed that such sentences are truth functions of their constituents. This assumption, however, does not entail that the use of 'not', 'if', 'and', 'or' always conforms to their truth-functional reading. For example, when one says 'Alf ate haggis and drank a digestive herb tea', one typically means not only that Alf performed two actions, but also that the first action precedes the second. This is why it is not equally appropriate to say 'Alf drank a digestive herb tea and ate haggis'. Yet if 'and' is read truth-functionally, the two sentences have the same truth conditions. Another example is the following. If Alf is talking with Clay and knows that Betty is at home because he just called her, it is appropriate for Alf to say 'Betty is at home', but it is not equally appropriate to say 'Betty is at home or in a restaurant'. Yet if 'or' is read truth-functionally and the first sentence is true, the second sentence is true as well.

One way to explain these apparent divergences is to appeal to the distinction drawn by Paul Grice between *what is said* and *what is implicated*. According to

---

[5]Wittgenstein [68], 4.31–5.1311, pp. 91–113.

Grice, what is said by uttering a sentence in a context depends on the meaning of the words that occur in the sentence and possibly on features of the context that fix their content. What is implicated, instead, goes beyond what is said, and may depend on general linguistic conventions or specific features of the conversation in which the utterance takes place. If this distinction is granted, one may claim that what is said by uttering 'Alf ate haggis and drank a digestive herb tea' is simply that two events occurred, because the suggested temporal relation is part of what is implicated. In other terms, 'Alf ate haggis and drank a digestive herb tea' and 'Alf drank a digestive herb tea and ate haggis' say the same thing, but they implicate different things. Similarly, one may claim that the reason why it is inappropriate for Alf to utter 'Betty is at home or in a restaurant' is that, in his conversation with Clay, that utterance would be taken with the implicature that Alf does not know which disjunct is true. In other terms, even though the disjunction is true, it would be misleading to assert it.[6]

4.3   Brackets

The complex formulas considered so far result from the combination of one connective with one or two sentence letters. But a complex formula can include more connectives, or more occurrences of the same connective. The brackets (,) are auxiliary symbols that enable us to construct such a formula without ambiguity. For example, 'Alf is bald and Betty owns a Fiat or Clay owns an Alfa Romeo' is structurally ambiguous, because it can be read either as a conjunction whose second conjunct is a disjunction, that is, $p \land (q \lor r)$, or as a disjunction whose first disjunct is a conjunction, that is, $(p \land q) \lor r$. Here the brackets make the difference, because they resolve the ambiguity in different ways.

Note that the two readings of 'Alf is bald and Betty owns a Fiat or Clay owns an Alfa Romeo' are not equivalent, that is, they yield different truth conditions. For example, if p is false and r is true, $p \land (q \lor r)$ is false but $(p \land q) \lor r$ is true. Thus, if Alf is not bald and Clay owns an Alfa Romeo, the sentence is false on the first reading but true on the second reading. Here is an analogy: $(2 \times 1) + n$ is not equivalent to $2 \times (1 + n)$. For example, their results differ if $n = 1$.

The general rule that will be adopted for brackets is that they must be added whenever a complex formula is formed by means of $\supset, \land, \lor$. This rule will be accompanied by two notational conventions. One is that outer brackets may always be omitted. For example, $p \land (q \lor r)$ and $(p \land q) \lor r$ are respectively abbreviations of $(p \land (q \lor r))$ and $((p \land q) \lor r)$. The other is that inner brackets may be omitted when they divide two occurrences of $\land$ or $\lor$. For example, instead of writing $(p \land q) \land r$ one may write $p \land q \land r$, and instead of writing $(p \lor q) \lor r$ one may write $p \lor q \lor r$. The reason is that $(p \land q) \land r$ and $p \land (q \land r)$, just as $(p \lor q) \lor r$ and $p \lor (q \lor r)$,

---

[6]Grice [21].

cannot have different truth values. To use again our arithmetic analogy, $(2 + 1) + n$ is equal to $2 + (1 + n)$ for every n. This is why we may simply write $2 + 1 + n$.

4.4 Expressive Completeness

The class of sentences that can be represented in L is rather wide. Here are two examples that show how L captures the meaning of natural language constructions other than those considered above. The first example is *exclusive disjunction*. As we saw in Sect. 4.2, $\vee$ is inclusive in the sense that $p \vee q$ is true when p and q are both true. But sometimes 'or' does not merely express a disjunction in this sense, for what is asserted is not only that at least one disjunct is true, but also that at most one disjunct is true. When you are told that hamburgers come either with salad or with fries, the disjunction is meant to be exclusive. In order to account for this use of 'or', no further symbol is needed, because an exclusive disjunction can be represented as a conjunction formed by an inclusive disjunction and the negation of the conjunction of its disjuncts, that is, as $(p \vee q) \wedge {\sim}(p \wedge q)$.

The second example is the *biconditional*, a complex sentence formed by two sentences by means of 'if and only if' or a semantically equivalent expression. The two constituents of a biconditional are called *left-hand side* and *right-hand side*. For example, 'You pass the logic exam if and only if you studied a lot' is a biconditional. Its left-hand side and right-hand are respectively 'You pass the logic exam' and 'You studied a lot'. The key to grasp the meaning of this biconditional is to understand the difference between 'if' and 'only if'. On the one hand, 'You pass the logic exam if you studied a lot' states a sufficient condition: in order to pass the exam, it suffices to study a lot. On the other, 'You pass the logic exam only if you studied a lot' states a necessary condition: in order to pass the exam it is necessary to study a lot, although it may not be enough. Therefore, these two sentences are correctly paraphrased as 'If you studied a lot, you pass the logic exam' and 'If you pass the logic exam, you studied a lot'. The biconditional amounts to their conjunction. More generally, a biconditional is formalized as $(p \supset q) \wedge (q \supset p)$, which can be abbreviated as $p \equiv q$.

What the two examples considered have in common is that in both cases the complex sentence can be described as a truth function of its constituents, and there is a formula of L that realizes that function, that is, for any assignment of truth values to the sentences letters that occur in the formula, the truth value of the formula is the value of the function for that assignment. The following truth functions, which are realized by $(p \vee q) \wedge {\sim}(p \wedge q)$ and $p \equiv q$, correspond to the exclusive reading of 'or' and to 'if and only if':

$\langle\langle 1, 1\rangle, 0\rangle$
$\langle\langle 1, 0\rangle, 1\rangle$
$\langle\langle 0, 1\rangle, 1\rangle$
$\langle\langle 0, 0\rangle, 0\rangle$

$\langle\langle 1, 1\rangle, 1\rangle$
$\langle\langle 1, 0\rangle, 0\rangle$
$\langle\langle 0, 1\rangle, 0\rangle$
$\langle\langle 0, 0\rangle, 1\rangle$

Similar considerations hold for any complex sentence that can be described as a truth function of its constituents. More generally, L is able to realize *any* truth function, regardless of whether it corresponds to some natural language expression. L is *expressively complete* in the sense that, for every truth function, it includes some formula that realizes that function. To recognize this fact, consider an arbitrary truth function:

$\langle\langle 1, 1, 1\rangle, 0\rangle$
$\langle\langle 1, 1, 0\rangle, 1\rangle$
$\langle\langle 1, 0, 1\rangle, 0\rangle$
$\langle\langle 1, 0, 0\rangle, 1\rangle$
$\langle\langle 0, 1, 1\rangle, 0\rangle$
$\langle\langle 0, 1, 0\rangle, 0\rangle$
$\langle\langle 0, 0, 1\rangle, 1\rangle$
$\langle\langle 0, 0, 0\rangle, 0\rangle$

To construct a formula α that realizes this function it suffices to take three sentence letters p, q, r and assume that they are the atomic formulas that occur in α, so that the first three numbers in each row indicate the values of p, q, r, while the fourth number indicates the value of α. The cases in which α is true are the second, the fourth, and the seventh. Consider the second. If p, q, r are respectively true, true, false, then $p \wedge q \wedge \sim r$ is true. Now consider the fourth. If p, q, r are respectively true, false, false, then $p \wedge \sim q \wedge \sim r$ is true. Finally, consider the seventh. If p, q, r are respectively false, false, true, then $\sim p \wedge \sim q \wedge r$ is true. Now take the disjunction $(p \wedge q \wedge \sim r) \vee (p \wedge \sim q \wedge \sim r) \vee (\sim p \wedge \sim q \wedge r)$. This disjunction is true in the three cases considered, that is, the second, the fourth, and the seventh, while it is false in the other five cases. So, we have found α. The same method can be applied to any truth function, that is, one can construct a formula that realizes the function by forming appropriate conjunctions and combining them in a disjunction.

Since the expressive completeness of L essentially depends on the fact that L includes $\sim, \supset, \wedge, \vee$ as logical constants, we can say that $\{\sim, \supset, \wedge, \vee\}$ is an *adequate set of connectives*, that is, a set of connectives by means of which we can express any truth function.

4.5 Truth-Functionality and Substitutivity

Although L can formally represent a wide class of sentences, its expressive capacity is limited in one important respect: in natural languages, not all sentential operators are truth-functional. When a complex sentence α is a truth function of its constituents, it conforms to the principle of *Substitutivity*: any expression which occurs in α can be substituted with another expression that has the same extension without affecting α's truth value. Assuming that the extension of a sentence is its truth value, this is to say that any sentence which occurs in α can be substituted with another sentence that has the same truth value without affecting α's truth value. So it suffices to recognize that some complex sentences violate Substitutivity to see that they are not truth functions of their constituents.

Here are some examples of violation of Substitutivity. The sentence 'Alf feels sick because he ate haggis' includes 'Alf feels sick' and 'Alf ate haggis' as constituents. Suppose that this sentence is true, and that the same goes for its constituents. If it is raining and we substitute 'Alf ate haggis' with 'It is raining', we easily get a false sentence, namely, 'Alf feels sick because it is raining'.

Similarly, the sentence 'Alf believes that it is raining' includes 'It is raining' as a constituent. Suppose that this sentence is true, and that Alf's belief is false because it is sunny. If we replace 'It is raining' with 'It is snowing', which is false as well, we get a sentence that is presumably false, that is, 'Alf believes that it is snowing'.

Finally, the sentence 'Necessarily, 2+2 = 4' includes '2+2 = 4' as a constituent. Clearly, both sentences are true. But if it is raining and we substitute '$2 + 2 = 4$' with 'It is raining', we get a false sentence, that is, 'Necessarily, it is raining'.

Since the sentences considered violate Substitutivity, the sentential operators they contain are not truth-functional. In general, the grammar of a natural language includes many constructions that are not truth-functional, so cannot be represented by means of the logical constants of L.

4.6 Formalization in a Propositional Language

Formalization in a language L is a process that can ideally be divided into two steps. First, the sentences to be formalized are paraphrased by using expressions that correspond to the logical constants of L, where this is possible. Then, the sentences that occur in the paraphrase, as output of the first step, are replaced by formulas of L. Although in practice these two steps tend to merge into a single mental act, it is heuristically useful to learn them separately.

In the case of L, the first step requires that the sentences to be formalized are paraphrased in terms of 'not', 'if', 'and', 'or', where this is possible. As 'where this is possible' implies, not every sentence is amenable to this kind of treatment. Simple sentences do not contain connectives because they are not formed by other sentences. Moreover, as explained in Sect. 4.5, some complex sentences are formed by sentential operators that are not truth-functional. So, the method to be adopted is the following: when one understands that a sentence can be paraphrased by using truth-functional operators, one paraphrases it in the way illustrated; instead, when one realizes that no such paraphrase is feasible, one leaves the sentence as it is.

Once the initial sentences are paraphrased, the truth-functional operators occurring in the paraphrase are to be replaced by the correspondent logical constants of L, and the sentences which do not contain such operators are to be replaced by sentence letters.

When one assigns sentence letters to sentences, one assumes that different sentence letters must be associated with different sentences, while the same sentence letter must be associated with the same sentence, if it occurs more than once. For example, if the paraphrase includes two sentences, say 'It is raining' and 'It is snowing', one will use p for every occurrence of 'It is raining' and q for every occurrence of 'It is snowing'. The reason is that normally different sentences have different truth conditions, so it is possible that one of them is true and the other is false. Since each sentence letter can be evaluated as true or false independently of the others, p and q can have different truth values.

Of course, it possible that two distinct sentences have the same truth conditions. For example, 'It is indeed raining' has the same truth conditions as 'It is raining'. Note, however, that the assumption we are considering—that different sentence letters must be associated with different sentences—concerns the second step of the process of formalization. Since the input of the second step is the output of the first step, the sentences to which sentence letters are to be assigned are not the initial sentences, but the result of a paraphrase of those sentences which makes their truth conditions explicit. Thus, in the case of 'It is raining' and 'It is indeed raining' it is reasonable to presume that their equivalence is made explicit at an earlier stage by eliminating the expression 'indeed' from the latter, hence that they can be represented by the same sentence letter.

Exercises

4.1 Are the following sentences equivalent?

(a) If it is raining, it is cold
(b) If it is not cold, it is not raining

4.2 Show the difference by using brackets:

(a) Either it is not raining or it is cold
(b) It is not the case that either it is raining or it is cold

4.3 The following function corresponds to the expression 'not both', as it gives 1 only when it is not the case that both constituents are true.

$$\langle\langle 1, 1\rangle, 0\rangle$$
$$\langle\langle 1, 0\rangle, 1\rangle$$
$$\langle\langle 0, 1\rangle, 1\rangle$$
$$\langle\langle 0, 0\rangle, 1\rangle$$

Find a formula that realizes this function.

4.4 Formalize the following sentences:

(a) It is raining
(b) If it is not raining, it is raining

4.5 Explain why the formulas that represent (a) and (b) in Exercise 4.4 realize the same truth function.

4.6 If $*$ were a connective that stands for 'not both', would $\{\sim, \supset, \wedge, \vee, *\}$ be an adequate set of connectives?

4.7 Paraphrase the following sentences by using 'if':

(a) It's not cold, if it is raining
(b) It is raining only if it is not cold
(c) It is not cold, provided that it is raining

4.8 Formalize the sentences paraphrased in Exercises 4.1 and 4.7.

4.9 Formalize Tisias' argument (Exercise 1.6).

4.10 Formalize the following argument:

If I have 3 euros, I can buy an ice cream. But if the ice cream shop is closed, I cannot buy it. Therefore, either I don't have 3 euros, or the ice cream shop is open.

Chapter 5
The Language L

5.1 Formation Rules

Chapter 4 introduced the symbols of L, explained their meaning, and illustrated how they can be used to formalize sentences of a natural language. Now it is time to define L in a rigorous way by making fully explicit its syntax and its semantics.

Let us start with the formation rules of L, which inductively define the set of formulas of L. In general, an *inductive definition* of a set A is structured in two parts: the first—the *basis of the induction*—fixes some initial elements of A; the second—the *induction step*—specifies some operations that, if applied to elements of A, produce elements of A. These two parts, together with the tacit assumption that nothing else belongs to A, define A as the smallest set containing the initial elements and closed under the operations specified, where 'closed' means that those operations cannot take you from objects that belong to A to objects that do not belong to A. For example, the set of natural numbers is inductively defined as follows:

1. 0 is a natural number;
2. if n is a natural number, then $n + 1$ is a natural number.

Clause 1 sets 0 as the initial element of $\mathbb{N}$. Clause 2 specifies an operation, the successor operation, that, if applied to an element of $\mathbb{N}$, yields another element of $\mathbb{N}$. On the assumption that nothing else belongs to $\mathbb{N}$, we get that $\mathbb{N}$ is the smallest set containing 0 and closed under the successor operation.

Here are the rules that inductively define the set of formulas of L:

Definition 5.1
1. $p, q, r \ldots$ are formulas;
2. if α is a formula, $\sim\alpha$ is a formula;
3. if α and β are formulas, $(\alpha \supset \beta)$ is a formula;

© The Author(s), under exclusive license to Springer Nature Switzerland AG 2021   45
A. Iacona, *LOGIC: Lecture Notes for Philosophy, Mathematics, and Computer Science*, Springer Undergraduate Texts in Philosophy,
https://doi.org/10.1007/978-3-030-64811-4_5

4. if α and β are formulas, $(\alpha \wedge \beta)$ is a formula;
5. if α and β are formulas, $(\alpha \vee \beta)$ is a formula.

The basis of the induction, clause 1, says that sentence letters are formulas. As we saw in Sect. 4.1, these are the atomic formulas of L. The induction step is constituted by clauses 2–5, each of which specifies an operation that, if applied to formulas, yields other formulas. On the assumption that nothing else is a formula, the set of formulas of L is defined as the smallest set containing the atomic formulas and closed under the operations specified.

5.2   Syntactic Trees

Any formula of L is constructed by applying a finite number of times clauses 2–5 of Definition 5.1, so it contains a finite number of occurrences of connectives. Here we talk about occurrences of connectives, rather than connectives, because the same connective can occur more than once in a formula. For example, $\sim\sim p$ contains two occurrences of $\sim$, which means that it is constructed by applying clause 2 twice. The *complexity* of a formula is the number of occurrences of connectives it contains. Thus, p has complexity 0, $\sim p$ has complexity 1, $\sim\sim p$ has complexity 2, and so on.

The structure of a formula can be described in a perspicuous way by tracing its "syntactic history", that is, by showing how it is built from an initial set of sentence letters. To do so it suffices to draw a *syntactic tree*, that is, a tree-like diagram where each node is occupied by a formula and is connected to other nodes by straight lines. The tree branches downward, so that the initial node, *the root*, is the top node and is occupied by the formula itself, while the terminal nodes, the *leaves*, are the lowest nodes and are occupied by the sentence letters that feature as its constituents.

The three diagrams below are examples of syntactic trees. The first represents the construction of $\sim\sim p$. In this case the root has complexity 2, and there is only one leaf. The second represents the construction of $p \vee q$. In this case the root has complexity 1, and there are two leaves because $\vee$ is a binary connective. The third, which is slightly more articulated, represents the construction of $\sim(p \vee q) \wedge r$. In this case the root has complexity 3. The first division leads to two formulas, $\sim(p \vee q)$ and r. The former has complexity 2, the latter has complexity 0. From $\sim(p \vee q)$ we go to another formula of complexity 1, $p \vee q$ and from this, through a further division, we get to two formulas of complexity 0, p and q.

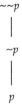

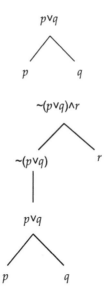

In general, to every formula we can associate a tree whose nodes are the parts of the formula that are themselves formulas. As long as we go down from the root to the leaves, the complexity of the formulas will decrease. To each step corresponds one of the formation rules of L. Therefore, by retracing the tree from the leaves to the root we see the mechanism of construction of the initial formula.

5.3 Scope

To conclude this outline of the syntax of L, we will consider an important syntactic notion that applies to L as well as to other languages.

Definition 5.2 The *scope* of the occurrence of a connective in a formula is the smallest formula that contains that occurrence.

Consider again the formula $\sim\sim p$. In this formula, the scope of the first occurrence of $\sim$ is $\sim\sim p$, while the scope of the second is $\sim p$. When a connective occurs only once in a formula, we can simply talk about the scope of the connective in the formula. For example, in $\sim(p \vee q) \wedge r$ the scope of $\vee$ is $p \vee q$, the scope of $\sim$ is $\sim(p \vee q)$, and the scope of $\wedge$ is $\sim(p \vee q) \wedge r$.

When two occurrences of connectives in a formula are such that the scope of one of them is included in the scope of the other, we say that the former occurrence is subordinate to the latter. For example, in $\sim\sim p$ the second occurrence of $\sim$ is subordinate to the first, and in $\sim(p \vee q) \wedge r$, $\vee$ is subordinate to $\sim$, while both $\vee$ and $\sim$ are subordinate to $\wedge$. Thus, any formula that is not atomic contains one occurrence of a connective which is not subordinate to any other occurrence. This is the *main connective* of the formula. Thus, in $\sim\sim p$ the main connective is the first occurrence of $\sim$, while in $\sim(p \vee q) \wedge r$ the main connective is $\wedge$.

The method of syntactic trees provide a clear visual representation of this hierarchy. In the syntactic tree of a formula, we can see that an occurrence of a connective is subordinate to another because its scope occupies a lower node with respect to the scope of the other, in the same branch. The main connective appears only in the root, because it corresponds to the last stage in the construction of the formula.

5.4   Interpretation

Now we will turn to the semantics of L. To define a semantics for a language is to define a set of interpretations that make its formulas true or false. An interpretation of L is a *valuation*, that is, an assignment of truth values to the atomic formulas of L:

Definition 5.3   An *interpretation* of L is a function that assigns 1 or 0 to each atomic formula of L.

An interpretation so understood represents a possible combination of truth values of simple sentences, such as 'Snow is white', 'It is raining', and so on. That is, it represents a way things might be.

From Definition 5.3 it turns out that, for every atomic formula α and every interpretation V, either α is true in V or it is false in V. The truth value of α in V is nothing but the value assigned to α by V. Since V does not assign truth values to complex formulas, in order to have a definition of truth in V that holds for every α it must be taken into account that complex formulas are truth functions of their constituents. The definition goes as follows, where $[\alpha]_V$ indicates the truth value of α in V:

Definition 5.4
1. If α is an atomic formula, $[\alpha]_V = 1$ iff $V(\alpha) = 1$;
2. $[\sim\alpha]_V = 1$ iff $[\alpha]_V = 0$;
3. $[\alpha \supset \beta]_V = 1$ iff $[\alpha]_V = 0$ or $[\beta]_V = 1$;
4. $[\alpha \wedge \beta]_V = 1$ iff $[\alpha]_V = 1$ and $[\beta]_V = 1$;
5. $[\alpha \vee \beta]_V = 1$ iff $[\alpha]_V = 1$ or $[\beta]_V = 1$.

Let it be agreed that an interpretation V *verifies* a formula α when $[\alpha]_V = 1$, and that V *falsifies* α when $[\alpha]_V = 0$. Verification and falsification can also be defined for sets of formulas: V verifies a set of formulas Γ when it verifies all the formulas in Γ, while it falsifies Γ when it falsifies at least some formulas in Γ.

5.5   Truth Tables

To calculate the truth value of a formula in an interpretation it suffices to follow
the syntactic tree of the formula. If one starts from the truth values of the leaves,
one can determine the truth value of each node in the tree, until one reaches the
root. Consider the formula $\sim(p \vee q) \wedge r$. Suppose that the values of p, q, r are
respectively $1, 0, 1$. As illustrated in Sect. 5.2, the formula to which p and q are
immediately subordinated is $p \vee q$. So we can assign 1 to $p \vee q$, in accordance with
clause 5 of Definition 5.4. Then we go up to $\sim(p \vee q)$, which gets 0 by clause 2
of Definition 5.4. Finally, from $\sim(p \vee q)$ and r we reach the root, $\sim(p \vee q) \wedge r$,
which gets 0 by clause 4 of Definition 5.4. The truth value of $\sim(p \vee q) \wedge r$ can be
calculated in the same way for any other combination of truth values of p, q, r.

The standard way to display the combinations of truth values that can be assigned
to the sentence letters in a formula is to draw a *truth table* that has a row for each
assignment. The simplest case is that in which the formula contains a single sentence
letter, say p. In this case the possible assignments are two, as in the truth table of $\sim p$:

p	$\sim p$
1	0
0	1

If the sentence letters are two, say p and q, the possible assignments are four. For
each of the two values that p can get, there are two values that q can get. Here are
the truth tables of $p \supset q$, $p \wedge q$, and $p \vee q$:

p	q	$p \supset q$
1	1	1
1	0	0
0	1	1
0	0	1

p	q	$p \wedge q$
1	1	1
1	0	0
0	1	0
0	0	0

p	q	$p \vee q$
1	1	1
1	0	1
0	1	1
0	0	0

If the sentence letters are three, the possible assignments are eight, and so on. In general, for n sentence letters, there are 2^n assignments of truth values. So the truth table of a formula with n sentence letters contains 2^n rows.

The invention and popularization of truth tables is traditionally attributed to Wittgenstein, who employed them in his *Tractatus Logico-Philosophicus*. But the use of matrices such as those illustrated above goes back at least to Charles Peirce. Moreover, Emil Post developed the same method concurrently but autonomously.[1]

Once we draw the truth table of a formula, we can calculate the truth value of the formula for every assignment of truth values to its sentence letters. For example, consider again the formula $\sim(p \vee q) \wedge r$. The truth table of this formula is the following:

p	q	r	$\sim(p \vee q) \wedge r$
1	1	1	0
1	1	0	0
1	0	1	0
1	0	0	0
0	1	1	0
0	1	0	0
0	0	1	1
0	0	0	0

The first row shows that $\sim(p \vee q) \wedge r$ is false if p, q, r are true. That is, for any V, if $V(p) = 1$, $V(q) = 1$, and $V(r) = 1$, then $[\sim(p \vee q) \wedge r]_V = 0$. Similarly, the other rows treat the other cases. In general, for any α, the truth table of α provides unmistakable information about the interpretations that verify α and those that falsify α. That is, it tells us how are the interpretations in which α is true, if they exist, and how are the interpretations in which α is false, if they exist.

Exercises

5.1 For each sequence of symbols, say if it is a formula:

(a) $p \sim q$
(b) $\supset p$
(c) $p \vee \sim q$

---

[1] Wittgenstein [68], 4.31–4.442, pp. 93–95. Charles Sanders Peirce (1839–1914) was an American logician and philosopher who wrote voluminously on a very wide range of topics. He articulated truth tables in an unpublished manuscript composed in 1893. Truth table matrices have also been discovered on the verso of a page of a text typed by Russell in 1912. Emil Leon Post (1897–1954) was a Polish-born American logician and mathematician, best known for his contributions to computability theory. He outlined the method of truth tables in Post [51].

5.2 Explain why any sequence of symbols which contains more left brackets than right brackets is not a formula.

5.3 Can a formula have two distinct syntactic trees?

5.4 What is the scope of $\vee$ in $\sim\sim(p \vee \sim q)$?

5.5 Indicate the main connective of $\sim(p \supset q) \vee r$.

5.6 Assuming that $V(p) = 1$ and $V(q) = 0$, calculate the value of the following formulas in V:

(a) $p \vee (p \supset q)$
(b) $p \supset \sim q$
(c) $\sim p \vee (p \wedge q)$

5.7 Draw the truth table of the following formulas:

(a) $\sim\sim p$
(b) $\sim q \supset \sim p$
(c) $\sim p \vee q$

5.8 Is there an interpretation that verifies every sentence letter?

5.9 Is there a sentence letter that is verified by all interpretations?

5.10 Is there an interpretation that verifies every formula?

Chapter 6
Logical Consequence in L

6.1 Definition of Logical Consequence

As anticipated in Sect. 3.4, there are two ways to characterize a set of valid forms expressible in a language: one is semantic, the other is syntactic. This chapter outlines the semantic method, which hinges on the notion of *logical consequence*. A formula α is a logical consequence of a set of formulas Γ when every interpretation that verifies Γ also verifies α. That is,

Definition 6.1 $\Gamma \vDash \alpha$ iff there is no interpretation that verifies Γ but falsifies α.

The symbol $\vDash$ indicates that α logically follows from Γ. For example, $\{p \supset q, p\} \vDash q$, since there is no interpretation that verifies $p \supset q$ and p but falsifies q. Or equivalently, omitting curly brackets, $p \supset q, p \vDash q$. The symbol $\nvDash$, instead, indicates that there is no logical consequence. One can write $\Gamma \nvDash \alpha$ to assert the existence of a *counterexample*, that is, an interpretation that verifies Γ but falsifies α.

Note that, since Γ is any set of formulas, it can contain a single formula β or even no formulas at all. In the first case one can say that α is a logical consequence of β, and write $\beta \vDash \alpha$. The second case is that in which $\Gamma = \emptyset$ and α is true in all interpretations. In this case one can simply write $\vDash \alpha$, and call α *valid*. For example, $\vDash p \vee \sim p$. A valid formula represents a logical truth, that is, a sentence that is true in virtue of its logical form. More specifically, a logical truth expressible in a propositional language is called *tautology*.

Note also that, although Definition 6.1 concerns argument forms, that is, ordered pairs of sets of formulas and formulas, the notion of logical consequence also applies, derivatively, to the arguments that instantiate those forms. If $\Gamma \vDash \alpha$, and Δ/β is an argument that instantiates Γ/α, one can say that β is a logical consequence of Δ.

© The Author(s), under exclusive license to Springer Nature Switzerland AG 2021 53
A. Iacona, *LOGIC: Lecture Notes for Philosophy, Mathematics, and Computer Science*, Springer Undergraduate Texts in Philosophy,
https://doi.org/10.1007/978-3-030-64811-4_6

6.2   Other Logical Properties and Relations

In Sect. 2.4 we considered four basic informal notions: entailment, consistency, equivalence, and contradiction. Logical consequence is a formal counterpart of entailment, where possibilities are replaced by interpretations. This section shows that consistency, equivalence, and contradiction also have formal counterparts defined in terms of the semantics of L.

The formal counterpart of consistency is *satisfiability*:

Definition 6.2   A set of formulas Γ is *satisfiable* iff some interpretation verifies Γ.

If Γ is not satisfiable, that is, no interpretation verifies Γ, then Γ is *unsatisfiable*. For example, $\{p, q\}$ is satisfiable, while $\{p, q, \sim p\}$ is unsatisfiable.

The formal counterpart of equivalence is *logical equivalence*:

Definition 6.3   Two formulas α and β are *logically equivalent* iff they have the same value in every interpretation.

Since α and β have the same value in every interpretation just in case $\alpha \vDash \beta$ and $\beta \vDash \alpha$, one can write $\alpha \vDash\!\dashv \beta$ to express this relation. Here are three interesting examples of logical equivalence. The first is *De Morgan's Laws*: $\sim(\alpha \vee \beta) \vDash\!\dashv \sim\alpha \wedge \sim\beta$, and $\sim(\alpha \wedge \beta) \vDash\!\dashv \sim\alpha \vee \sim\beta$. Given Double Negation, we also get $\sim(\sim\alpha \vee \sim\beta) \vDash\!\dashv \alpha \wedge \beta$, and $\sim(\sim\alpha \wedge \sim\beta) \vDash\!\dashv \alpha \vee \beta$.[1]

The second example is Contraposition. This principle, which was phrased in terms of entailment in Sect. 2.5, can also be phrased as follows: if $\alpha \supset \beta$ is true, then $\sim\beta \supset \sim\alpha$ is true. Given Double Negation, we also get that if $\sim\beta \supset \sim\alpha$ is true, then $\alpha \supset \beta$ is true, which is to say that $\alpha \supset \beta \vDash\!\dashv \sim\beta \supset \sim\alpha$.

The third example is *Exportation*: $(\alpha \wedge \beta) \supset \gamma \vDash\!\dashv \alpha \supset (\beta \supset \gamma)$. Exportation holds because the only case in which $(\alpha \wedge \beta) \supset \gamma$ is false is that in which α and β are true and γ is false, which is exactly the case in which $\alpha \supset (\beta \supset \gamma)$ is false.

The formal counterpart of contradiction is defined as follows:

Definition 6.4   Two formulas α and β are *contradictory* iff they have different values in every interpretation.

This is to say that $\alpha \vDash \sim\beta$ and $\beta \vDash \sim\alpha$. For example, p and $\sim p$ are contradictory, and the same goes for $p \supset q$ and $p \wedge \sim q$.

---

[1] Augustus De Morgan (1806–1871) was a British logician and mathematician who studied at the University of Cambridge and taught at University College, London. He made several important contributions to logic, which include the formulation of the laws that bear his name.

6.3 Important Facts About Logical Consequence

Logical consequence exhibits properties that are analogous to the properties of entailment outlined in Sect. 2.5. Let us begin with Reflexivity, Monotonicity, and Cut.

Theorem 6.1 $\alpha \vDash \alpha$

Proof Trivially, any interpretation that verifies α verifies α.   □

Theorem 6.2 *If* $\Gamma \vDash \alpha$ *and* $\Gamma \subseteq \Delta$, *then* $\Delta \vDash \alpha$.

Proof Assume that $\Gamma \vDash \alpha$ and $\Gamma \subseteq \Delta$. Since $\Gamma \subseteq \Delta$, any interpretation that verifies Δ verifies Γ. Since $\Gamma \vDash \alpha$, any interpretation that verifies Γ verifies α.   □

Theorem 6.3 *If* $\Gamma \vDash \alpha$ *and* $\Delta \cup \{\alpha\} \vDash \beta$, *then* $\Gamma \cup \Delta \vDash \beta$.

Proof Assume that $\Gamma \vDash \alpha$ and $\Delta \cup \{\alpha\} \vDash \beta$. Now suppose that a given interpretation verifies $\Gamma \cup \Delta$. Since that interpretation verifies Γ, by the first assumption it verifies α. Since it also verifies Δ, it verifies $\Delta \cup \{\alpha\}$. By the second assumption, then, it verifies β.   □

As in the case of entailment, Theorems 6.1 and 6.2 imply that $\Gamma \vDash \alpha$ whenever $\alpha \in \Gamma$.

The following theorem concerns Proof by Contradiction:

Theorem 6.4 *If* $\Gamma \cup \{\alpha\} \vDash \beta$ *and* $\Gamma \cup \{\alpha\} \vDash \sim\beta$, *then* $\Gamma \vDash \sim\alpha$.

Proof Assume that $\Gamma \cup \{\alpha\} \vDash \beta$ and $\Gamma \cup \{\alpha\} \vDash \sim\beta$. Then no interpretation verifies $\Gamma \cup \{\alpha\}$. For if some interpretation verified $\Gamma \cup \{\alpha\}$, the same interpretation would verify β and $\sim\beta$, which is impossible. It follows that every interpretation that verifies Γ falsifies α, hence verifies $\sim\alpha$.   □

A fifth theorem corresponds to Theorem 2.5:

Theorem 6.5 $\Gamma \vDash \sim\alpha$ *iff* $\Gamma \cup \{\alpha\}$ *is unsatisfiable.*

Proof Assume that $\Gamma \vDash \sim\alpha$. Then, every interpretation that verifies Γ falsifies α. Therefore, $\Gamma \cup \{\alpha\}$ is unsatisfiable. Now assume that $\Gamma \cup \{\alpha\}$ is unsatisfiable. Then, as explained in the proof of Theorem 6.4, every interpretation that verifies Γ falsifies α, hence verifies $\sim\alpha$.   □

Finally, the following two theorems correspond to Theorems 2.6 and 2.7:

Theorem 6.6 *If* Γ *is unsatisfiable, then* $\Gamma \vDash \alpha$, *for every* α.

Proof Assume that Γ is unsatisfiable. Then there is no interpretation that verifies Γ. So, for any α, there is no interpretation that verifies Γ but falsifies α.   □

Theorem 6.7 *If* $\vDash \alpha$, *then* $\Gamma \vDash \alpha$, *for any* Γ.

Proof Assume that α is true in all interpretations. Then, for any Γ, there is no interpretation that verifies Γ but falsifies α.   □

Note that the converse of Theorem 6.7 holds as well: if $\Gamma \vDash \alpha$ for any Γ, then $\vDash \alpha$. If α were false in some interpretation, $\sim\!\alpha$ would be true in that interpretation, so there would be at least one Γ such that $\Gamma \nvDash \alpha$, namely, $\{\sim\!\alpha\}$. Moreover, note that $\Gamma \vDash \alpha$ for any Γ if and only if $\emptyset \vDash \alpha$. This simply follows from Theorem 6.7 and the fact that $\emptyset \vDash \alpha$ is equivalent to $\vDash \alpha$.

6.4   Logical Consequence as a Test for Validity

The notion of logical consequence can be employed to test arguments. Suppose that an argument Γ/α is adequately formalized in L as Δ/β, where Δ is a set of formulas that represents Γ and β is a formula that represents α. If one knows that $\Delta \vDash \beta$, one can conclude that Γ/α is valid. Similarly, if one knows that $\Delta \nvDash \beta$, one can conclude that Γ/α is not valid in virtue of formal properties expressible in L. Even though this does not rule out that Γ/α is valid, as noted in Sect. 3.2, it is still something.

How can one know that $\Delta \vDash \beta$? By means of truth tables. Consider the following argument:

(1)   It is not the case that it is raining and snowing
(2)   It is raining
(3)   It is not snowing

This argument is adequately formalized in L as $\sim\!(p \wedge q)$, $p/\!\sim\!q$. So, the question is whether $\sim\!(p \wedge q)$, $p \vDash \sim\!q$. To answer this question we can draw a truth table which enables us to calculate the value of each of the formulas that occur in the schema for each assignment of values to p and q:

p	q	$\sim\!(p \wedge q)$	p	$\sim\!q$
1	1	0	1	0
1	0	1	1	1
0	1	1	0	0
0	0	1	0	1

Now it suffices to go through the rows where $\sim\!(p \wedge q)$ and p are both true, and check if $\sim\!q$ is true in those rows. As the table shows, there is only one case in which $\sim\!(p \wedge q)$ and p are both true, the second. Since $\sim\!q$ is true in that case, there is no counterexample. This means that $\sim\!(p \wedge q)$, $p \vDash \sim\!q$.

Most of the times it is not necessary to write down all the rows and check each of them. To shorten the procedure, one may reason "backwards" and try to find a counterexample that shows that $\Delta \nvDash \beta$. In the case of the argument above, this means that one may start by considering the case in which $\sim\!q$ is false, to see whether it is possible that in that case $\sim\!(p \wedge q)$ and p are both true. This way one reasons only on the first and third row of the table. So, the options to be considered are two: $\sim(p \land q)$ is false and p is true, $\sim(p \land q)$ is true and p is false. In neither case the formulas are both true.

Note that, when $\Delta = \emptyset$, the procedure outlined boils down to a truth table for a single formula. So it becomes a test for logical truth. For example, 'Either it is raining or it is not raining' is a tautology, in that it is true no matter whether it is raining or not. This sentence instantiates Excluded Middle, and is formalized in L as $p \lor \sim p$. So we can check that $\vDash p \lor \sim p$ by means of a truth table.

6.5 Effective Computability

This last section introduces the notion of *effective computability*, which can be spelled out informally as follows:

Definition 6.5 An *effective method* for solving a problem is a procedure for computing the answer that, if followed correctly and as far as may be necessary, it is bound to give the right answer, and no wrong answers, in a finite number of steps.

The idea expressed by this definition is that an effective computation involves executing an algorithm that successfully terminates. An algorithm is a set of step-by-step instructions, with each step clearly specified in advance, so that its execution requires a determinate sequence of discrete procedures, and there is no room left for imagination, intuition, or any other fallible ability. The algorithm successfully terminates when its execution produces the right sort of output in a finite number of steps.

An example of effective computation is addition. Given any two numbers n and m, the rule by means of which we compute $n + m$ is a purely mechanical procedure that requires a finite number of steps. This is to say that the addition function is effectively computable. More generally,

Definition 6.6 A function F is *effectively computable* iff there is an effective method to compute the value of F for any argument.

To put it another way, an effectively computable function is a function that in principle could be computed by a machine, where 'in principle' means that we leave aside any limitation that depends on the size or speed of the machine.

We often use algorithmic routines not only to compute the values of a function but also to establish whether a property or relation holds. In the case of numerical properties and relations this boils down to the same thing, for a numerical property or relation is definable in terms of a *characteristic function*: for any numerical property P, there is a function C_P such that if n is P, then $C_P(n) = 0$, otherwise $C_P(n) = 1$ (or the other way round, the choice of values is entirely arbitrary), and for any numerical relation R, there is a function C_R such that if R obtains between m and n, then $C_R(m, n) = 0$, otherwise $C_R(m, n) = 1$. Therefore, any procedure to compute the value of the characteristic function of a numerical property or relation is *ipso facto* a procedure to decide whether the property or relation obtains.

More generally, the notion of effective computability applies to any property or relation, for it applies to the set that constitutes its extension. The following definition holds for any set:

Definition 6.7 A set Γ is *decidable* iff there is an effective method to tell, for any x, whether or not $x \in \Gamma$.

It is easy to see that any finite set is decidable. If Γ is finite, one can list all its elements and check, for each of them, whether it is x. If $\Gamma = \emptyset$, decidability is assumed by convention. An infinite set can be decidable as well. For example, the set of primes is decidable because there is an algorithm that tells us, for every number, whether it is prime. Another example is the set of formulas of L: for any finite sequence of symbols of L, Definition 5.1 tells us whether it is a formula of L.

Now we can state one important fact about the semantics of L:

Theorem 6.8 *For any finite set of formulas Γ, the set of logical consequences of Γ is decidable.*

Proof For any finite set of formulas Γ and any formula α, there is an effective method to decide whether $\Gamma \vDash \alpha$, the method of truth tables. Therefore, for any formula α, there is an effective method to decide whether α belongs to the set of logical consequences of Γ.   □

This fact is important because any argument that we may want to represent in L is constituted by a finite set of sentences, so it is formalized by means of a finite set of formulas Γ and a formula α. Since the validity of the argument can be tested by checking whether $\Gamma \vDash \alpha$, as explained in Sect. 6.4, this means that, for any argument that we may want to represent in L, the semantics of L provides an effective method to test its validity. Note that Theorem 6.8 entails that the set of valid formulas of L is decidable, for the latter is nothing but the set of logical consequences of Γ for $\Gamma = \emptyset$.

The quest for a mechanical procedure to test arguments is a leitmotif of the history of logic. In the thirteenth century, Ramon Llull aspired to construct a system of signs capable of generating conclusions, which could serve as a tool for winning Muslims to the Christian faith.[2] A long time later, Thomas Hobbes described reasoning as a computation which essentially consists in adding and subtracting ideas.[3] And the ultimate aim of Leibniz's *characteristica universalis* was to put reasoning on a firmer basis by reducing it to a matter of calculation: he prophesized that, once in possession of a formal method for drawing conclusions, men of good

---

[2]Ramon Llull (c.1232–c.1315) was a Catalan philosopher, mystic and poet. He is best known as the inventor of *Ars Magna*, which he understood as the art of finding truth, see Llull [45].

[3]Thomas Hobbes (1588–1679) was an English philosopher, scientist, and historian, best known for his political philosophy. He expressed his view about logic in Hobbes [26], 1.2.

will desiring to settle a dispute will use their pens and calculate.[4] Theorem 6.8 shows that, at least as far as propositional logic is concerned, it is realistic to expect a correlation between formality and decidability. Note that this is not quite the same thing as to say that a propositional language provides a mechanical procedure for settling disputes, as Leibniz desired, since people discuss in natural languages, and the formalization of their arguments is *not* a mechanical process. Still, decidability is far from trivial, as we shall see, because it does not hold for more complex languages.

Exercises

6.1 Can a set formed by a single atomic formula be unsatisfiable?

6.2 Explain why $\alpha \vDash \beta$ if and only if $\alpha \supset \beta$ is a tautology.

6.3 Show by means of truth tables that affirming the consequent and denying the antecedent (Sect. 3.2) are invalid forms.

6.4 Check the validity of Tisias' argument (Exercise 1.6) by using a truth table.

6.5 Show by means of truth tables that the following are tautologies:

(a) $p \supset p$
(b) $\sim(p \wedge \sim p)$
(c) $p \vee \sim p$

6.6 Show what follows by means of truth tables:

(a) $p \wedge p \Dashv\vDash p$
(b) $p \vee p \Dashv\vDash p$
(c) $p \wedge q \Dashv\vDash q \wedge p$
(d) $p \vee q \Dashv\vDash q \vee p$

6.7 Prove De Morgan's Laws, Contraposition, and Exportation by means of truth tables.

6.8 Explain why $\alpha \Dashv\vDash \beta$ if and only if $\vDash \alpha \equiv \beta$.

6.9 Explain why $\sim(\alpha \wedge \beta)$ is a tautology if α and β are contradictory.

6.10 Is logical consequence a transitive relation?

---

[4]Leibniz [36], p. 184, Leibniz [37], p. 30.

Chapter 7
The System G

7.1 Derivation

This chapter outlines a natural deduction system in L called **G**. As explained in
Sect. 3.4, a natural deduction system is constituted by a set of inference rules that
are taken to be intuitively correct. Assuming our definition of validity as necessary
truth preservation, this is to say that the rules of **G** necessarily preserve truth. But it
is important to understand that an intuitively correct inference rule may equally be
described without appealing to the notion of truth. An antirealist may consistently
treat the rules of **G** as rules that necessarily preserve assertibility: if one is justified
to assert the premises, then one is justified to assert the conclusion. As we will see,
G is defined without any reference to the semantics of L.[1]

A valid reasoning is represented in **G** as a *derivation* of a formula α from a set
of formulas Γ:

Definition 7.1 A *derivation of α from* Γ is a finite sequence of formulas that ends
with α such that (i) each formula in the sequence is an assumption or is obtained
from other formulas that precede it by means of some inference rule, and (ii) α
depends only on assumptions that belong to Γ.

Three clarifications are needed to fully grasp this definition. First, any formula
can occur as an assumption in a derivation of α from Γ. This is why (i) does not
imply that the formulas that occur as assumptions belong to Γ. The key difference
between assumptions and formulas obtained by means of inference rules is that the
former do not depend on other formulas. An assumption depends only on itself.

Second, (ii) requires that α depends only on assumptions that belong to Γ. Since
the derivation can include assumptions that do not belong to Γ, this means that

---

[1] I call this system **G** because it is very similar to that presented in Gentzen [18].

© The Author(s), under exclusive license to Springer Nature Switzerland AG 2021
A. Iacona, *LOGIC: Lecture Notes for Philosophy, Mathematics, and Computer
Science*, Springer Undergraduate Texts in Philosophy,
https://doi.org/10.1007/978-3-030-64811-4_7

α must not depend on such assumptions. As we will see, some inference rules involve *auxiliary assumptions*, that is, formulas that are considered hypothetically just to show their consequences. Auxiliary assumptions are used temporarily and then *discharged*, that is, they do not form part of the baggage of premises that we carry when we get to the conclusion.

Third, (ii) does *not* require that α depends on all the formulas that belong to Γ. Γ can include formulas that do not occur among the assumptions on which α depends. That is, it can happen that the elements of Γ that occur in the derivation of α belong to a subset of Γ smaller than Γ.

A derivation will be written as a vertical sequence of numbered lines, where the number of each line is used to refer to the formula which occurs in the line. Thus, if the derivation is constituted by n formulas $\beta_1, \ldots, \beta_n$, it will have n lines. This vertical sequence will be enriched with further signs to the right and to the left of each formula β_i, where $1 \leq i \leq n$. The notation to the right of β_i provides an explicit justification of the appearance of β_i at that stage of the derivation. If β_i is an assumption, it will be indicated with an A; if β_i is obtained from other formulas that occur at earlier lines by means of an inference rule, we will write the name of the rule and the numbers of the lines. These numbers, which we will call *right numbers*, are analogous to the numbers used in Sect. 1.3, but they involve reference to specific inference rules. To the left of β_i, instead, we will write numbers separated by a comma, for example 1, 3, 4, that indicate the lines on which β_i depends. These numbers will be called *left numbers*.

7.2   Rules for $\sim$

G has eight inference rules: I$\sim$, E$\sim$, I$\supset$, E$\supset$, I$\wedge$, E$\wedge$, I$\vee$, E$\vee$. The letters I and E stand respectively for 'introduction' and 'elimination', because each rule is understood either as a legitimate way to obtain formulas which contain a given occurrence of a connective from formulas which do not contain that occurrence, or as a legitimate way to obtain formulas which do not contain a given occurrence of a connective from formulas which contain that occurrence.

Let us start with the rules for $\sim$. E$\sim$ is stated as follows:

E$\sim$ From $\sim\sim\alpha$ one can derive α.

This rule expresses in syntactic terms the claim that $\sim\sim\alpha$ entails α, which directly follows from Double Negation. Given E$\sim$, if you have a derivation of $\sim\sim\alpha$, you can extend it to a derivation of α by adding one line. α will depend on the same assumptions on which $\sim\sim\alpha$ depends. The notation is very simple: only one right number is required, which indicates the line of $\sim\sim\alpha$. As to the left numbers, they are the same as those of $\sim\sim\alpha$. So, E$\sim$ is used as follows:

z (n) $\sim\sim\alpha$

          .

z (m) α E~ n

For example, here is a derivation of $\sim p$ from $\sim\sim\sim p$:

1   (1) $\sim\sim\sim p$ A
1   (2) $\sim p$ E~ 1

I~ is more complex, as it involves one auxiliary assumption:

I~ If assuming α (given other assumptions) one can derive β and $\sim\beta$, then (from those assumptions) one can derive $\sim\alpha$.

The principle that underpins this rule is Proof by Contradiction: if α (given other assumptions) entails β and $\sim\beta$, then α can be rejected (on the basis of those assumptions). Here 'entails' is replaced by 'one can derive': to say that from α (given other assumptions) one can derive β and $\sim\beta$ is to say that, for some Γ, there is a derivation of β from $\Gamma \cup \{\alpha\}$ and there is a derivation of $\sim\beta$ from $\Gamma \cup \{\alpha\}$. Obviously, it may happen that $\Gamma = \emptyset$, so that $\Gamma \cup \{\alpha\} = \{\alpha\}$, and this is why the expression 'given other assumptions' is bracketed in the formulation of the rule.

     I~ is used as follows:

n (n) α A

                      .

z (m) β

                      .

x (o) $\sim\beta$

                      .

$(z + x) - n$ (p) $\sim\alpha$ I~ n, m, o

Since I~ takes three formulas as input and gives one formula as output, it requires three right numbers to indicate respectively the line of α, the line of β, and the line of $\sim\beta$. As to the left numbers, the important thing to bear in mind is that $\sim\alpha$ does not depend on α, for α is discharged. So, $\sim\alpha$ depends on all the assumptions on which β and $\sim\beta$ depend except α. Here z stands for the numbers that indicate the assumptions on which β depends, and x stands for the numbers that indicate the assumptions on which $\sim\beta$ depends. The symbols $+$ and $-$ in the last line indicate that the left numbers in that line result from adding z to x and then subtracting n, even though we are not talking about addition and subtraction properly understood, for the result is not a number but a sequence of numbers separated by commas. For example, here is a derivation of $\sim q$ from p and $\sim p$:

1	(1)	p	A
2	(2)	$\sim p$	A
3	(3)	q	A
1,2	(4)	$\sim q$	I$\sim$ 3,1,2

In this case, α is q, β is p, and $\sim\beta$ is $\sim p$. (4) depends only on (1) and (2), because (3) is discharged. Note that (1) and (2) occur as assumptions, so they are not obtained from (3). That is, (3) plays no role in the derivation of (1) and (2). But you don't have to worry about this. I$\sim$ contemplates the possibility that α is inert in that it plays no role in the derivation of β and $\sim\beta$. In general, given a set of formulas that includes a contradiction, one can always infer the negation of one of the formulas in the set from the remaining formulas. This accords with the idea that, if $\Gamma \cup \{\alpha\}$ is an inconsistent set of sentences, then Γ entails $\sim\alpha$ (see Theorem 2.5).

7.3 Rules for $\supset$

$\supset$ is similar to $\sim$ in that it has a very simple elimination rule and a more complex introduction rule. E$\supset$ is nothing but Modus Ponens:

E$\supset$ From $\alpha \supset \beta$ and α one can derive β.

In this case β depends on the same assumptions on which $\alpha \supset \beta$ and α depend. So E$\supset$ is used as follows:

x	(n)	$\alpha \supset \beta$	
		.	
z	(m)	α	
		.	
$x + z$	(o)	β	E$\supset n, m$

For example, here is a derivation of q from $r \supset p, p \supset q, r$:

1	(1)	$r \supset p$	A
2	(2)	$p \supset q$	A
3	(3)	r	A
1,3	(4)	p	E$\supset$ 1,3
1,2,3	(5)	q	E$\supset$ 2,4

I$\supset$ is more complex in that it involves one auxiliary assumption:

I$\supset$ If assuming α (given other assumptions) one can derive β, then (from those assumptions) one can derive $\alpha \supset \beta$.

To say that assuming α (given other assumptions) one can derive β is to say that, for some Γ, there is a derivation of β from $\Gamma \cup \{\alpha\}$. The formula $\alpha \supset \beta$ thus obtained will depend on Γ. So I$\supset$ is used as follows:

n (n) α A

               .

z (m) β

               .

$z - n$ (o) $\alpha \supset \beta$ I$\supset n, m$

Beside $\alpha \supset \beta$ there are two right numbers, which respectively indicate the line of α and the line of β. The left numbers $z - n$, instead, indicate the assumptions on which β depends except α, because α is discharged. For example, consider the following derivation of $p \supset q$ from $\sim p$:

1   (1) $\sim p$ A
2   (2) p A
3   (3) $\sim q$ A
1,2   (4) $\sim\sim q$ I$\sim$ 3,2,1
1,2   (5) q E$\sim$ 4
1   (6) $p \supset q$ I$\supset$ 2,5

As in the case of I$\sim$, it is not necessary that β is obtained from α. That is, I$\supset$ contemplates the possibility that α is inert. For example, the use of I$\supset$ in the following derivation of $p \supset q$ from q is correct:

1   (1) q A
2   (2) p A
1   (3) $p \supset q$ I$\supset$ 2,1

Here (2) plays no role in the derivation of (1). If one thinks about the truth table of $\supset$, this derivation makes perfect sense: if q is true, then $p \supset q$ must be true.

7.4 Rules for ∧

In the case of $\wedge$, neither of the two rules involves auxiliary assumptions. E$\wedge$ is very simple:

E$\wedge$ From $\alpha \wedge \beta$ one can derive α, and one can derive β.

In this case the formula obtained, α or β, depends on the assumptions on which $\alpha \wedge \beta$ depends. So E$\wedge$ is used as follows:

x   (*n*)   α ∧ β

.

x   (*m*)   α   E∧ *n*

Or alternatively:

x   (*n*)   α ∧ β

.

x   (*m*)   β   E∧ *n*

The right number *n* indicates the line of α ∧ β. Instead, the left numbers are those of α ∧ β. For example, here is a derivation of (*p* ∧ *q*) ⊃ *r* from *p* ⊃ (*q* ⊃ *r*):

1	(1)	*p* ⊃ (*q* ⊃ *r*)	A
2	(2)	*p* ∧ *q*	A
2	(3)	*p*	E∧ 2
2	(4)	*q*	E∧ 2
1,2	(5)	*q* ⊃ *r*	E⊃ 1,3
1,2	(6)	*r*	E⊃ 5,4
1	(7)	(*p* ∧ *q*) ⊃ *r*	I⊃ 2,6

I∧ is equally simple:

I∧ From α and β one can derive α ∧ β.

The conjunction obtained will depend on all the assumptions on which its conjuncts depend. So I∧ is used as follows:

x   (*n*)   α

.

z   (*m*)   β

.

x + *z*   (*o*)   α ∧ β   I∧ *n*, *m*

The right numbers *n*, *m* indicate respectively the line of α and the line of β. The left numbers *x* + *z* indicate the assumptions on which α and β depend. For example, I∧ is used in the following derivation of *p* ⊃ (*q* ⊃ *r*) from (*p* ∧ *q*) ⊃ *r*:

1	(1)	$(p \wedge q) \supset r$	A
2	(2)	p	A
3	(3)	q	A
2,3	(4)	$p \wedge q$	I∧ 2,3
1,2,3	(5)	r	E⊃ 1,4
1,2	(6)	$q \supset r$	I⊃ 3,5
1	(7)	$p \supset (q \supset r)$	I⊃ 2,6

One interesting implication of the two rules just illustrated concerns inert assumptions. In Sect. 7.2 we saw that I∼ can be employed as follows:

1	(1)	p	A
2	(2)	$\sim p$	A
3	(3)	q	A
1,2	(4)	$\sim q$	I∼ 3,1,2

Here the contradiction that leads to (4) is obtained without using (3). Similarly, in Sect. 7.3 we saw that I⊃ can be used as follows:

1	(1)	q	A
2	(2)	p	A
1	(3)	$p \supset q$	I⊃ 2,1

Here (1) is obtained without using (2). As noted in Sects. 7.2 and 7.3, one way to see that the derivations of this kind are acceptable is to think that they correspond to valid forms. But independently of such considerations, I∧ and E∧ show that there is a trivial way to transform any derivation in which a given assumption is inert into a derivation in which that assumption is not inert. For example, the first of the two derivations considered can be extended as follows:

1	(1)	p	A
2	(2)	$\sim p$	A
3	(3)	q	A
1,3	(4)	$q \wedge p$	I∧ 3,1
1,3	(5)	p	E∧ 4
1,2	(6)	$\sim q$	I∼ 3,5,2

In this derivation, (5) is obtained from (3). The same goes for the second derivation, which can be extended as follows:

1	(1)	q	A
2	(2)	p	A
1,2	(3)	$p \wedge q$	I∧ 2,1
1,2	(4)	q	E∧ 3
1	(5)	$p \supset q$	I⊃ 2,4

Here (4) is obtained from (2). In general, for any derivation in which an assumption is inert, there is another derivation in which the same assumption is not inert. This is just another way of saying that there is nothing wrong with inert assumptions.

7.5   Rules for ∨

In the case of ∨, the introduction rule is the easy one, while the elimination rule involves two auxiliary assumptions. I∨ is phrased as follows:

I∨ From α, or from β, one can derive $\alpha \vee \beta$.

Here $\alpha \vee \beta$ depends on the same assumptions on which α, or β, depends. So I∨ is used as follows:

x	(n)	α	
		.	
x	(m)	$\alpha \vee \beta$	I∨ n

Or alternatively:

x	(n)	β	
		.	
x	(m)	$\alpha \vee \beta$	I∨ n

The right number n indicates the line of α, or β. The left numbers, instead, are the same as those of α, or β. For example, I∨ is used in the following derivation of $\sim p \vee q$ from $p \supset q$:

1	(1)	$p \supset q$	A
2	(2)	$\sim(\sim p \vee q)$	A
3	(3)	p	A
1,3	(4)	q	E⊃ 1,3
1,3	(5)	$\sim p \vee q$	I∨ 4
1,2	(6)	$\sim p$	I∼ 3,5,2
1,2	(7)	$\sim p \vee q$	I∨ 6
1	(8)	$\sim\sim(\sim p \vee q)$	I∼ 2,7,2
1	(9)	$\sim p \vee q$	E∼ 8

E∨ is more complex. The idea that underlies this rule is that if one has a reason to accept a disjunction, and each of its disjuncts, taken separately, entails a given sentence, then one has a reason to accept that sentence. Think about Tisias' argument: Tisias considers both the hypothesis that Córax taught him to persuade anyone of anything and the negation of that hypothesis, and observes that both horns of the dilemma yield the conclusion that he does not have to pay.

E∨   Given $\alpha \vee \beta$, if assuming α (given other assumptions) one can derive γ, and assuming β (given other assumptions) one can derive γ, then (from the assumptions other than α used in the first case and the assumptions other than β used in the second case) one can derive γ.

E∨ requires two auxiliary assumptions: α and β. One has to show that, for some Γ, there is a derivation of γ from $\Gamma \cup \{\alpha\}$, and that, for some Δ, there is a derivation of γ from $\Delta \cup \{\beta\}$. Then, given $\alpha \vee \beta$, one can obtain γ from $\Gamma \cup \Delta$, that is, from the assumptions other than α (if they exist) used in the first derivation and from the assumptions other than β (if they exist) used in the second derivation. In other terms, γ will depend on the assumptions on which $\alpha \vee \beta$ depends, on the assumptions on which the first occurrence of γ depends except α, and on the assumptions on which the second occurrence of γ depends except β. So E∨ is used as follows:

x	(n)	$\alpha \vee \beta$	
		.	
m	(m)	α	A
		.	
y	(o)	γ	
		.	
p	(p)	β	A
		.	
z	(q)	γ	
		.	
$x, (y-m), (z-p)$	(r)	γ	E∨ n, m, o, p, q

The five numbers beside the third occurrence of γ indicate respectively the line of $\alpha \vee \beta$, the line of α, the line of the first occurrence of γ, the line of β, and the line of the second occurrence of γ. The left numbers, instead, indicate the assumptions on which $\alpha \vee \beta$ depends, the assumptions on which the first occurrence of γ depends except α, and the assumptions on which the second occurrence of γ depends except β. This means that α and β are discharged. For example, here is a derivation of $p \supset q$ from $\sim p \vee q$:

1   (1) $\sim p \vee q$ A
2   (2) p A
3   (3) $\sim p$ A
4   (4) $\sim q$ A
2,3   (5) $\sim\sim q$ I$\sim$ 4,2,3
2,3   (6) q E$\sim$ 5
7   (7) q A
1,2   (8) q E$\vee$ 1,3,6,7,7
1   (9) $p \supset q$ I$\supset$ 2,8

Note that E$\vee$ requires neither that the derivation of γ from $\Gamma \cup \{\alpha\}$ precedes the derivation of γ from $\Delta \cup \{\beta\}$ nor that the two derivations end at different lines, that is, that the first two occurrences of γ are distinct. To avoid confusion with the left numbers, it must be clear that, when one calculates the assumptions on which the third occurrence of γ depends, one must proceed as follows: first, calculate the assumptions on which the first occurrence of γ depends; second, calculate the assumptions on which the second occurrence of γ depends; third, put them together. This means that the subtraction of the number of α is to be made in the first step and the subtraction of the number of β is to be made in the second step. The two subtractions are not to be made at the end, after putting together the assumptions on which the third occurrence of γ depends.

Exercises

7.1 Derive q from p and $\sim p$.

7.2 Derive $p \supset q$ from $p \supset (p \supset q)$.

7.3 Derive $\sim p$ from $p \supset q$ and $p \supset \sim q$.

7.4 Derive p from $\sim p \supset p$.

7.5 Derive $q \wedge p$ from $p \wedge q$.

7.6 Derive $\sim(p \supset \sim q)$ from $p \wedge q$.

7.7 Derive $q \vee p$ from $p \vee q$.

7.8 Derive q from $p \vee q$ and $\sim p$.

7.9 Derive $(p \supset q) \wedge (r \supset q)$ from $(p \vee r) \supset q$.

7.10 Derive $(p \vee r) \supset q$ from $(p \supset q) \wedge (r \supset q)$.

Chapter 8
Derivability in G

8.1 Derivability and Related Notions

To say that a formula α is *derivable* from a set of formulas Γ in a system S is to say that there is a derivation of α from Γ in S. That is,

Definition 8.1 $\Gamma \vdash \alpha$ in S iff there is a derivation of α from Γ in S.

The symbol $\vdash$ indicates derivability. Accordingly, one can write $\Gamma \nvdash \alpha$ to say that α is not derivable from Γ. If $\Gamma \vdash \alpha$ and Γ contains a single formula β, one can say that α is derivable from β, and write $\beta \vdash \alpha$ without curly brackets.

Derivability is a formal counterpart of entailment which differs from logical consequence in that it is syntactic rather than semantic. As we have seen, the notion of derivation is defined in terms of a deductive apparatus and involves no reference to the interpretation of the language.

Just as one can define a syntactic analogue of logical consequence, one can define syntactic analogues of satisfiability, logical equivalence, and contradiction, given any system S.

Definition 8.2 A set of formulas Γ is *consistent* in S iff there is no formula α such that $\Gamma \vdash \alpha$ and $\Gamma \vdash \sim\alpha$ in S.

Definition 8.3 Two formulas α and β are *interderivable* in S iff $\alpha \vdash \beta$ and $\beta \vdash \alpha$ in S.

Definition 8.4 Two formulas α and β are *contradictory* in S iff $\alpha \vdash \sim\beta$ and $\beta \vdash \sim\alpha$ in S.

© The Author(s), under exclusive license to Springer Nature Switzerland AG 2021
A. Iacona, *LOGIC: Lecture Notes for Philosophy, Mathematics, and Computer Science*, Springer Undergraduate Texts in Philosophy,
https://doi.org/10.1007/978-3-030-64811-4_8

Definitions 8.1–8.4 hold for any system, so they apply to **G**. From now on the symbol ⊢ will be used without making explicit reference to the intended system, unless it is necessary to avoid ambiguity. Moreover, the symbol ⊣⊢ will be used to indicate interderivability.

If $\Gamma \vdash \alpha$ and $\Gamma = \emptyset$, one can write $\vdash \alpha$, which means that there is a *proof* of α. A proof is a derivation in which the last formula depends on no assumption. For example, the following derivation is a proof in **G**:

1	(1)	$\sim p$	A
2	(2)	$\sim\sim p$	A
1	(3)	$\sim\sim\sim p$	I$\sim$ 2,1,2
	(4)	$\sim p \supset \sim\sim\sim p$	I$\supset$ 1,3

Here (4) depends on no assumption, for (1) is discharged by applying I$\supset$ and (2) is discharged by applying I$\sim$. This proof shows that $\vdash \sim p \supset \sim\sim\sim p$. A provable formula is a *theorem*. Theorems are the syntactic counterpart of valid formulas, that is, they are formulas that can be justified independently of any assumption.

Note that the terms 'proof' and 'theorem' may be used in two distinct ways. In one sense, a proof is a sound reasoning phrased in the metalanguage, such as those indicated by the symbol □, and a theorem is an assertion that is justified by means of such a reasoning. In the other sense, a proof is a sequence of formulas that satisfies certain syntactic constraints, and a theorem is a formula for which there is such a sequence. It is important to be aware of this distinction, because one thing is to prove an assertion *about* a system, quite another thing is to prove a formula *in* a system.

8.2   Important Facts About Derivability

Derivability, just like logical consequence, exhibits properties that are analogous to the properties of entailment considered in Sect. 2.5. First, consider Reflexivity, Monotonicity, and Cut.

Theorem 8.1 $\alpha \vdash \alpha$

Proof If one simply assumes α, one trivially derives α. The sequence that contains α as its only formula is a derivation of α from α.   □

Theorem 8.2   *If* $\Gamma \vdash \alpha$ *and* $\Gamma \subseteq \Delta$, *then* $\Delta \vdash \alpha$.

Proof Assume that there is a derivation of α from Γ, and let d be such derivation. Assume that $\Gamma \subseteq \Delta$. Then d is a derivation of α from Δ, because all the assumptions on which α depends belong to Γ.   □

Theorem 8.3   *If* $\Gamma \vdash \alpha$ *and* $\Delta \cup \{\alpha\} \vdash \beta$, *then* $\Gamma \cup \Delta \vdash \beta$.

Proof Assume that there is a derivation d of α from Γ and that there is a derivation d' of β from $\Delta \cup \{\alpha\}$. If we eliminate α from the assumptions in d'—provided that

α occurs in d' as an assumption—and add the rest of the sequence to d starting after α, we obtain a derivation of β from $\Gamma \cup \Delta$.   □

As in the case of entailment and logical consequence, Theorems 8.1 and 8.2 entail that $\Gamma \vdash \alpha$ when $\alpha \in \Gamma$. Moreover, Theorem 8.3 entails that derivability is a transitive relation.

The following theorem shows that Proof by Contradiction holds in virtue of I$\sim$:

Theorem 8.4 *If $\Gamma \cup \{\alpha\} \vdash \beta$ and $\Gamma \cup \{\alpha\} \vdash \sim\beta$, then $\Gamma \vdash \sim\alpha$.*

Proof Suppose that β and $\sim\beta$ are obtained by using assumptions in $\Gamma \cup \{\alpha\}$. Then one can apply I$\sim$ and obtain $\sim\alpha$ from the assumptions in Γ.   □

A fifth theorem is analogous to Theorems 2.5 and 6.5:

Theorem 8.5 *$\Gamma \vdash \sim\alpha$ iff $\Gamma \cup \{\alpha\}$ is inconsistent.*

Proof Assume that $\Gamma \vdash \sim\alpha$. By Monotonicity (Theorem 8.2) we get that $\Gamma \cup \{\alpha\} \vdash \sim\alpha$. Since $\alpha \in \Gamma \cup \{\alpha\}$, we also get that $\Gamma \cup \{\alpha\} \vdash \alpha$. So $\Gamma \cup \{\alpha\}$ is inconsistent. Now assume that $\Gamma \cup \{\alpha\}$ is inconsistent. Then, for some β, one can derive β and $\sim\beta$ from $\Gamma \cup \{\alpha\}$. By Theorem 8.4, this entails that $\Gamma \vdash \sim\alpha$.   □

Finally, the two theorems below are analogous to Theorems 2.6 and 6.6 and to Theorems 2.7 and 6.7 respectively:

Theorem 8.6 *If Γ is inconsistent, then $\Gamma \vdash \alpha$, for any α.*

Proof Assume that Γ is inconsistent, that is, $\Gamma \vdash \beta$ and $\Gamma \vdash \sim\beta$ for some β. By Monotonicity (Theorem 8.2) it follows that, for any α, $\Gamma\cup\{\sim\alpha\} \vdash \beta$ and $\Gamma\cup\{\sim\alpha\} \vdash \sim\beta$. But if one can derive β and $\sim\beta$ from $\Gamma \cup \{\sim\alpha\}$, one can derive $\sim\sim\alpha$ from Γ by means of I$\sim$. Consequently, one can derive α from Γ by means of E$\sim$.   □

Theorem 8.7 *If $\vdash \alpha$, then $\Gamma \vdash \alpha$, for any Γ.*

Proof This directly follows from Monotonicity (Theorem 8.2).   □

Note that the converse of Theorem 8.7 holds as well: if $\Gamma \vdash \alpha$ for any Γ, then $\emptyset \vdash \alpha$, which means that $\vdash \alpha$.

8.3 Some Tips

Derivations, like truth tables, can be checked in a mechanical way. The set of derivations in **G** is decidable in the sense that, for any finite sequence of formulas, there is an effective method to tell whether that sequence is a derivation: just check each formula in the sequence and see whether the conditions specified in the definition are satisfied. However, derivations differ from truth tables in one important respect: there is no easy recipe to find derivations. Drawing a truth table is like performing an arithmetical operation, that is, all you need to do is to follow the instructions correctly. Instead, finding a derivation is like solving a problem of

geometry where you start from some data—say, the side of a triangle or one of its
angles—and you must find the missing information. Derivations, like problems of
geometry, require skills that can be acquired only with practice.

Although no set of instructions can guarantee the result, some strategy may help.
To construct a derivation of α from Γ, the first step is to list all the formulas in Γ as
assumptions. For example, suppose that you want to derive $p \wedge r$ from $p \wedge q$ and
$q \supset r$. In this case the derivation will contain $p \wedge q$ and $q \supset r$ as assumptions, so
you may start as follows:

1 (1) $p \wedge q$ A
2 (2) $q \supset r$ A

The second step is to write α at the end of the derivation, for α must occur as the
last formula. Thus, in our example you may write $p \wedge r$ at the end of the sequence:

1 (1) $p \wedge q$ A
2 (2) $q \supset r$ A

    .

( ) $p \wedge r$

Once the formulas in Γ and α are set out, you have to conjecture how to get to α by
reasoning on the main connective of α. In the example considered α is a conjunction,
so it is reasonable to presume that it is obtained by means of I$\wedge$ from two formulas
that occur at earlier lines, that is, p and r. Since p can be directly obtained from
$p \wedge q$, you may write as follows:

1 (1) $p \wedge q$ A
2 (2) $q \supset r$ A
1 (3) p E$\wedge$ 1

    .

( ) $p \wedge r$

The other formula, r, can be obtained by means of the assumption (2) if one applies
E$\supset$, so the derivation may be completed as follows:

1   (1) $p \wedge q$ A
2   (2) $q \supset r$ A
1   (3) p E$\wedge$ 1
1   (4) q E$\wedge$ 1
1,2 (5) r E$\supset$ 2,4
1,2 (6) $p \wedge r$ I$\wedge$ 3,5

Of course, if the main connective of α were $\sim$, it would be reasonable to presume
that α is obtained by means of I$\sim$, and the same goes for $\supset$ and $\vee$. When the
conjectured rules require auxiliary assumptions, the latter will be listed after the
formulas in Γ. This method of "backwards" reasoning will not solve all your
problems, but at least it will help you to make some progress.

8.4 Derived Rules

G has been defined by stating eight inference rules: I$\sim$, E$\sim$, I$\supset$, E$\supset$, I$\wedge$, E$\wedge$, I$\vee$, E$\vee$. But there is a sense in which **G** includes more than eight rules. Taking I$\sim$, E$\sim$, I$\supset$, E$\supset$, I$\wedge$, E$\wedge$, I$\vee$, E$\vee$ as primitive, other rules can be derived from them. This section explains what derived rules are.

Let us call *sequent* an expression of the form $\beta_1, \ldots \beta_n \vdash \alpha$, which says that α is derivable from $\beta_1, \ldots \beta_n$. A sequent is true if there is a derivation of the kind required. For example, $p \supset q, \sim q \vdash \sim p$ says that $\sim p$ is derivable from $p \supset q$ and $\sim q$. So it is made true by the following derivation:

1	(1)	$p \supset q$	A
2	(2)	$\sim q$	A
3	(3)	p	A
1,3	(4)	q	E$\supset$ 1,3
1,2	(5)	$\sim p$	I$\sim$ 3,4,2

Note that, since provability is a special case of derivability, an expression of the form $\vdash \alpha$ is also a sequent. For example, $\vdash p \supset p$ is made true by the following proof:

1	(1)	p	A
	(2)	$p \supset p$	I$\supset$ 1,1

Given a sequent s, a *substitution* of s is a sequent obtained by uniformly replacing one or more sentence letters in s with formulas, where 'uniformly' means that the same sentence letter is always replaced by the same formula. For example, $p \supset (r \wedge s), \sim(r \wedge s) \vdash \sim p$ is a substitution of $p \supset q, \sim q \vdash \sim p$.

Given two sequents s and s', if s is true and s' is a substitution of s, then s' is also true. For example, $p \supset (r \wedge s), \sim(r \wedge s) \vdash \sim p$ is made true by a derivation similar to that outlined above:

1	(1)	$p \supset (r \wedge s)$	A
2	(2)	$\sim(r \wedge s)$	A
3	(3)	p	A
1,3	(4)	$r \wedge s$	E$\supset$ 1,3
1,2	(5)	$\sim p$	I$\sim$ 3,4,2

More generally, every sequent that instantiates the schema $\alpha \supset \beta, \sim\beta \vdash \sim\alpha$ is true. The proof is provided by following derivation schema:

1   (1) $\alpha \supset \beta$ A
2   (2) $\sim\beta$ A
3   (3) α A
1,3   (4) β E$\supset$ 1,3
1,2   (5) $\sim\alpha$ I$\sim$ 3,4,2

Since one can always derive $\sim\alpha$ from $\alpha \supset \beta$ and $\sim\beta$, Modus Tollens holds in **G** as a derived rule:

MT From $\alpha \supset \beta$ and $\sim\beta$ one can derive $\sim\alpha$.

To see how MT can be employed, consider the following derivation of $\sim q \supset \sim p$ from $p \supset q$:

1   (1) $p \supset q$ A
2   (2) $\sim q$ A
3   (3) p A
1,3   (4) q E$\supset$ 1,3
1,2   (5) $\sim p$ I$\sim$ 3,4,2
1   (6) $\sim q \supset \sim p$ I$\supset$ 2,5

If MT is added to the set of rules presented in Chapter 7, one can construct a shorter derivation of $\sim q \supset \sim p$ from $p \supset q$:

1   (1) $p \supset q$ A
2   (2) $\sim q$ A
1,2   (3) $\sim p$ MT 1,2
1   (4) $\sim q \supset \sim p$ I$\supset$ 2,3

The same holds for theorems. For example, since every sequent of the form $\vdash \alpha \supset \alpha$ is provable, it is a derived rule of **G** that every formula of the form $\alpha \supset \alpha$ is a theorem.

8.5   Other Natural Deduction Systems

G is not the only natural deduction system of propositional logic. In this last section we will consider two kinds of alternatives to **G**, in order to show the variety of natural deduction systems that can be defined in a propositional language.

   The first category includes systems that differ from **G** because they are based on a different language. We saw in Sect. 4.4 that L is expressively complete, which is definitely a virtue. But L is not the only expressively complete propositional language, for different sets of connectives are equally adequate. On the one hand, any superset of $\{\sim, \supset, \wedge, \vee\}$ is adequate (see Exercise 4.6). On the other—and this is even more interesting—a smaller set of connectives can be adequate as well. In particular, consider $\{\sim, \supset\}$. Since $\alpha \wedge \beta \equiv\!\models \sim(\alpha \supset \sim\beta)$ and $\alpha \vee \beta \equiv\!\models \sim\alpha \supset \beta$, it can be shown that every truth function is realized by some formula which does not contain connectives other than $\sim$ and $\supset$. This means that a language L^- that has $\sim$ and $\supset$ as its only logical constants is expressively complete. Accordingly, one can define a system $\mathbf{G}^-$ in L^- whose only inference rules are I$\sim$, E$\sim$, I$\supset$, E$\supset$.

The second category includes systems that differ from $\mathbf{G}$ in that they have different inference rules. Here the distinction between primitive and derived rules becomes relevant. For as long as the underlying assumptions about the meaning of the connectives are the same, the differences between these systems essentially concern the choice of the primitive rules. Consider for example a system S in L that differs from $\mathbf{G}$ in that it includes MT as a primitive rule. Since MT is derivable in $\mathbf{G}$, for every derivation in S in which MT occurs, there is a derivation in $\mathbf{G}$ in which MT does not occur, as illustrated in Sect. 8.4. Conversely, a system may not include one of the rules of $\mathbf{G}$ among its primitive rules, provided that it includes other rules from which that rule can be derived.[1]

More generally, a natural deduction system in L can be equivalent to $\mathbf{G}$ in the following sense:

Definition 8.5 Two systems S and S$'$ in a language L are *deductively equivalent* iff, for every set of formulas Γ of L and every formula α of L, $\Gamma \vdash \alpha$ in S iff $\Gamma \vdash \alpha$ in S$'$.

To say that S and S$'$ are deductively equivalent is to say that they have exactly the same deductive power. In order to have a system that is not deductively equivalent to $\mathbf{G}$, hence substantively differs from $\mathbf{G}$, one should replace some of the rules of $\mathbf{G}$ by rules that are not derivable in $\mathbf{G}$, or from which the rules of $\mathbf{G}$ are not derivable. But that would no longer be a classical system of propositional logic.[2]

Exercises

8.1 Show by means of a derivation that Tisias reasons validly.

8.2 Show that Excluded Middle and Non-Contradiction are provable in $\mathbf{G}$:

(a) $\sim(p \wedge \sim p)$
(b) $p \vee \sim p$

---

[1]Lemmon [39] adopts a natural deduction system that includes MT among the primitive rules.
[2]Priest [53], chapters 5–10, provides a survey of non-classical logics.

8.3 From Chapter 7 we get what follows:

(a) $(p \wedge q) \supset r \dashv\vdash p \supset (q \supset r)$ (Sect. 7.4).
(b) $p \wedge q \dashv\vdash q \wedge p$ (Exercise 7.5)
(c) $p \vee q \dashv\vdash q \vee p$ (Exercise 7.7)
(d) $p \supset q \dashv\vdash {\sim}p \vee q$. (Sect. 7.5)
(e) $(p \supset q) \wedge (r \supset q) \dashv\vdash (p \vee r) \supset q$ (Exercises 7.9 and 7.10)

Verify that (a)–(e) are also cases of logical equivalence.

8.4 Show that $p \wedge p \dashv\vdash p$.

8.5 Show that $p \dashv\vdash {\sim}p \supset p$.

8.6 Prove what follows:

$\Gamma \vdash \alpha$ if and only if $\Gamma \cup \{{\sim}\alpha\}$ is inconsistent.

8.7 Show that the following holds:

(a) $p \vee q \vdash {\sim}({\sim}p \wedge {\sim}q)$
(b) ${\sim}({\sim}p \wedge {\sim}q) \vdash p \vee q$.
(c) $p \wedge q \vdash {\sim}({\sim}p \vee {\sim}q)$
(d) ${\sim}({\sim}p \vee {\sim}q) \vdash p \wedge q$.

8.8 Show that De Morgan's Laws hold at the syntactic level.

8.9 Given the rules of **G**, can we obtain a derived rule according to which from $\alpha \vee \beta$ one can derive ${\sim}({\sim}\alpha \wedge {\sim}\beta)$?

8.10 Provide an inductive definition of the formulas of L^-.

Chapter 9
The System L

9.1 Axioms and Inference Rule

This chapter outlines an axiomatic system called **L**. The language of **L** is L^-, the fragment of **L** whose logical constants are $\sim$ and $\supset$. So, **L** may be regarded as an axiomatic version of G^-, the poor cousin of **G** considered in Sect. 8.5.[1]

The axioms of **L** are the formulas of L^- that instantiate the following schemas:

A1 $\alpha \supset (\beta \supset \alpha)$
A2 $(\alpha \supset (\beta \supset \gamma)) \supset ((\alpha \supset \beta) \supset (\alpha \supset \gamma))$
A3 $(\sim\alpha \supset \sim\beta) \supset (\beta \supset \alpha)$

A1–A3 are tautological schemas, in that every formula that instantiates them is a tautology. The unique inference rule of **L** is Modus Ponens:

MP From $\alpha \supset \beta$ and α one can derive β.

A derivation in **L** of a formula α from a set of formulas Γ is defined as follows:

Definition 9.1 A *derivation of α from* Γ is a finite sequence of formulas that ends with α such that each of the formulas in the sequence instantiates A1–A3 or belongs to Γ or is obtained by means of MP from formulas that precede it.

Here is a very simple example of derivation in **L**:

(1) $p \supset q$ A
(2) p A
(3) q MP 1,2

---

[1] I call this system **L** because its choice of axioms comes from Łukasiewicz [44], even though A1 and A2 already appeared in Frege [14].

© The Author(s), under exclusive license to Springer Nature Switzerland AG 2021   79
A. Iacona, *LOGIC: Lecture Notes for Philosophy, Mathematics, and Computer Science*, Springer Undergraduate Texts in Philosophy,
https://doi.org/10.1007/978-3-030-64811-4_9

Note that there are no left numbers, because this system does not contemplate the possibility of auxiliary assumptions: every assumption made in the course of a derivation counts until the end. A proof is a derivation with no assumptions, such as the following:

(1) $p \supset ((p \supset p) \supset p)$ A1
(2) $(p \supset ((p \supset p) \supset p)) \supset ((p \supset (p \supset p)) \supset (p \supset p))$ A2
(3) $(p \supset (p \supset p)) \supset (p \supset p)$ MP 2,1
(4) $p \supset (p \supset p)$ A1
(5) $p \supset p$ MP 3,4

As in the case of a natural deduction system, any result obtained by means of a derivation can be generalized:

Theorem 9.1 $\alpha \supset \beta, \alpha \vdash \beta$

Proof Like the first derivation above, replacing p and q with α and β.   □

Theorem 9.2 $\vdash \alpha \supset \alpha$

Proof Like the second derivation above, replacing p with α.   □

A direct consequence of Definition 9.1 is that Reflexivity, Monotonicity, and Cut hold in **L**, just as they hold in **G⁻**.

Theorem 9.3 $\alpha \vdash \alpha$

Proof Like the proof of Theorem 8.1.   □

Theorem 9.4 *If* $\Gamma \vdash \alpha$ *and* $\Gamma \subseteq \Delta$, *then* $\Delta \vdash \alpha$.

Proof Like the proof of Theorem 8.2.   □

Theorem 9.5 *If* $\Gamma \vdash \alpha$ *and* $\Delta \cup \{\alpha\} \vdash \beta$, *then* $\Gamma \cup \Delta \vdash \beta$.

Proof Like the proof of Theorem 8.3.   □

From now on, Theorems 9.3–9.5 will be taken for granted without explicitly mentioning them.

The following theorems also holds:

Theorem 9.6 *If* $\alpha \in \Gamma$, *then* $\Gamma \vdash \alpha$.

Proof From Theorems 9.3 and 9.4.   □

Theorem 9.7 *If* $\Gamma \vdash \alpha \supset \beta$ *and* $\Gamma \vdash \alpha$, *then* $\Gamma \vdash \beta$.

Proof If $\Gamma \vdash \alpha$ and $\Gamma \vdash \alpha \supset \beta$, then one can construct a derivation from Γ that contains α and $\alpha \supset \beta$ and that ends with β, where β is obtained by using MP.   □

Since Theorem 9.7 directly follows from the fact that **L** includes MP, from now on the same label MP will be used to refer to it. Note that, when $\Gamma = \emptyset$, we simply have that if $\vdash \alpha$ and $\vdash \alpha \supset \beta$, then $\vdash \beta$.

L is analogous to **G**$^-$ in two important respects. First, its language is decidable, that is, for every finite sequence of symbols, there is an effective method to check whether that sequence is a formula of **L**. Second, the set of derivations in **L** is decidable, that is, for any finite sequence of formulas, there is an effective method to check whether that sequence is a derivation in **L**. A third feature of **L** is that the set of its axioms is decidable, that is, for every formula of **L**, there is an effective method to check whether that formula instantiates A1–A3. Thus, **L** satisfies the following definition:

Definition 9.2 A system S is *effectively axiomatized* iff the language of S is decidable, the set of axioms of S is decidable, and the set of derivations in S is decidable.

A significant difference between **G**$^-$ and **L** is that in **L** it is harder to find derivations. Consider the formula $p \supset p$. To prove this formula in **G**$^-$, two lines are enough (Sect. 8.4). Instead, as we have seen, a proof of $p \supset p$ in **L** requires a different reasoning. The difference is not simply a matter of length. The fact is that in **L** one must go through a more devious path: surely, the proof above is not the first thing that comes to mind. Yet this difference must not be mistaken for a difference of deductive power. The aim of the rest of the chapter is to show that in **L** one can obtain the same results that one can obtain in **G**$^-$.

9.2 Deduction Theorem

This section outlines a basic theorem about **L**, the *deduction theorem*, which is a cornerstone of its deductive power. The deduction theorem, proved in 1930 by Jacques Herbrand, expresses a general property of derivability that **L** shares with a wide class of axiomatic systems. In particular, the proof set out below holds for any system that includes A1–A3 and MP.[2]

The proof method that will be employed—*proof by induction*—rests on the following principle: given a set A defined by induction, that is, in the way illustrated in Sect. 5.1, if a condition C holds for the initial elements of A and is closed under the operations through which the other elements of A are obtained, then C holds for all the elements of A. According to this principle, called *Induction Principle*, the claim that C holds for all the elements of A can be justified in two steps. The basis of the induction shows that C holds for the initial elements of A. The induction step then shows that the operations through which the other elements of A are obtained preserve C. This is done by assuming as induction hypothesis that C holds for some

---

[2]Jacques Herbrand (1908–1931) was a brilliant French mathematician who tragically died at the age 23 in a mountaineering accident in the Alps. He outlined the proof of the theorem in his doctoral dissertation, Herbrand [23].

arbitrary elements of A, and showing that, under that assumption, C holds for the objects obtained from them by means of the operations.

To illustrate this method, consider the fact, recalled in Euclid's proof of the existence of infinitely many primes (Sect. 1.3), that every $n > 1$ is a product of primes. This fact can be proved by induction. First assume that $n = 2$. In this case n is a product of primes, because 2 is prime, and every number is a multiple of itself. Now assume, for any $n > 1$, that every number less than or equal to n is a product of primes. Either $n + 1$ is prime or it is not. If it is, then obviously it is a product of primes. If it is not, then it admits some divisor other than itself and 1, so it is the product of two numbers i and k greater than 1. Since i and k are less than $n + 1$, by the induction hypothesis they are both products of primes. This means that $n + 1$ is a product of products of primes, hence a product of primes.

In this example, the induction starts from 2 because the proof concerns the set of natural numbers greater than 1. But similar proofs can be given for other subsets of $\mathbb{N}$, including $\mathbb{N}$ itself, so the induction can start from 0, from 1, or from any natural number. The important fact is that in all such cases the induction step is phrased as follows: if the condition to be proved holds for every number less than or equal to n, then it holds for $n + 1$. The proofs by induction that will be offered from now on share this feature, as they concern sets whose elements can be "measured" by means of natural numbers. Since every formula of a language has a finite complexity, in that it is formed by n symbols for some n, we can reason by induction on its complexity. Similarly, since every derivation in a system has a finite length, in that it is formed by n formulas for some n, we can reason by induction on its length.

Now it is time to state the deduction theorem and its proof:

Theorem 9.8 *If $\Gamma \cup \{\alpha\} \vdash \beta$, then $\Gamma \vdash \alpha \supset \beta$.*

Proof We reason by induction on the length of the derivation of β from $\Gamma \cup \{\alpha\}$. The induction starts from $n = 1$ because the shortest derivation is constituted by a single formula.

Basis. Assume that there is a derivation of β from $\Gamma \cup \{\alpha\}$ of length 1. Three cases are possible.

Case 1: β is an axiom. In this case there is a derivation of $\alpha \supset \beta$ from Γ:

(1) $\beta \supset (\alpha \supset \beta)$ A1
(2) β
(3) $\alpha \supset \beta$ MP 1,2

Here the blank in the second line can be filled by A1, A2, or A3.

Case 2: $\beta \in \Gamma$. In this case there is a derivation of $\alpha \supset \beta$ from Γ, the same considered in case 1 but with A in line (2).

Case 3: $\beta = \alpha$. In this case $\alpha \supset \beta = \alpha \supset \alpha$. Since Theorem 9.2 entails that $\Gamma \vdash \alpha \supset \alpha$, there is a derivation of $\alpha \supset \beta$ from Γ.

Step. Assume that the conditional to be proved holds for every derivation of length less than or equal to n, and that there is a derivation of β from $\Gamma \cup \{\alpha\}$ of length $n + 1$. The possible cases are four. The first three are those treated in the basis, the fourth is that in which β is obtained by means of MP from two formulas $\gamma \supset \beta$ and γ. In the latter case, since $\gamma \supset \beta$ and γ precede β, there is a derivation of $\gamma \supset \beta$ from $\Gamma \cup \{\alpha\}$ whose length is at most n, and the same goes for γ. So, by the induction hypothesis, $\Gamma \vdash \alpha \supset (\gamma \supset \beta)$ and $\Gamma \vdash \alpha \supset \gamma$. Moreover, from A2 we get that $\Gamma \vdash (\alpha \supset (\gamma \supset \beta)) \supset ((\alpha \supset \gamma) \supset (\alpha \supset \beta))$. Therefore, two applications of MP suffice to conclude that $\Gamma \vdash \alpha \supset \beta$. □

Here is an example of how the deduction theorem can be employed to obtain further results:

Theorem 9.9 $\alpha \supset \beta, \beta \supset \gamma \vdash \alpha \supset \gamma$

Proof If we assume $\alpha \supset \beta, \beta \supset \gamma, \alpha$, we can derive γ by applying MP twice. So, $\alpha \supset \beta, \beta \supset \gamma, \alpha \vdash \gamma$. From this and the deduction theorem (Theorem 9.8) we get that $\alpha \supset \beta, \beta \supset \gamma \vdash \alpha \supset \gamma$. □

Note that Theorem 9.9 yields that if $\vdash \beta \supset \gamma$, then $\alpha \supset \beta \vdash \alpha \supset \gamma$. This follows from Cut (Theorem 9.5), provided that $\Gamma = \emptyset$, $\alpha = \beta \supset \gamma$, and $\Delta = \{\alpha \supset \beta\}$. Similarly, if $\vdash \alpha \supset \beta$, then $\beta \supset \gamma \vdash \alpha \supset \gamma$. Again, take Cut (Theorem 9.5), and let $\Gamma = \emptyset$, $\alpha = \alpha \supset \beta$, and $\Delta = \{\beta \supset \gamma\}$. Moreover, from Theorem 9.9 we get that if $\vdash \alpha \supset \beta$ and $\vdash \beta \supset \gamma$, then $\vdash \alpha \supset \gamma$. For the second assumption entails that $\alpha \supset \beta \vdash \alpha \supset \gamma$, as noted above, hence $\vdash (\alpha \supset \beta) \supset (\alpha \supset \gamma)$ by the deduction theorem (Theorem 9.8). From this and the first assumption we get $\vdash \alpha \supset \gamma$ by MP.

9.3 Explosion, Double Negation, Contraposition

Now we will go through some syntactic results which depend on the deduction theorem (Theorem 9.8). Let us start with the following theorem, which says that a conditional holds whenever its antecedent does not hold:

Theorem 9.10 $\vdash \sim\alpha \supset (\alpha \supset \beta)$

Proof

(1) $\vdash \sim\alpha \supset (\sim\beta \supset \sim\alpha)$ A1
(2) $\vdash (\sim\beta \supset \sim\alpha) \supset (\alpha \supset \beta)$ A3
(3) $\vdash \sim\alpha \supset (\alpha \supset \beta)$ T 9.9 1,2

□

Note that this is not a proof in **L** but a proof *about* **L**. What it establishes is a syntactic fact about **L** expressed by using the metalinguistic symbol $\vdash$. In this proof, the letter T abbreviates 'theorem'. That is, the justification of (3) is that Theorem 9.9 holds in **L**. The same convention will be adopted in the following proofs.

Now we can prove Explosion:

Theorem 9.11 $\alpha, \sim\alpha \vdash \beta$

Proof

(1) $\alpha, \sim\alpha \vdash \alpha$ T 9.6
(2) $\alpha, \sim\alpha \vdash \sim\alpha$ T 9.6
(3) $\alpha, \sim\alpha \vdash \sim\alpha \supset (\alpha \supset \beta)$ T 9.10
(4) $\alpha, \sim\alpha \vdash \alpha \supset \beta$ MP 3,2
(5) $\alpha, \sim\alpha \vdash \beta$ MP 4,1

□

The following two theorems, instead, express Double Negation:

Theorem 9.12 $\vdash \sim\sim\alpha \supset \alpha$

Proof

(1) $\vdash \sim\sim\alpha \supset (\sim\alpha \supset \sim\sim\sim\alpha)$ T 9.10
(2) $\vdash (\sim\alpha \supset \sim\sim\sim\alpha) \supset (\sim\sim\alpha \supset \alpha)$ A3
(3) $\vdash \sim\sim\alpha \supset (\sim\sim\alpha \supset \alpha)$ T 9.9 1,2
(4) $\vdash (\sim\sim\alpha \supset (\sim\sim\alpha \supset \alpha)) \supset ((\sim\sim\alpha \supset \sim\sim\alpha) \supset (\sim\sim\alpha \supset \alpha))$ A2
(5) $\vdash (\sim\sim\alpha \supset \sim\sim\alpha) \supset (\sim\sim\alpha \supset \alpha)$ MP 4,3
(6) $\vdash \sim\sim\alpha \supset \sim\sim\alpha$ T 9.2
(7) $\vdash \sim\sim\alpha \supset \alpha$ MP 5,6

□

Theorem 9.13 $\vdash \alpha \supset \sim\sim\alpha$

Proof

(1) $\vdash \sim\sim\sim\alpha \supset \sim\alpha$ T 9.12
(2) $\vdash (\sim\sim\sim\alpha \supset \sim\alpha) \supset (\alpha \supset \sim\sim\alpha)$ A3
(3) $\vdash \alpha \supset \sim\sim\alpha$ MP 2,1

□

Here are three further theorems concerning the interaction between $\sim$ and $\supset$, the third of which expresses Contraposition.

Theorem 9.14 $\sim\sim\alpha, \alpha \supset \beta \vdash \sim\sim\beta$

Proof

(1) $\sim\sim\alpha$ A
(2) $\alpha \supset \beta$ A
(3) $\vdash \sim\sim\alpha \supset \alpha$ T 9.12
(4) α MP 3,1
(5) β MP 2,4
(6) $\vdash \beta \supset \sim\sim\beta$ T 9.13
(7) $\sim\sim\beta$ MP 6,5

$\square$

Theorem 9.15 $\vdash (\alpha \supset \beta) \supset (\sim\sim\alpha \supset \sim\sim\beta)$

Proof From Theorem 9.14, by applying the deduction theorem (Theorem 9.8) twice. $\square$

Theorem 9.16 $\vdash (\alpha \supset \beta) \supset (\sim\beta \supset \sim\alpha)$

Proof

(1) $\vdash (\alpha \supset \beta) \supset (\sim\sim\alpha \supset \sim\sim\beta)$ T 9.15
(2) $\vdash (\sim\sim\alpha \supset \sim\sim\beta) \supset (\sim\beta \supset \sim\alpha)$ A3
(3) $\vdash (\alpha \supset \beta) \supset (\sim\beta \supset \sim\alpha)$ T 9.9 1,2

$\square$

9.4 Substitution of Equivalents

The theorems proved in the previous section can be used to derive a rule that will make our life easier, *Substitution of Equivalents*. This rule says that if two formulas γ and γ' are provably equivalent, then we can replace γ with γ' in any formula α:

SE If α contains γ, α' differs from α only in having γ' instead of γ at one or more places, and $\vdash \gamma \equiv \gamma'$, then $\vdash \alpha \equiv \alpha'$.

Proof We reason by induction on the complexity of α, assuming that the three conditions stated in the antecedent are satisfied. The induction starts from $n = 0$ because atomic formulas have complexity 0.

   Basis. Assume that α is atomic. Then $\alpha = \gamma$ and $\alpha' = \gamma'$. So, $\vdash \alpha \equiv \alpha'$ because $\vdash \gamma \equiv \gamma'$ by hypothesis.

Step. Assume that the conditional to be proved holds for every formula of complexity less than or equal to n, and that α has complexity $n + 1$. The possible cases are two.

Case 1: α has the form $\sim\beta$. In this case, $\alpha' = \sim\beta'$. By the induction hypothesis $\vdash \beta \equiv \beta'$. By Theorem 9.16, $\vdash (\beta \supset \beta') \supset (\sim\beta' \supset \sim\beta)$ and $\vdash (\beta' \supset \beta) \supset (\sim\beta \supset \sim\beta')$. It follows that $\vdash \sim\beta \supset \sim\beta'$ and $\vdash \sim\beta' \supset \sim\beta$.

Case 2: α has the form $\beta \supset \delta$. In this case, $\alpha' = \beta' \supset \delta$ or $\alpha' = \beta \supset \delta'$ or $\alpha' = \beta' \supset \delta'$. Suppose that $\alpha' = \beta' \supset \delta$. By the induction hypothesis, $\vdash \beta \equiv \beta'$. So, by Theorem 9.9, $\beta \supset \delta \vdash \beta' \supset \delta$ and $\beta' \supset \delta \vdash \beta \supset \delta$. By the deduction theorem (Theorem 9.8) it follows that $\vdash (\beta \supset \delta) \supset (\beta' \supset \delta)$ and $\vdash (\beta' \supset \delta) \supset (\beta \supset \delta)$. Now suppose that $\alpha' = \beta \supset \delta'$. By the induction hypothesis, $\vdash \delta \equiv \delta'$. So, by Theorem 9.9, $\beta \supset \delta \vdash \beta \supset \delta'$ and $\beta \supset \delta' \vdash \beta \supset \delta$. By the deduction theorem (Theorem 9.8) it follows that $\vdash (\beta \supset \delta) \supset (\beta \supset \delta')$ and $\vdash (\beta \supset \delta') \supset (\beta \supset \delta)$. Finally, suppose that $\alpha' = \beta' \supset \delta'$. Given what has been said about the first two suppositions, we obtain that $\vdash (\beta \supset \delta) \supset (\beta' \supset \delta')$ and $\vdash (\beta' \supset \delta') \supset (\beta \supset \delta)$ through the same kind of reasoning.   □

A direct corollary of SE is that, if $\vdash \alpha$, and α' is obtained from α in the way explained, then $\vdash \alpha'$. For example, Theorems 9.12 and 9.13 show that $\vdash \alpha \equiv \sim\sim\alpha$. Therefore, we can always replace α with $\sim\sim\alpha$ in a theorem, or the other way round. Similarly, A3 and Theorem 9.16 show that $\vdash (\alpha \supset \beta) \equiv (\sim\beta \supset \sim\alpha)$. Therefore, we can always replace $\alpha \supset \beta$ with $\sim\beta \supset \sim\alpha$ in a theorem, or the other way round. The proofs of the following theorems illustrate this use of SE.

Theorem 9.17 $\vdash (\alpha \supset \sim\beta) \supset (\beta \supset \sim\alpha)$

Proof

(1) $\vdash (\sim\sim\alpha \supset \sim\beta) \supset (\beta \supset \sim\alpha)$ A3
(2) $\vdash (\alpha \supset \sim\beta) \supset (\beta \supset \sim\alpha)$ SE 1

                                                                                                      □

Theorem 9.18 $\vdash \alpha \supset (\sim\beta \supset \sim(\alpha \supset \beta))$

Proof

(1) $\alpha \supset \beta, \alpha \vdash \beta$ T 9.1
(2) $\alpha \vdash (\alpha \supset \beta) \supset \beta$ T 9.8 1
(3) $\vdash \alpha \supset ((\alpha \supset \beta) \supset \beta)$ T 9.8 2
(4) $\vdash \alpha \supset (\sim\beta \supset \sim(\alpha \supset \beta))$ SE 3

                                                                                                      □

Theorem 9.19 $\vdash (\sim\alpha \supset \alpha) \supset (\beta \supset \alpha)$

Proof   □

(1) $\vdash \sim\alpha \supset (\alpha \supset \sim\beta)$ T 9.10

(2) $\vdash (\sim\alpha \supset (\alpha \supset \sim\beta)) \supset ((\sim\alpha \supset \alpha) \supset (\sim\alpha \supset \sim\beta))$ A2

(3) $\vdash (\sim\alpha \supset \alpha) \supset (\sim\alpha \supset \sim\beta)$ MP 2,1

(4) $\vdash (\sim\alpha \supset \alpha) \supset (\beta \supset \alpha)$ SE 3

9.5   Reductio Ad Absurdum

Now we will prove two further theorems in order to show that **L** licenses *reductio ad absurdum*:

Theorem 9.20 $\vdash (\sim\alpha \supset \alpha) \supset \alpha$

Proof

(1) $\vdash (\sim\alpha \supset \alpha) \supset ((\sim\alpha \supset \alpha) \supset \alpha)$ T 9.19

(2) $\vdash ((\sim\alpha \supset \alpha) \supset ((\sim\alpha \supset \alpha) \supset \alpha)) \supset (((\sim\alpha \supset \alpha) \supset$
     $(\sim\alpha \supset \alpha)) \supset ((\sim\alpha \supset \alpha) \supset \alpha))$ A2

(3) $\vdash ((\sim\alpha \supset \alpha) \supset (\sim\alpha \supset \alpha)) \supset ((\sim\alpha \supset \alpha) \supset \alpha)$ MP 1,2

(4) $\vdash (\sim\alpha \supset \alpha) \supset (\sim\alpha \supset \alpha)$ T 9.2

(5) $\vdash (\sim\alpha \supset \alpha) \supset \alpha$ MP 3,4   □

Theorem 9.21 $\vdash (\alpha \supset \sim\alpha) \supset \sim\alpha$

Proof

(1) $\vdash (\sim\sim\alpha \supset \sim\alpha) \supset \sim\alpha$ T 9.20

(2) $\vdash (\alpha \supset \sim\alpha) \supset \sim\alpha$ SE 1   □

Proof by Contradiction can now be stated as follows:

Theorem 9.22 $\vdash (\alpha \supset \beta) \supset ((\alpha \supset \sim\beta) \supset \sim\alpha)$

Proof

(1) $\alpha \supset \beta, \beta \supset \sim\alpha \vdash \alpha \supset \sim\alpha$ T 9.9

(2) $\vdash (\alpha \supset \sim\alpha) \supset \sim\alpha$ T 9.21

(3) $\alpha \supset \beta, \beta \supset \sim\alpha \vdash \sim\alpha$ MP 2,1

(4) $\alpha \supset \beta \vdash (\beta \supset \sim\alpha) \supset \sim\alpha$ T 9.8 3

(5) $\vdash (\alpha \supset \beta) \supset ((\beta \supset \sim\alpha) \supset \sim\alpha)$ T 9.8 4

(6) $\vdash (\alpha \supset \beta) \supset ((\alpha \supset \sim\beta) \supset \sim\alpha)$ SE 5

□

Theorem 9.22 corresponds to the first of the two kinds of *reductio* introduced in Sect. 1.3: if α entails β and $\sim\beta$, then $\sim\alpha$ holds. To express the second, we need the following theorem:

Theorem 9.23 $\vdash (\sim\alpha \supset \beta) \supset ((\sim\alpha \supset \sim\beta) \supset \alpha)$

If $\sim\alpha$ entails β and $\sim\beta$, then α holds. In Sect. 2.5 we saw that these two kinds of *reductio* are equivalent on the assumption that $\sim\sim\alpha$ amounts to α. Since **L** warrants this assumption, Theorem 9.23 is provable as well.

9.6 Deductive Equivalence Between **G⁻** and **L**

This section—*dulcis in fundo*—shows that **G⁻** and **L** are deductively equivalent, that is, $\Gamma \vdash \alpha$ in **G⁻** if and only if $\Gamma \vdash \alpha$ in **L**. We will consider the two parts of the biconditional separately, first the left-to-right direction and then the right-to-left direction.

Theorem 9.24 *If* $\Gamma \vdash \alpha$ *in* **G⁻**, *then* $\Gamma \vdash \alpha$ *in* **L**.

Proof We reason by induction on the length of the derivation in **G⁻** of α from Γ.

Basis. Assume that in **G⁻** there is a derivation of α from Γ of length 1. In this case $\alpha \in \Gamma$. So $\Gamma \vdash \alpha$ in **L** by Theorem 9.6.

Step. Assume that the conditional to be proved holds for every derivation in **G⁻** of length less than or equal to n and that there is a derivation in **G⁻** of α from Γ of length $n + 1$. Two cases are possible.

Case 1: α is an assumption. In this case, again, $\alpha \in \Gamma$, so $\Gamma \vdash \alpha$ in **L** by Theorem 9.6.

Case 2: α is obtained from previous formulas. In this case there are four options, given that **G⁻** has four inference rules.

(a) α is obtained by means of I$\sim$. In this case α has the form $\sim\beta$ and is preceded by β, which occurs as an assumption, and by two formulas γ and $\sim\gamma$. So, both γ and $\sim\gamma$ are derivable from $\Gamma \cup \{\beta\}$ in a number of steps less than or equal to n. By the induction hypothesis it follows that $\Gamma \cup \{\beta\} \vdash \gamma$ and $\Gamma \cup \{\beta\} \vdash \sim\gamma$ in **L**. By the deduction theorem (Theorem 9.8), then, $\Gamma \vdash \beta \supset \gamma$ and $\Gamma \vdash \beta \supset \sim\gamma$ in **L**. Since Theorem 9.22 entails that $\Gamma \vdash (\beta \supset \gamma) \supset ((\beta \supset \sim\gamma) \supset \sim\beta)$ in **L**, by using MP twice we get that $\Gamma \vdash \sim\beta$ in **L**.

(b) α is obtained by means of E$\sim$. In this case $\sim\sim\alpha$ precedes α in the derivation. So in **G⁻** there is a derivation of $\sim\sim\alpha$ from Γ of length less than or equal to n. By the induction hypothesis it follows that $\Gamma \vdash \sim\sim\alpha$ in **L**. Since Theorem 9.12 entails that $\Gamma \vdash \sim\sim\alpha \supset \alpha$ in **L**, by MP we get that $\Gamma \vdash \alpha$ in **L**.

(c) α is obtained by means of I$\supset$. In this case α has the form $\beta \supset \gamma$ and is preceded by β, which occurs as an assumption, and by γ. So, in **G⁻** there is a derivation of γ from $\Gamma \cup \{\beta\}$ of length less than or equal to n. By the induction hypothesis, then $\Gamma \cup \{\beta\} \vdash \gamma$ in **L**. By the decuction theorem (Theorem 9.8) it follows that $\Gamma \vdash \beta \supset \gamma$ in **L**.

(*d*) α is obtained by means of E$\supset$. In this case $\beta \supset \alpha$ and β precede α. So in $\mathbf{G}^-$ there are derivations of $\beta \supset \alpha$ and β from Γ of length less than or equal to n. By the induction hypothesis, then $\Gamma \vdash \beta \supset \alpha$ and $\Gamma \vdash \beta$ in $\mathbf{L}$. Therefore, by MP, $\Gamma \vdash \alpha$ in $\mathbf{L}$. □

Theorem 9.25 *If* $\Gamma \vdash \alpha$ *in* $\mathbf{L}$, *then* $\Gamma \vdash \alpha$ *in* $\mathbf{G}^-$.

Proof We reason by induction on the length of the derivation in $\mathbf{L}$ of α from Γ.

Basis. Assume that in $\mathbf{L}$ there is a derivation of α from Γ of length 1. Two cases are possible.

Case 1: $\alpha \in \Gamma$. In this case obviously $\Gamma \vdash \alpha$ in $\mathbf{G}^-$.

Case 2: α is an axiom. In this case $\vdash \alpha$ in $\mathbf{G}^-$, for every instance of A1–A3 is provable in $\mathbf{G}^-$. Therefore, $\Gamma \vdash \alpha$ in $\mathbf{G}^-$.

Step. Assume that the conditional to be proved holds for every derivation in $\mathbf{L}$ of length less than or equal to n, and that there is a derivation in $\mathbf{L}$ of α from Γ of length $n+1$. In this derivation, α is an assumption, or an axiom, or a formula inferred from previous formulas. The first two cases are treated in the basis. In the third case, α is obtained by means of MP, which implies that $\beta \supset \alpha$ and β are derivable from Γ in a number of steps less than or equal to n. By the induction hypothesis it follows that $\Gamma \vdash \beta \supset \alpha$ and $\Gamma \vdash \beta$ in $\mathbf{G}^-$. Since $\mathbf{G}^-$ includes E$\supset$, we get that $\Gamma \vdash \alpha$ in $\mathbf{G}^-$. □

Theorems 9.24 and 9.25 show that $\mathbf{G}^-$ and $\mathbf{L}$ have exactly the same deductive power. In general, the choice between a natural deduction system and an axiomatic system does not have substantial consequences from the deductive point of view.

9.7 Systems and Theories

Let us close the chapter with a terminological distinction that is important to bear in mind, the distinction between 'system' and 'theory'. Although these two terms are sometimes treated as synonyms, very often they are not. There are contexts in which we want to talk of sets of derivable formulas without making reference to any specific system, because we are not primarily interested in the deductive process but only in its output. The term 'theory' may be used in such contexts to indicate a set of derivable formulas. More precisely, a theory is a set of formulas that is *deductively closed* in the following sense:

Definition 9.3 A *theory* T is a set of formulas such that, for every α, if $T \vdash \alpha$, then $\alpha \in T$.

Since the converse conditional is trivial, that is, if $\alpha \in T$, then $T \vdash \alpha$, we get that $\alpha \in T$ if and only if $T \vdash \alpha$. This means that belonging to T and being a theorem of T are one and the same thing.

It is easy to see that, for any set of formulas Γ, there is a theory T such that $\Gamma \subseteq T$, namely, the theory that includes all and only the formulas derivable from Γ. For example, if Γ contains two formulas α and $\alpha \supset \beta$, then T will contain α, $\alpha \supset \beta$, β,

$\sim\sim\beta$, and so on. In other words, T is the *deductive closure* of Γ. Just as any set of formulas has a deductive closure, any theory is the deductive closure of some set of formulas. Trivially, every theory is the deductive closure of itself.

Note that a theory may contain only formulas that are provable in a system S, in which case it reduces to the set of theorems of S. If $\Gamma = \emptyset$, the deductive closure of Γ is the set of formulas which are derivable from $\emptyset$. Since two deductively equivalent systems have the same theorems, this means that two deductively equivalent systems determine one and the same theory. In the specific case considered, **G**$^-$ and **L** are different systems which determine one and the same theory.

The term 'propositional logic' is often used generically without making reference to any specific system. The term so understood designates what **G**$^-$, **L**, and other deductively equivalent systems have in common, that is, it designates a theory rather than a system.

Exercises

9.1 Prove the following theorem about **L**:

Theorem 9.26 *If $\alpha, \beta \vdash \gamma$ and $\alpha, \gamma \vdash \delta$, then $\alpha, \beta \vdash \delta$.*

9.2 In the proof of Theorem 9.25, case 2 of the basis, it is assumed that every instance of A1–A3 is a theorem of **G**$^-$. Justify this assumption by providing the corresponding proofs in **G**$^-$.

9.3 Does the deduction theorem hold for **G**$^-$ as well?

9.4 Prove Theorem 9.23.

9.5 Explain why in **L** we have that $\vdash \alpha \supset \beta$ iff $\alpha \vdash \beta$.

9.6 Explain why in **L** we have that $\vdash \alpha \equiv \beta$ iff $\alpha \dashv\vdash \beta$.

9.7 Prove the following theorems about **L**:

Theorem 9.27 $\vdash \sim(\alpha \supset \beta) \supset \alpha$

Theorem 9.28 $\vdash \sim(\alpha \supset \beta) \supset \sim\beta$

9.8 Prove the following theorems about **L**:

Theorem 9.29 $\Gamma \cup \{\alpha\}$ *is inconsistent iff* $\Gamma \vdash \sim\alpha$.

Theorem 9.30 $\Gamma \cup \{\sim\alpha\}$ *is inconsistent iff* $\Gamma \vdash \alpha$.

9.9 Explain why the following theorem holds for **G**$^-$ and for **L**:

Theorem 9.31 $\Gamma \vdash \alpha$ *iff there is a finite subset Δ of Γ such that $\Delta \vdash \alpha$.*

9.10 Prove that if a set of formulas is consistent, the same goes for its deductive closure.

Chapter 10
Consistency, Soundness, Completeness

10.1 Consistency of L

This chapter deals with three key properties of systems: *consistency*, *soundness*, and *completeness*. As we shall see, **L** has these three properties, and the same goes for any other system that is deductively equivalent to **L**, such as **G⁻**.

Consistency is defined in terms of derivability, just like the property of sets of formulas introduced in Sect. 8.1:

Definition 10.1 A system S is *consistent* iff there is no formula α such that $\vdash \alpha$ and $\vdash \sim\alpha$ in S.

A system S is *inconsistent* when it is not consistent, that is, when a contradiction is provable in S. Consistency may be regarded as a minimal condition that a system must satisfy in order to be non-trivial. Inconsistency amounts to triviality in the following sense: as long as it is granted that anything follows from a contradiction, an inconsistent system is a system in which one can prove anything.

To prove that **L** is consistent it suffices to show that every axiom of **L** is valid, and consequently that every theorem of **L** is valid.

Theorem 10.1 $\vDash \alpha \supset (\beta \supset \alpha)$

Proof This theorem holds because A1 is a tautological schema. As is easy to check by means of a truth table, the schema is true for any combination of values of α and β. ☐

Theorem 10.2 $\vDash (\alpha \supset (\beta \supset \gamma)) \supset ((\alpha \supset \beta) \supset (\alpha \supset \gamma))$

Proof The proof is analogous to that of Theorem 10.1. ☐

Theorem 10.3 $\vDash (\sim\alpha \supset \sim\beta) \supset (\beta \supset \alpha)$

Proof The proof is analogous to that of Theorems 10.1 and 10.2. ☐

© The Author(s), under exclusive license to Springer Nature Switzerland AG 2021
A. Iacona, *LOGIC: Lecture Notes for Philosophy, Mathematics, and Computer Science*, Springer Undergraduate Texts in Philosophy,
https://doi.org/10.1007/978-3-030-64811-4_10

Theorem 10.4 *If* $\vdash \alpha$, *then* $\vDash \alpha$.

Proof Assume that $\vdash \alpha$. Then α is obtained by means of A1–A3 and MP. By Theorems 10.1–10.3, all the formulas that instantiate A1–A3 are valid. Moreover, MP preserves validity, because for every interpretation, if $\beta \supset \gamma$ and β are true in that interpretation, then γ is true in that interpretation. Therefore, $\vDash \alpha$.   □

Theorem 10.5 *In* **L** *it is not the case that* $\vdash \alpha$ *and* $\vdash \sim\alpha$ *for some* α.

Proof Suppose that $\vdash \alpha$. By Theorem 10.4 it follows that $\vDash \alpha$. But then $\nvDash \sim\alpha$, for $\sim\alpha$ is false whenever α is true. So, by Theorem 10.4, $\nvdash \sim\alpha$.   □

10.2   Definitions of Soundness and Completeness

We have seen that there are two ways to characterize a set of valid forms expressible in **L**. One employs the semantic notion of logical consequence, in that it picks out the set of ordered pairs Γ/α such that $\Gamma \vDash \alpha$. The other employs the syntactic notion of derivability, in that it picks out the set of ordered pairs Γ/α such that $\Gamma \vdash \alpha$. So it is natural to ask whether these two ways are equivalent, that is, whether they pick out the same set of ordered pairs. The two properties that will be considered now concern precisely this equivalence:

Definition 10.2 A system S is *sound* iff, if $\Gamma \vdash \alpha$ in S, then $\Gamma \vDash \alpha$.

Definition 10.3 A system S is *complete* iff, if $\Gamma \vDash \alpha$, then $\Gamma \vdash \alpha$ in S.

As we shall see, **L** is sound and complete: derivability in **L** entails logical consequence, and logical consequence entails derivability in **L**. Before proving these two facts, however, it is useful to recognize that soundness and completeness can be phrased in terms of satisfiability and consistency, as the following theorems show.

Theorem 10.6 **L** *is sound iff every satisfiable set of formulas of* **L** *is consistent.*

Proof Assume that **L** is sound. Let Γ be any set of formulas of **L**, and suppose that Γ is inconsistent, that is, $\Gamma \vdash \alpha$ and $\Gamma \vdash \sim\alpha$ for some α. By the soundness of **L** it follows that $\Gamma \vDash \alpha$ and $\Gamma \vDash \sim\alpha$. So Γ is unsatisfiable, for otherwise some interpretation would verify α and $\sim\alpha$. This shows that if Γ is satisfiable, then Γ is consistent. Now assume that every satisfiable set of formulas of **L** is consistent. Suppose that $\Gamma \vdash \alpha$. Then $\Gamma \cup \{\sim\alpha\}$ is inconsistent by Theorem 9.30, so it is unsatisfiable. But if no interpretation verifies Γ and $\sim\alpha$, then no interpretation verifies Γ without verifying α, which means that $\Gamma \vDash \alpha$.   □

Theorem 10.7 **L** *is complete iff every consistent set of formulas of* Γ *is satisfiable.*

Proof Assume that **L** is complete. Let Γ be any set of formulas of **L**, and suppose that Γ is unsatisfiable. Then $\Gamma \vDash \alpha$ and $\Gamma \vDash \sim\alpha$ for some α. By the completeness of **L** we get that $\Gamma \vdash \alpha$ and $\Gamma \vdash \sim\alpha$. This shows that if Γ is consistent, then Γ is satisfiable. Now assume that every consistent set of formulas of **L** is satisfiable.

Suppose that $\Gamma \nvdash \alpha$. Then $\Gamma \cup \{\sim\alpha\}$ is consistent, given Theorem 9.30. So $\Gamma \cup \{\sim\alpha\}$ is satisfiable. This means that some interpretation verifies Γ but falsifies α, hence $\Gamma \nvDash \alpha$. Therefore, if $\Gamma \vDash \alpha$, then $\Gamma \vdash \alpha$. □

One last distinction must be drawn between completeness and *negation-completeness*, a syntactic property defined in terms of negation:

Definition 10.4 A system S is *negation-complete* iff, for every formula α of S, either $\vdash \alpha$ or $\vdash \sim\alpha$ in S.

A similar definition applies to theories:

Definition 10.5 A theory T is *negation-complete* iff, for every formula α of the language of T, either $T \vdash \alpha$ or $T \vdash \sim\alpha$.

Since T is deductively closed by definition, this is to say that either $\alpha \in T$ or $\sim\alpha \in T$. Note that Definitions 10.4 and 10.5 imply that negation-completeness is distinct from completeness. Unfortunately, the word 'completeness' occurs in both cases. These usages are now entirely entrenched, so you just have to learn to live with them.

10.3 Soundness of **L**

The soundness of **L** can easily be proved on the basis of Theorem 10.4.

Theorem 10.8 *If* $\Gamma \vdash \alpha$ *in* **L**, *then* $\Gamma \vDash \alpha$.

Proof Assume that $\Gamma \vdash \alpha$. Then, by Theorem 9.31, there is a finite subset Δ of Γ such that $\Delta \vdash \alpha$. Either $\Delta = \emptyset$ or $\Delta \neq \emptyset$. If $\Delta = \emptyset$, then $\vdash \alpha$. By Theorem 10.4 it follows that $\vDash \alpha$, so that $\Gamma \vDash \alpha$. If $\Delta \neq \emptyset$, then $\Delta = \{\beta_1, \ldots, \beta_n\}$ for some n, and $\beta_1, \ldots, \beta_n \vdash \alpha$. If we apply the deduction theorem (Theorem 9.8) n times we get that $\vdash \beta_1 \supset (\ldots (\beta_n \supset \alpha))$. By Theorem 10.4 it follows that $\vDash \beta_1 \supset (\ldots (\beta_n \supset \alpha))$. So there is no interpretation that verifies $\beta_1, \ldots, \beta_n$ but falsifies α. This means that $\Delta \vDash \alpha$. Therefore, $\Gamma \vDash \alpha$. □

10.4 Completeness of **L**

The completeness theorem requires a more articulated reasoning. The proof method employed here is due to Kurt Gödel, who established the first completeness result in 1930, and was then refined by Leon Henkin.[1] The structure of the proof is as

---

[1] Kurt Friedrich Gödel (1906–1978) was an extraordinarily gifted Austrian-Hungarian logician who started his academic career at the University of Vienna and then moved to the United States, where he got a position at Princeton University. He established several results of great importance,

follows. First it is shown that if a set of formulas of **L** is consistent, there is a theory that includes it as a subset and enjoys certain properties. Then it is shown that a theory with those properties is satisfiable, so the same goes for the initial set. This justifies the conclusion that every consistent set of formulas of **L** is satisfiable, which amounts to the completeness of **L**.

The first part of the proof hinges on a result known as *Lindenbaum's lemma*, which was first published by Alfred Tarski and attributed to Adolf Lindenbaum.[2] Let us start with two definitions:

Definition 10.6 An *extension* of a set of formulas Γ is a set of formulas Γ' such that $\Gamma \subseteq \Gamma'$.

Definition 10.7 A set of formulas Γ is *maximally consistent* iff Γ is consistent and, for every formula α, either $\alpha \in \Gamma$ or $\Gamma \cup \{\alpha\}$ is inconsistent.

In other words, Γ is maximally consistent when there is no consistent extension of Γ other than Γ itself: no formula can be added to Γ without losing consistency. Note that Definitions 10.6 and 10.7 hold for sets of formulas in general, so they apply to theories as well.

Lindenbaum's lemma says that every consistent set of formulas has a maximally consistent extension:

Theorem 10.9 *If a set of formulas Γ is consistent, then there is a maximally consistent extension of Γ.*

Proof Let Γ be a consistent set of formulas. Given an enumeration $\langle \alpha_1, \alpha_2, \alpha_3 \ldots \rangle$ of the formulas of the language of Γ, let $\langle \Gamma_0, \Gamma_1, \Gamma_2 \ldots \rangle$ be an infinite sequence of sets of formulas defined by induction as follows:

(i) $\Gamma_0 = \Gamma$;

(ii) for every n, $\begin{cases} \Gamma_{n+1} = \Gamma_n \cup \{\alpha_{n+1}\} & \text{if the latter is consistent} \\ \Gamma_{n+1} = \Gamma_n & \text{otherwise} \end{cases}$

Let $\Gamma_\infty = \Gamma_0 \cup \Gamma_1 \cup \Gamma_2 \ldots$. The following reasoning shows that Γ_∞ is consistent. First, each of the sets in the sequence $\langle \Gamma_0, \Gamma_1, \Gamma_2 \ldots \rangle$ is consistent, because (i)

---

among which the famous incompleteness theorems that are usually associated with his name (see Chapter 19). He proved the completeness theorem in his doctoral dissertation, Gödel [19]. Leon Albert Henkin (1921–2006) was an American logician who worked at the University of California, Berkeley. In Henkin [22] he provided a simplified version of Gödel's proof, which has become standard.

[2] Alfred Tarski (1902–1983) was a Polish logician who started his academic career at the University of Warsaw, then, at the outbreak of World War II, moved to the United States and settled in Berkeley, at the University of California. He is well known for his works on model theory, algebraic logic, and the foundations of mathematics. The proof of the lemma is in Tarski [62]. Adolf Lindenbaum (1904–1941) was a Polish logician who studied in Warsaw and collaborated closely with Tarski. He also had to leave Warsaw in 1939, due to his Jewish origin and his political orientation, but his decision to remain in Poland proved fatal, because two years later he was arrested by the Gestapo and shot to death.

entails that Γ_0 is consistent, and (ii) entails that, for every n, if Γ_n is consistent, then Γ_{n+1} is consistent as well. Now suppose that Γ_∞ is inconsistent. Then, for some β, we have both a derivation of β from Γ_∞ and a derivation of $\sim\beta$ from Γ_∞. Each of the two derivations contains a finite set of the formulas that have been added to Γ to obtain Γ_∞. Let α_m be the formula among them with the highest number in the enumeration $\langle\alpha_1, \alpha_2, \alpha_3 \dots\rangle$. Then the two derivations are also derivations of β and $\sim\beta$ from Γ_m, so there is an inconsistent set in the sequence $\langle\Gamma_0, \Gamma_1, \Gamma_2 \dots\rangle$, contrary to what has been proved.

Since $\Gamma \subseteq \Gamma_\infty$ and Γ_∞ is consistent, in order to prove that Γ has a maximally consistent extension it suffices to show that, for every α, either $\alpha \in \Gamma_\infty$ or $\Gamma_\infty \cup \{\alpha\}$ is inconsistent. Let α_{n+1} be any formula in the enumeration. Either $\Gamma_n \cup \{\alpha_{n+1}\}$ is consistent or it is inconsistent. If it is consistent, then $\Gamma_{n+1} = \Gamma_n \cup \{\alpha_{n+1}\}$, so $\alpha_{n+1} \in \Gamma_\infty$. If it is inconsistent, instead, $\Gamma_n \cup \{\alpha_{n+1}\} \vdash \beta$ and $\Gamma_n \cup \{\alpha_{n+1}\} \vdash \sim\beta$ for some β. Since $\Gamma_n \subseteq \Gamma_\infty$, it follows that $\Gamma_\infty \cup \{\alpha_{n+1}\} \vdash \beta$ and $\Gamma_\infty \cup \{\alpha_{n+1}\} \vdash \sim\beta$. $\qquad\square$

A direct corollary of this theorem is that every consistent set of formulas is a subset of a consistent and negation-complete theory:

Theorem 10.10 *If a set of formulas* Γ *is consistent, then there is a theory T which is a consistent and negation-complete extension of* Γ.

Proof Assume that Γ is consistent. By Lindenbaum's lemma (Theorem 10.9), there is a set Γ' such that $\Gamma \subseteq \Gamma'$ and Γ' is maximally consistent. Let T be the deductive closure of Γ'. T is an extension of Γ because $\Gamma \subseteq \Gamma'$ and $\Gamma' \subseteq$ T. Since Γ' is consistent, T is consistent as well (see Exercise 9.10). So it suffices to show that T is negation-complete. Take any formula α. Suppose that $\alpha \notin$ T. Then $\Gamma' \nvdash \alpha$, being T the deductive closure of Γ'. It follows that $\alpha \notin \Gamma'$. Since Γ' is maximally consistent, $\Gamma' \cup \{\alpha\}$ is inconsistent. By Theorem 9.29, this entails that $\Gamma' \vdash \sim\alpha$, so that $\sim\alpha \in$ T. Therefore, either $\alpha \in$ T or $\sim\alpha \in$ T. $\qquad\square$

Theorem 10.10 holds for a wide class of systems, as is shown by the fact that the proof of Lindenbaum's lemma (Theorem 10.9) does not depend on specific features of the deductive apparatus of **L**. As far as **L** is concerned, Theorem 10.10 entails that every consistent set of formulas of **L** is a subset of a consistent and negation-complete theory. Thus, in order to prove that every set of formulas of **L** is satisfiable it suffices to prove that every consistent and negation-complete theory in the language of **L** is satisfiable. This is the second part of the proof.

Theorem 10.11 *If T is a consistent and negation-complete theory in the language of* **L**, *then T is satisfiable.*

Proof Let T be a consistent and negation-complete theory in the language of **L**. Let V be an interpretation that assigns 1 to all the sentence letters that belong to T and 0 to all the sentence letters that do not belong to T. Now it will be shown by induction on the complexity of a formula α that $[\alpha]_V = 1$ iff $T \vdash \alpha$.

Basis. Assume that α is an atomic formula. Then $[\alpha]_V = 1$ iff $T \vdash \alpha$ simply because V is defined this way.

Step. Assume that the biconditional to be proved holds for any formula of complexity less than or equal to n, and consider a formula α of complexity $n + 1$.

Case 1: α has the form $\sim\beta$. Suppose that $[\sim\beta]_V = 1$. Then $[\beta]_V = 0$. By the induction hypothesis it follows that $T \nvdash \beta$. Since T is negation-complete, $T \vdash \sim\beta$. Now suppose that $T \vdash \sim\beta$. Then $T \nvdash \beta$, because T is consistent. By the induction hypothesis it follows that $[\beta]_V = 0$. So, $[\sim\beta]_V = 1$.

Case 2: α has the form $\beta \supset \gamma$. Suppose that $[\beta \supset \gamma]_V = 0$, that is, $[\beta]_V = 1$ and $[\gamma]_V = 0$. By the induction hypothesis we get that $T \vdash \beta$ and $T \nvdash \gamma$, which entails that $T \vdash \sim\gamma$, given that T is negation-complete. Since $T \vdash \beta \supset (\sim\gamma \supset \sim(\beta \supset \gamma))$ by Theorem 9.18, we get that $T \vdash \sim(\beta \supset \gamma)$. Since T is consistent, $T \nvdash \beta \supset \gamma$. Now suppose that $T \nvdash \beta \supset \gamma$. Then $T \vdash \sim(\beta \supset \gamma)$, given that T is negation-complete. By Theorems 9.27 and 9.28, $T \vdash \sim(\beta \supset \gamma) \supset \beta$ and $T \vdash \sim(\beta \supset \gamma) \supset \sim\gamma$. It follows by MP that $T \vdash \beta$ and $T \vdash \sim\gamma$. Since T is consistent, $T \nvdash \gamma$. By the induction hypothesis, then, $[\beta]_V = 1$ and $[\gamma]_V = 0$, which means that $[\beta \supset \gamma]_V = 0$. $\square$

Theorem 10.12 *If $\Gamma \vDash \alpha$, then $\Gamma \vdash \alpha$ in **L**.*

Proof Assume that Γ is a consistent set of formulas of **L**. By Theorem 10.10, there is a maximally consistent theory T such that $\Gamma \subseteq T$. By Theorem 10.11, T is satisfiable. So, Γ is satisfiable as well. By Theorem 10.7, this means that if $\Gamma \vDash \alpha$, then $\Gamma \vdash \alpha$ in **L**. $\square$

10.5   Extension to **G⁻**

We have seen that **L** is consistent, sound, and complete. Now it will be shown that the same results hold for **G⁻**, given the deductive equivalence between **G⁻** and **L**.

Theorem 10.13 *In **G⁻** it is not the case that $\vdash \alpha$ and $\vdash \sim\alpha$ for some α.*

Proof Suppose that $\vdash \alpha$ in **G⁻**. By Theorem 9.24 it follows that $\vdash \alpha$ in **L**. From this and Theorem 10.4 we get that $\vDash \alpha$. But then $\nvDash \sim\alpha$. So, by Theorem 10.4 again, $\nvdash \sim\alpha$ in **L**, hence by Theorem 9.24 $\nvdash \sim\alpha$ in **G⁻**. $\square$

Theorem 10.14 *If $\Gamma \vdash \alpha$ in **G⁻**, then $\Gamma \vDash \alpha$.*

Proof Assume that $\Gamma \vdash \alpha$ in **G⁻**. By Theorem 9.24 it follows that $\Gamma \vdash \alpha$ in **L**. From this and Theorem 10.8 we get that $\Gamma \vDash \alpha$. $\square$

Theorem 10.15 *If $\Gamma \vDash \alpha$, then $\Gamma \vdash \alpha$ in **G⁻**.*

Proof Assume that $\Gamma \vDash \alpha$. By Theorem 10.12 it follows that $\Gamma \vdash \alpha$ in **L**. From this and Theorem 9.25 we get that $\Gamma \vdash \alpha$ in $\mathbf{G}^-$.   □

More generally, the results just proved can be extended to any axiomatic or natural deduction system of propositional logic which is deductively equivalent to **L**.

Exercises

10.1 Explain why a system S is consistent only if some formula of S is not a theorem.

10.2 Explain why some formula of a system S is not a theorem only if S is consistent.

10.3 Explain why a theory T is consistent and negation-complete only if T is maximally consistent.

10.4 Explain why a theory T is maximally consistent only if T is consistent and negation-complete.

10.5 Is **L** negation-complete?

10.6 Is $\mathbf{G}^-$ negation-complete?

10.7 Is the set of valid formulas of **L** decidable?

10.8 Is the set of theorems of **L** decidable?

10.9 Is the set of theorems of $\mathbf{G}^-$ decidable?

10.10 In order to prove Theorem 10.11, all that need be shown is that T is satisfied, namely, that, for every α, if $\alpha \in$ T, then $[\alpha]_V = 1$. So why don't we just prove this conditional by induction, instead of proving the corresponding biconditional?

Chapter 11
Quantification

11.1 Quantified Sentences

Although propositional logic provides a formal account of a wide class of valid arguments, its explanatory power is limited. Many arguments are valid in virtue of formal properties that do not depend on the truth-functional structure of their premises and conclusion, so their validity is not explainable in propositional logic. Here is an example:

(1) Socrates is a philosopher
(2) Something is a philosopher

(1) The Coliseum is material
(2) Something is material

These two arguments are valid for the same reason: if it is true that a given object has a certain property, then it must be true that something has that property. This fact has nothing to do with truth-functionality. Consider the first argument. Since (1) and (2) are distinct simple sentences, in a propositional language they are represented by different sentence letters, say p and q. But p/q is not a valid form, given that $p \nvDash q$. The same goes for the second.

Predicate logic can explain the validity of the two arguments above, and of many other arguments in which the legitimacy of the inference depends on the internal structure of simple sentences. These arguments do not exhaust the range of cases that exceed the expressive resources of propositional logic. An argument can be valid in virtue of other structural features, as in the following case:

© The Author(s), under exclusive license to Springer Nature Switzerland AG 2021
A. Iacona, *LOGIC: Lecture Notes for Philosophy, Mathematics, and Computer Science*, Springer Undergraduate Texts in Philosophy,
https://doi.org/10.1007/978-3-030-64811-4_11

(1)   Necessarily, everything is material

(2)   Everything is material

The validity of this argument hinges on the meaning of 'necessarily', which is not a truth-functional operator, as noted in Sect. 4.5. The only way to formalize (1) and (2) in a propositional language is, again, to assign different sentence letters to them, thus obtaining an invalid form. Chapter 20 will show how 'necessarily' can be treated at the formal level. But for the moment we will leave aside such operators, which fall outside the domain of predicate logic, and focus on the internal structure of simple sentences.

There are various kinds of simple sentences. Some, such as 'Socrates is a philosopher', are about specific objects and their properties or relations. Others, instead, concern properties or relations without referring to specific objects. The sentences of the latter kind—*quantified sentences*—are about sets of objects rather than specific objects. For example, 'Something is a philosopher' says something about the property of being a philosopher without referring to a specific individual. In order to explain the validity of the first argument above we need a proper analysis of this sentence. More generally, in order to explain the validity of the inferences that hinge on the internal structure of simple sentences it is essential to clarify the logical form of quantified sentences.

Predicate logic focuses on two basic kinds of quantified sentences, *universal* and *existential* sentences. The former typically begin with quantifier expressions such as 'all', 'every' or 'any', while the latter typically begin with quantifier expressions such as 'there is', 'at least one' or 'some'. For example, 'Everything is material' is a universal sentence, while 'Something is a philosopher' is an existential sentence. Here 'something' is understood as 'at least one thing'. Normally it is assumed that the truth of an existential sentence requires the existence of at least one object that satisfies the condition specified.

These two kinds of quantified sentences are basic in the sense that a considerable part of the assertions that involve some form of quantification are expressible by means of sentences of one or the other kind. This does not mean that they are the only kinds of quantified sentences. Beside 'all', 'every', 'any', 'there is', 'at least one' and 'some', English contains other quantifier expressions: 'many', 'few', 'more than half of', and so on. But a comprehensive analysis of quantifier expressions goes beyond the scope of the present work.[1]

---

[1] Peters and Westerståhl [49] provides a rigorous and thorough treatment of a wide variety of quantifier expressions.

11.2   A Brief Historical Survey

The study of quantified sentences goes back to the origins of logic itself. The first systematic treatment of quantification is Aristotle's theory of syllogism, outlined in *Prior Analytics* (c. 350 BC). A syllogism, as Aristotle understands it, is a valid argument formed by two premises and one conclusion, each of which contains two "terms", such as 'man', 'animal', or 'mortal'. Here is an example:

(1)   Every animal is mortal
(2)   Every man is an animal
(3)   Every man is mortal

In a syllogism, the legitimacy of the inference depends on the relation between the two terms that occur in the conclusion and a third term that occurs in the premises, called "middle term". For example, in the argument above the middle term is 'animal'.[2]

Aristotle uses schematic letters to indicate arbitrary terms. For example, the following schema represents the kind of syllogism instantiated by the argument above:

Every *A* is *B*, Every *C* is *A*/Every *C* is *B*

By means of schemas of this kind, Aristotle provides a classification of syllogisms based on a distinction between "figures", which depend on the different relations in which the middle term stands to the other two terms.

Aristotle's syllogistic initiated a tradition of logical investigations that produced many important results, as its influence lasted for more than two millennia. Yet it has some unsurmountable limitations. First, the way in which quantified sentences are represented is not purely formal but semi-formal, given that it involves natural language expressions. Formalization as is it understood now was not contemplated by Aristotle. Second, it is reasonable to expect that an adequate analysis of the internal structure of simple sentences can be integrated with the truth-functional analysis of complex sentences that grounds propositional logic. But there is no obvious way to combine Aristotle's schemas with propositional logic. Third, many valid arguments involving quantified sentences are left unexplained, such as the following:

(1)   Every philosopher has read some old book
(2)   Every philosopher has read some book

Since (1) is a sentence of the form 'Every *A* is *B*', where *B* stands for 'has read some old book', if one wants to represent this argument, one has to use a different variable for 'has read some book', say *C*. But the schema 'Every *A* is *B*/Every *A*

---

[2] Aristotle, *Prior Analytics*, 41b36.

is C' is invalid. More generally, the method of representation adopted by Aristotle is unable to capture the structure of sentences in which quantification occurs in predicate position.

The theory of quantification outlined in Frege's *Begriffsschrift* overcomes these limitations. The key of Frege's method of formalization is the hypothesis that sentences have function-argument structure. To illustrate, consider the expression $S(1)$, where S stands for 'successor'. This expression denotes the number 2. Its denotation is the result of the combination of the denotation of S with the denotation of 1. According to Frege, 'Socrates is a philosopher' is analogous to $S(1)$: the name 'Socrates' denotes Socrates, and the predicate 'philosopher' denotes a function that applies to Socrates. More precisely, 'philosopher' denotes a function P such that, for every object x, $P(x) = 1$ if x is a philosopher, and $P(x) = 0$ otherwise. The truth value of 'Socrates is a philosopher', which Frege identifies with its denotation, is the result of the combination of the denotation of 'Socrates' and the denotation of 'philosopher', namely, the value that P takes for Socrates as argument.[3]

Now let us turn to quantified sentences. Frege draws a distinction between *first-level functions*, which take objects as arguments, and *second-level functions*, which take first-level functions as arguments. His view is that expressions such as 'everything' and 'something' denote second-level functions. Consider 'Everything is material'. According to Frege, 'material' denotes a first-level function M such that, for every object x, $M(x) = 1$ if x is material, and $M(x) = 0$ otherwise, while 'everything' denotes a second-level function E such that, for every first-level function F, $E(F) = 1$ if $F(x) = 1$ for every x, and $E(F) = 0$ otherwise. So the truth value of 'Everything is material' is the result of the combination of E and M. In other terms, this sentence says that 'material' has the property of being true of every object. To express this, Frege employs variables as follows:

For every x, x is material.

The same idea can be applied to 'Every animal is mortal', where the universal quantification is restricted by the predicate 'animal'. This sentence says that 'mortal' has the property of being true of every animal, namely, of every object of which 'animal' is true. Accordingly, it is paraphrased as follows:

For every x, if x is an animal, x is mortal.

The case of existential quantification is analogous. According to Frege, 'something' denotes a second-level function S such that, for every first-level function F, $S(F) = 1$ if $F(x) = 1$ for some x, and $S(F) = 0$ otherwise. Thus, the truth value of 'Something is material' is the result of the combination of S and M. In other words, 'Something is material' says that 'material' has the property of being true of some object:

---

[3] Frege [14]. The view that predicates denote functions from objects to truth values, which is not explicitly stated in *Begriffsschrift*, is outlined in Frege [15].

For some x, x is material.

The same idea can be applied to sentences where the existential quantification is restricted by some predicate, such as 'Some philosophers are wise'. According to Frege, this sentence is to be paraphrased as follows:

For some x, x is a philosopher and x is wise.

Frege's analysis of quantification overcomes the three limitations that affect Aristotle's syllogistic. First, it enables us to formally represent quantified sentences without using natural language expressions. As noted in Sect. 3.3, the language defined in his *Begriffsschrift* is the first formal language properly understood. Second, it integrates with propositional logic, as it is easy to see if one thinks that 'if' and 'and' occur respectively in the paraphrases suggested. Third, it provides an adequate formal treatment of a class of quantified sentences that includes not only the sentences studied in the Aristotelian tradition, such as 'Every animal is mortal', but also a variety of more complex sentences whose logical properties had not been properly elucidated within that tradition. For example, 'Every philosopher has read some old book' and 'Every philosopher has read some book' are paraphrased as follows:

For every x, if x is a philosopher, then for some y such that y is a book and y is old, x has read y.

For every x, if x is a philosopher, then for some y such that y is a book, x has read y.

As we shall see, this paraphrase enables us to explain why the former sentence entails the latter. More generally, any quantified sentence in which universal or existential quantification occurs in predicate position can adequately be represented by means of variables in the way illustrated. The innovative force of Frege's method of formalization crucially depends on this capacity.

11.3 Existential Import

According to Frege's analysis of quantification, 'Every A is B' has no existential import: it can happen that A is an empty predicate—a predicate whose extension is $\emptyset$—hence that, for every x, 'if x is A, x is B' is true no matter whether x is B. In other terms, if A is empty, 'Every A is B' is vacuously true.

To grasp the implications of this fact, consider the sentences 'Every unicorn has teeth' and 'No unicorn has teeth'. These sentences are to be paraphrased as follows:

For every x, if x is a unicorn, x has teeth.
For every x, if x is a unicorn, x lacks teeth.

Since there are no unicorns, both statements are vacuously true.

This outcome may cause some puzzlement, for our first naïve reaction is to think that 'Every unicorn has teeth' and 'No unicorn has teeth' are inconsistent. We are inclined to reason as follows: if B and C are incompatible predicates, then 'Every A is B' contradicts 'Every A is C'. Since we tend to accept 'Every unicorn has teeth' on the basis of background information about unicorns, and 'lacks teeth' contradicts 'has teeth', we are naturally led to reject 'No unicorn has teeth'.

However, this inclination provides no conclusive evidence against Frege's analysis of quantification. Certainly, when A is not empty, it is true that 'Every A is B' contradicts 'Every A is C' if B and C are incompatible predicates. For example, 'Every horse has teeth' and 'Every horse lacks teeth' cannot both be true. But this does not guarantee that the same holds when A is empty. To see how our first naïve reaction can be overridden by more reflective considerations, two points may be taken into account.

First, if we endorsed a formal account of universal sentences that preserves existential import, we would get consequences that are no less puzzling, for some apparently true sentences would turn out false. For example, since no actual table is 2 km long, 'Every table 2 km long is longer than this table' would turn out false, while it is clearly true. It is implausible that the truth of this sentence depends on the existence of tables 2 km long, given that one can accept it without knowing whether such tables exist. In many cases we tend to use universal sentences this way, so the assumption that 'Every A is B' has existential import is no less in conflict with our unreflective inclinations.

Second, the impression that 'Every unicorn has teeth' is true and 'Every unicorn lacks teeth' is false clashes with other assumptions that are quite reasonable. If 'Every unicorn lacks teeth' is false, then 'Not every unicorn lacks teeth' must be true. But it is reasonable to grant, as Frege does, that 'Not every A is B' is equivalent to 'Some A is not B', so that 'Not every unicorn lacks teeth' is equivalent to 'Some unicorn has teeth'. Thus, rejecting 'Every unicorn lacks teeth' amounts to accepting 'Some unicorn has teeth', which entails the existence of unicorns. And we know that there are no unicorns.

11.4   Multiple Generality

As we have seen, one of the merits of Frege's analysis of quantification is that it enables us to elucidate the logical structure of sentences in which quantification occurs in predicate position. To fully appreciate the potential of this analysis, it is important to recognize that the same method can be applied to any case of *multiple generality*, that is, any case in which a quantified sentence contains more than one quantifier expression.

Quantifier expressions can be combined in various ways. Some sentences, such as 'Every philosopher has read some book', involve both universal and existential quantification, while others include distinct quantifier expressions of the same kind.

For example, 'The man who falls in love with every woman is unhappy' contains a double universal quantification:

For every x such that x is a man, and for every y such that y is a woman, if x falls in love with y, x is unhappy.

Instead, 'Alf has bought something and has exchanged it for something' contains a double existential quantification:

There is an x such that Alf has bought x and there is a y such that Alf has exchanged x for y.

Multiple generality is closely related to structural ambiguity, for a wide range of cases of structural ambiguity can be explained in terms of distinct combinations of quantifiers. A classical example is 'Every sailor loves a girl', which admits two readings:

For every x, if x is a sailor, there is a y such that y is a girl and x loves y.
There is an x such that x is a girl and, for every y, if y is a sailor, y loves x.

The second reading is stronger than the first, as it entails the first without being entailed by it.

To illustrate how a proper treatment of structural ambiguity can provide a deeper insight into the logical properties of natural language, let us consider a philosophically pregnant case. In the past, some theologicians have appealed to the following argument in order to justify their faith in God:

(1) Every thing has a cause
(2) There is a cause of every thing

However, the flaw of this argument becomes evident once it is made clear that (1) admits two readings:

For every x, there is a y such that y is the cause of x.
There is an x such that, for every y, x is the cause of y.

The second reading—which is also the intended reading of (2)—is stronger than the first: while the first is consistent with the possibility that different objects have different causes, the second rules out that possibility. Therefore, if (1) is understood in the first sense, which is the only intelligible sense in which it differs from (2), then (2) does not follow from (1).[4]

---

[4]This example is drawn from Frascolla [13], pp. 178–179.

11.5   Definite Descriptions

A *definite description* is an expression that is used to denote a single object in that it states a condition that is taken to be satisfied uniquely by that object. For example, 'the capital of Italy' is a definite description. This expression denotes Rome, because Rome is the unique object that is capital of Italy. As we shall see, the kind of paraphrase outlined in the previous sections can be applied to sentences containing definite descriptions.

Definite descriptions resemble proper names in many respects. There is an obvious sense in which 'The capital of Italy is charming' and 'Rome is charming' say the same thing, namely, that Rome has the property of being charming. However, definite descriptions are not exactly like proper names from the logical point of view. Consider the following argument:

(1)   The capital of Italy is charming
(2)   Something is capital of Italy and is charming

This argument is valid, and it is reasonable to expect that its validity is formally explainable. Independently of what city is actually the capital of Italy, if that city is charming, there must be an x such that x is capital of Italy and x is charming. Now consider the following argument:

(1)   Rome is charming
(2)   Something is capital of Italy and is charming

This argument is invalid, for the capital of Italy could be some ugly city other than Rome. To obtain (2), one needs a vital piece of information that cannot be extracted from a formal analysis of (1), namely, that Rome is the capital of Italy. This suggests that the logical properties of 'The capital of Italy is charming' significantly differ from those of 'Rome is charming'.

In his famous article *On Denoting* (1905), Russell suggested that the logical structure of sentences containing definite descriptions is more complex than it may appear. Although it may appear that 'the capital of Italy' is a genuine singular term, like 'Rome', in reality it is not. According to Russell, 'The capital of Italy is charming' is correctly paraphrased as follows:

For some x, x is capital of Italy, and for every y, if y is capital of Italy, $y = x$, and x is charming.

Since this paraphrase contains no singular term that refers to Rome, 'the capital of Italy' is a singular term only superficially, that is, it is not a singular term from the logical point of view.[5]

---

[5]Russell [55], p. 482.

Russell argues for his view by drawing attention to some problems that seem to arise if definite descriptions are treated as genuine singular terms. One of his arguments concerns empty definite descriptions, that is, definite descriptions which do not denote anything. For example, 'The present King of France is bald' seems meaningful, just like 'The capital of Italy is charming'. But since 'the present King of France' does not denote anything, we cannot say that 'The present King of France is bald' is meaningful in virtue of picking out some particular individual and ascribing a property to that individual. Some alternative explanation must be provided. One might be tempted to say that 'the present King of France' differs from 'the capital of Italy' only in that it denotes a different kind of object, that is, a nonexistent object. But such a move does not seem promising to Russell. His explanation is instead that 'The present King of France is bald' says what follows:

For some x, x is King of France, and for every y, if y is King of France, $y = x$, and x is bald.

So it is exactly as meaningful as 'The capital of Italy is charming'. The only difference between 'The present King of France is bald' and 'The capital of Italy is charming' is that the first sentence is false, because there is no King of France.[6]

A related argument concerns negative existential claims made by using sentences which contain empty definite descriptions. For example, since France is a republic, 'The present King of France does not exist' is intuitively true. But if 'the present King of France' were a genuine singular term, this sentence would say that the object denoted by 'the present King of France' has the property of not existing, which seems contradictory. Russell suggests the following paraphrase:

It is not the case that, for some x, x is King of France, and for every y, if y is King of France, $y = x$.

This way he provides a coherent explanation of the apparent truth of 'The present King of France does not exist'.[7]

Exercises

11.1 Rephrase each sentence in the passage quoted in Exercise 1.9

11.2 Set out the reasoning contained in the same passage in the way illustrated in Sect. 1.3.

11.3 Paraphrase the following sentences by using one variable:

(a) Whales are mammals

---

[6]Russell [55], pp. 482–484.
[7]Russell [55], pp. 485–490.

(b) Only silly people make silly jokes

(c) No cat likes swimming

11.4 Paraphrase 'Everything is identical to itself' by using one variable.

11.5 Paraphrase the following sentences:

(a) Every happy man has a shirt that suits him

(b) Some dogs like cats

(c) Everybody loves lovers

11.6 For each of the following sentences, show its ambiguity:

(a) Sophie only eats pesticide-free vegetables

(b) If Astrid gives 100 euros to a poor woman, she will be happy

(c) There is a natural number greater than any natural number

11.7 Explain how Russell's theory of descriptions accounts for the intuitive difference between the two arguments considered in Sect. 11.5.

11.8 Paraphrase the following sentences assuming Russell's theory of descriptions:

(a) The abominable snowman is hairy

(b) The abominable snowman does not exist

11.9 Assuming Russell's theory of descriptions, show that 'It is not the case that the present king of France is bald' admits two readings.

11.10 Assuming Russell's theory of descriptions, explain why 'Scott is the author of *Waverley*' is not a real identity statement, like 'Tully is Cicero'.

Chapter 12
The Symbols of Predicate Logic

12.1 Non-logical Expressions

This chapter introduces a predicate language called L_q. The alphabet of L_q is constituted by the following symbols:

$a, b, c \ldots$
$P, Q, R \ldots$
$\sim, \supset, \forall$
$x, y, z \ldots$
$(,)$

Let us start with the non-logical expressions. L_q has a denumerable set of *individual constants* $a, b, c \ldots$, which represent singular terms, and a denumerable set of *predicate letters* $P, Q, R \ldots$, which represent predicates. Each predicate letter has n places, for some n. One-place predicate letters represent monadic predicates, that is, predicates that apply to single objects and express properties. Two-place predicate letters represent dyadic predicates, that is, predicates that apply to ordered pairs of objects and express relations. Three-place predicate letters represent triadic predicates, and so on.

As we saw in Sect. 1.4, the extension of a singular term is the object it denotes, and the extension of a predicate is the set of objects to which it applies. Accordingly, an individual constant is interpreted by assigning an object to it, and a predicate letter is interpreted by assigning a set of objects to it. More specifically, one-place predicates letters are associated with sets of objects, two-place predicate letters are associated with sets of ordered pairs, three-place predicates are associated with ordered triples, and so on.

© The Author(s), under exclusive license to Springer Nature Switzerland AG 2021
A. Iacona, *LOGIC: Lecture Notes for Philosophy, Mathematics, and Computer Science*, Springer Undergraduate Texts in Philosophy,
https://doi.org/10.1007/978-3-030-64811-4_12

By combining predicate letters with individual constants, we can represent any sentence that asserts that a certain object has a certain property or that certain objects stand in a certain relation. For example, 'Socrates is a philosopher' is formalized as follows:

Ps

Here P is a one-place predicate letter that stands for 'philosopher' and s is an individual constant that stands for 'Socrates'. Instead, 'Othello loves Desdemona' is formalized as follows:

Lod

Here L is a two-place predicate letter that stands for 'loves', while o and d are individual constants that stand respectively for 'Othello' and 'Desdemona'. Note that, when we represent non-monadic predicates, the order of the individual constants matters: one thing is to say that Othello loves Desdemona, another thing is to say that Desdemona loves Othello.

A formula obtained by combining an n-place predicate letter and n individual constants is true or false depending on whether the objects denoted by the individual constants belong to the set denoted by the predicate letter. Thus, just as 'Socrates is a philosopher' is true if and only if Socrates belongs to the extension of 'philosopher', the first formula above is true if and only if the object denoted by s belongs to the set denoted by P. Similarly, just as 'Othello loves Desdemona' is true if and only if the ordered pair ⟨Othello, Desdemona⟩ belongs to the extension of 'loves', the second formula above is true if and only if the ordered pair formed by the objects denoted by o and d belongs to the set denoted by L.

12.2   Logical Constants and Auxiliary Symbols

The symbols $\sim, \supset, \forall$ are the logical constants of $\mathsf{L_q}$. $\sim$ and $\supset$ stand respectively for 'not' and 'if', as in a propositional language, and behave truth-functionally. For example, 'If Othello loves Desdemona, Socrates is not a philosopher' is formalized as follows:

Lod $\supset \sim Ps$

This formula is true if and only if its antecedent is false or its consequent is true.

$\forall$ is the *universal quantifier*, which means 'for every'. This symbol is used in combination with the variables $x, y, z \ldots$, which are auxiliary symbols.[1] Variables are exactly like individual constants from the syntactic point of view, in that they can be combined with predicate letters in the same way. For example, Px is a

---

[1]The symbol $\forall$ was introduced in Gentzen [18]. Frege expressed universal quantification in a different way.

formula, and the same goes for Lxd. This is why both individual constants and variables are classified as *terms*. But variables do not have denotation, at least not in the sense in which individual constants have denotation. An interpretation of L_q involves an assignment of objects to its individual constants, but it does not involve an assignment of objects to its variables. So, variables differ both from non-logical expressions, in that they do not have meaning relative to interpretations, and from logical constants, in that they do not have meaning independently of interpretations.

The semantic difference between variables and individual constants may be illustrated by means of an analogy. While individual constants are like names, variables are rather like pronouns, which refer to different things on different occasions. Px stands for something like 'It is a philosopher', a sentence that expresses no content—hence cannot be evaluated as true or false—unless it is specified what 'it' denotes: 'It is a philosopher' says something true if 'it' denotes Aristotle, while it says something false if 'it' denotes a banana.

To see how $\forall$ can be combined with variables, consider the sentence 'Everything is material'. This sentence says that, for every x, x is material. Accordingly, it is formalized as follows:

$\forall x M x$

Just as 'Everything is material' is true if and only if every object is material, this formula is true if and only if every x belongs to the extension of M.

To represent more complex universal sentences we need brackets. For example, 'All philosophers are wise' says that, for every x, if x is philosopher, then x is wise. Accordingly, it is formalized as follows:

$\forall x (Px \supset Wx)$

Here the brackets make clear that the universal quantifier applies to $Px \supset Wx$, not to Px. The formula above is true if and only if, for every x, if x belongs to the extension of P, then x belongs to the extension of W. The conventions about brackets that will be adopted are the same as in a propositional language (Sect. 4.3).

12.3 Other Symbols

The alphabet of L_q does not exhaust the symbolic apparatus of predicate logic. Even though we will focus on L_q in the next two chapters, it is important to know that a predicate language can include other symbols.

First, the set of sentential connectives can be larger. In particular, $\wedge$ and $\vee$ can be added to the alphabet of L_q. As noted in Sects. 4.4 and 8.5, these connectives are definable in terms of $\sim$ and $\supset$.

Second, a predicate language can include ∃, the *existential quantifier*, which means 'for some'.[2] This symbol enables us to represent existential sentences. For example, 'Something is material' says that there is at least one x such that x is material, so it is formalized as follows:

$\exists x\,Mx$

Similarly, 'Some philosophers are wise' says that there is at least one x such that x is philosopher and x is wise, so it is formalized as follows:

$\exists x(Px \wedge Wx)$

Asserting that something is material amounts to denying that everything is non-material. Therefore, 'Something is material' can equally be represented as follows:

$\sim\forall x\sim Mx$

Similarly, asserting that something is both philosopher and wise amounts to denying that every philosopher is not wise. Therefore, 'Some philosophers are wise' can equally be represented as follows:

$\sim\forall x(Px \supset \sim Wx)$

More generally, whatever can be expressed by means of ∃ can also be expressed by means of ∀, and whatever can be expressed by means of ∀ can also be expressed by means of ∃. One quantifier is sufficient to formalize any universal or existential sentence, provided that the language includes negation.

Note that in the formalization of 'All philosophers are wise' considered in Sect. 12.2, ∀ is combined with ⊃, while in the first formalization of 'Some philosophers are wise' above, ∃ is combined with ∧. In general, ∀ goes with ⊃, while ∃ goes with ∧. To avoid confusion, it suffices to realize that it would make no sense to do the opposite. A formula obtained by adding $\forall x$ to $Px \wedge Wx$ would not adequately represent 'All philosophers are wise', for it would be true if and only if $Px \wedge Wx$ is true of every x, so it would say that everything is a wise philosopher. A formula obtained by adding $\exists x$ to $Px \supset Wx$ would not adequately represent 'Some philosophers are wise', for it would be true if and only if $Px \supset Wx$ is true of some object, so it would say that something is not a philosopher or is wise. The inadequacy of the two representations becomes evident if we think that the first formula would require the existence of philosophers, while the second would not.

Finally, a predicate language can include =, the symbol of identity. This symbol resembles a two-place predicate letter in that it combines with two terms and denotes a relation. However, unlike a two-place predicate letter, = always denotes the same relation: its extension is always the set of ordered pairs in which the same object occurs twice. This means that a formula obtained by combining = with two terms

---

[2]The symbol ∃ appears in Russell and Whitehead [57], and derives from an inverted ϵ previously used by Peano.

expresses an identity statement. For example, 'Rome is Rome' can be represented as follows:

$$a = a$$

Note that $=$ does not precede the two terms, like a two-place predicate letter, that is, we do not write $= aa$. The negation of a formula of this kind is indicated by using the symbol $\neq$.

12.4   Numerical Expressions

So far we have considered some elementary cases of formalization in a predicate language. These last three sections deal with more complex cases in order to show the expressive potential of predicate logic. Let us begin with 'at least n'. When this expression occurs in a sentence and $n = 1$, the sentence can be formalized simply by means of $\exists$. For example, 'At least one object is material' has the same content as 'Something is material', so it is formalized in the way explained in Sect. 12.3. Now consider the case in which $n = 2$. In order to express the content of 'At least two objects are material', it is not enough to say that there is an x such that x is material and there is a y such that y is material, for nothing rules out that x and y refer to the same thing. So it must be indicated that x and y are distinct:

$$\exists x \exists y (Mx \wedge My \wedge x \neq y)$$

The case in which $n = 3$ is similar, that is, 'At least three objects are material' becomes

$$\exists x \exists y \exists z (Mx \wedge My \wedge Mz \wedge x \neq y \wedge x \neq z \wedge y \neq z)$$

More generally, any sentence that says that at least n objects satisfy a given condition can be formalized by combining $\exists$ and $=$ in the way illustrated.

The expression 'at most n' imposes a similar increase in complexity, but requires the symbol of identity even in the case in which $n = 1$. For example, 'At most one object is material' says that there are no distinct objects x and y such that both x and y are material. That is, if x and y are both material, they are the same object:

$$\forall x \forall y ((Mx \wedge My) \supset x = y)$$

Now consider the sentence 'At most two objects are material'. This sentence says that, for any x, y, z, if x, y, z are material, then either z is identical to x or z is identical to y, so it is formalized as follows:

$$\forall x \forall y \forall z ((Mx \wedge My \wedge Mz) \supset (z = x \vee z = y \vee x = y))$$

The case of 'At most three objects are material' is similar. More generally, any sentence that says that at most n objects satisfy a given condition can be formalized by combining $\forall$ and $=$ in the way illustrated.

What has been said about 'at least n' and 'at most n' implies that 'exactly n' can be also expressed by means of quantifiers. To say that exactly n objects satisfy a given condition is to say that at least n objects and at most n objects satisfy that condition. For example, 'Exactly one object is material' says that at least one and at most one object is material. So it is formalized as follows:

$$\exists x (Mx \wedge \forall y (My \supset y = x))$$

The cases in which $n > 1$ are treated in similar way, in accordance with the method illustrated.

Note that this representation of 'exactly one' is relevant for the formalization of sentences containing definite descriptions. According to Russell's theory of descriptions, 'The capital of Italy is charming' says that there is an x such that x is capital of Italy, and for every y such that y is capital of Italy, $y = x$, and x is charming. The first two conditions require the existence of exactly one capital of Italy. So, if Russell's theory is correct, this sentence is adequately formalized as follows:

$$\exists x (Ix \wedge \forall y (Iy \supset y = x) \wedge Cx)$$

12.5   Multiple Generality and Scope Ambiguity

Another interesting case is that in which different quantifier expressions are combined in the same sentence. As explained in Sect. 11.4, there is a close connection between multiple generality and structural ambiguity. For example, 'Every sailor loves a girl' admits two readings. On one reading, it says that, for every x, if x is a sailor, there is a y such that y is a girl and x loves y. On the other, it says that there is a x such that x is a girl and, for every y, if y is a sailor, y loves x. That is,

$$\forall x (Sx \supset \exists y (Gy \wedge Lxy))$$
$$\exists x (Gx \wedge \forall y (Sy \supset Lyx))$$

These two formulas differ in one crucial respect: in the first, $\exists$ occurs in the scope of $\forall$, while in the second, $\forall$ occurs in the scope of $\exists$. Therefore, 'Every sailor loves a girl' is an example of *scope ambiguity*. More generally, a case of scope ambiguity is a case in which the ambiguity of a sentence can be elucidated by means of two formal representations of the sentence that differ in the relation of subordination between two connectives.

Note that the notion of scope adopted here is that defined in Sect. 5.3, so it applies to any connective. Scope ambiguity does not specifically concern quantifiers.

For example, the case considered at the beginning of Sect. 4.3, which involves conjunction and disjunction, can equally be described as a case of scope ambiguity.

12.6 Existence

The last issue that deserves attention concerns the sentences that assert or deny the existence of one or more objects. The notion of existence is notoriously elusive, and there is no unique way to express it in a predicate language. On the one hand, ∃ is the existential quantifier, so it is reasonable to expect that this symbol plays some role in the formalization of sentences concerning existence. On the other, 'exists' is syntactically analogous to 'is red', so it can be represented by means of a one-place predicate letter E.

There are cases in which the existence predicate is definitely not an option. For example, 'Honest politicians exist' is adequately formalized as follows:

$\exists x (Px \land Hx)$

In this case it would be clearly inappropriate to treat 'exist' as predicate that expresses a property of honest politicians. If the statement conveyed by 'Honest politicians exist' were that every honest politician has such property—that is, for every x, if x is a honest politician, x exists—its truth would be compatible with the non-existence of honest politicians. Moreover, if there were no honest politicians, 'Honest politicians do not exist' would also be true, instead of being false, for it would mean that, for every x, if x is a honest politician, x does not exist.

Although in some cases the formalization of a sentence that asserts or denies the existence of one or more objects clearly does not require an existence predicate, in other cases there is no obvious way to go. For example, 'The abominable snowman does not exist' and 'Sherlock Holmes does not exist' differ from 'Honest politicians exist' in that they assert the existence of specific objects. In the first case, much depends on the theory of descriptions one adopts. As we have seen, Russell's theory implies that 'The abominable snowman does not exist' is formalized as follows:

$\sim\exists x (Ax \land \forall y (Ay \supset y = x))$

In second case, instead, the name 'Sherlock Holmes' seems to require an individual constant, which suggests the following formalization of 'Sherlock Holmes does not exist':

$\sim\exists x\, x = s$

However, this formalization yields an unpalatable result. Assuming that s denotes an object, it is true that there is an x such that x is identical to that object. So, this formula must be false. Yet there is a clear sense in which the sentence is true: Sherlock Holmes is not a real person.

There are different ways to cope with this fact. One is to say that there are two senses of 'exists': in one of them Sherlock Holmes exists, because it is an abstract entity of some kind, while in the other he does not exist, because it is not a real person. If ∃ is taken to express existence in the first sense, and E is understood in terms of the second, 'Sherlock Holmes does not exist' can be formalized as follows:

$$\exists x (x = s \wedge {\sim}Ex)$$

Or equivalently as follows:

$${\sim}Es$$

Another option is to extend Russell's theory of descriptions to proper names, or at least to some proper names, and say that 'Sherlock Holmes' is not a genuine singular term, like 'the abominable snowman'. On such a view, 'Sherlock Holmes does not exist' is formally similar to 'The abominable snowman does not exist'. In any case, the symbolic apparatus of predicate logic is to a good extent neutral with respect to the philosophical discussions concerning existence.[3]

Exercises

12.1 Formalize the following sentences:

(a) Desdemona loves Othello
(b) Desdemona is loved by Othello

12.2 Imagine a language which differs from L_q in that it only includes formulas containing individual constants, predicate letters, and the sentential connectives. Could such language express valid argument forms that are not expressible in L?

12.3 Formalize the following sentences by using ∀:

(a) Nothing is material
(b) If everything is material, nothing is spiritual
(c) If not everything is material, something is spiritual

12.4 Formalize the following sentences by using ∀:

(a) No philosopher is rich
(b) Some philosophers are not wise
(c) Only philosophers are wise

12.5 Formalize (b) and (c) of Exercise 12.3 by using ∀ and ∃.

---

[3] Sainsbury [58], ch. 4, provides a thorough treatment of some main issues concerning formalization in a predicate language.

12.6 Formalize (a) and (b) of Exercise 12.4 by using ∃.

12.7 Formalize the following sentences:

(a) Someone killed Desdemona
(b) Othello killed someone
(c) Othello killed himself

12.8 Formalize the two readings of the sentence considered in Exercise 11.9.

12.9 Formalize the sentences considered in Exercise 11.5.

12.10 Formalize the sentences considered in Exercise 11.6.

Chapter 13
The Language $\mathsf{L_q}$

13.1 Syntax

Now $\mathsf{L_q}$ will be defined in a rigorous way. Let us start with its formation rules:

Definition 13.1

1 If P is an n-place predicate letter and $t_1, \ldots, t_n$ are terms, $P t_1 \ldots t_n$ is a formula;
2 if α is a formula, $\sim\alpha$ is a formula;
3 if α and β are formulas, $(\alpha \supset \beta)$ is a formula;
4 if α is a formula and x is a variable, $\forall x\alpha$ is a formula.

Clause 1 defines the atomic formulas of $\mathsf{L_q}$. Here P indicates an arbitrary predicate letter. The indexed letters $t_1, \ldots, t_n$ refer to arbitrary terms. As explained in Sect. 12.2, a term is either an individual constant or a variable. So, for example, if M is one-place, Ma and Mx are formulas. Clauses 2 and 3 are like those of Definition 5.1. Clause 4 defines quantified formulas. Here, again, x indicates an arbitrary variable. From now on we will assume that individual constants, predicate letters, and variables can be used schematically to refer to arbitrary members of the respective categories.

Clause 4 requires some terminology. An occurrence of a variable in a formula is *bound* when it is in the scope of a quantifier immediately followed by the same variable, otherwise it is *free*. Similarly, a variable is bound in a formula when all its occurrences are bound, otherwise it is free. For example, x is bound in $\forall x Mx$, while it is free in Mx. A formula that contains free variables, such as Mx, is *open*. A formula that is not open, such as $\forall x Mx$, is *closed*. Therefore, when $\forall x$ is combined with an open formula α in which x is free, it has the effect of binding x, so that $\forall x\alpha$ is closed if α does not contain other free variables. Note that clause 4 does not require that α is an open formula in which x is free. It can happen that α is closed, or that α is open but with free variables other than x.

© The Author(s), under exclusive license to Springer Nature Switzerland AG 2021
A. Iacona, *LOGIC: Lecture Notes for Philosophy, Mathematics, and Computer Science*, Springer Undergraduate Texts in Philosophy,
https://doi.org/10.1007/978-3-030-64811-4_13

As in the case of a propositional language, the "syntactic history" of a formula of L$_q$ can be represented by means of a syntactic tree that shows the stages through which the formula is constructed from atomic formulas. A very simple example is the diagram below. In this case the root is $\sim\forall x Mx$, which has complexity 2, and there is a unique leaf, Mx, because both $\sim$ and $\forall$ apply to single formulas.

$$\sim\forall x Mx$$
$$|$$
$$\forall x Mx$$
$$|$$
$$Mx$$

In general, to every formula we can associate a diagram with the features illustrated in Sect. 5.2, which displays its internal hierarchy. In the syntactic tree of a formula, the occurrence of a connective is subordinate to another when its scope occupies a lower node with respect to the scope of the other, in the same branch.

Two final stipulations are in order. First, $(\alpha)_x^t$ indicates the formula obtained from α by replacing the variable x, wherever it occurs free, with the term t. That is,

Definition 13.2

1 If α is atomic, $(\alpha)_x^t$ is obtained by replacing x with t, if x occurs in α, otherwise $(\alpha)_x^t = \alpha$;

2 $(\sim\alpha)_x^t = \sim(\alpha)_x^t$;

3 $(\alpha \supset \beta)_x^t = (\alpha)_x^t \supset (\beta)_x^t$;

4 $(\forall y\alpha)_x^t = \forall y(\alpha)_x^t$ if $x \neq y$, while $(\forall y\alpha)_x^t = \forall y\alpha$ if $x = y$.

Second, *t is substitutable for x in α* when the following conditions hold:

Definition 13.3

1 If α is atomic, t is substitutable for x in α;

2 t is substitutable for x in $\sim\alpha$ iff t is substitutable for x in α;

3 t is substitutable for x in $\alpha \supset \beta$ iff t is substitutable for x in α and in β;

4 t is substitutable for x in $\forall y\alpha$ iff either x is not free in $\forall y\alpha$, or t is substitutable for x in α and $t \neq y$.

Clause 1 contemplates the possibility that x does not occur in α, in which case $(\alpha)_x^t = \alpha$. The same goes for clauses 2 and 3. In clause 4, the case in which x does not occur in $\forall y\alpha$ is one of the two cases that verify the first disjunct of the right-hand side. The other is that in which x is bound in $\forall y\alpha$. In both cases, $(\forall y\alpha)_x^t = \forall y\alpha$. Instead, if the first disjunct does not hold because x is free in $\forall y\alpha$, the condition that $t \neq y$ is intended to avoid that we get a bound variable by replacing x with t.

13.2   Basic Semantic Notions

A predicate language is syntactically more articulated than a propositional language, since it represents the internal structure of simple sentences by means of symbols that stand for their parts. This imposes a greater complexity at the semantic level, when it comes to specifying the conditions under which a formula is true in an interpretation. As we have seen, an interpretation of a propositional language is defined as an assignment of truth values to its atomic formulas, thus it suffices to indicate, for each connective, how the truth value of a formula containing that connective is determined by the truth values of its constituents. But in the case of a predicate language one cannot define an interpretation in the same way, and consequently one cannot give rules that, for each connective, decide how the truth value of a formula containing that connective is determined by the truth value of its constituents.

This limitation specifically concerns $\forall$. Take the formula $\forall x M x$. We want this formula to be true or false in any interpretation, because it represents a sentence to which we ascribe truth or falsity, such as 'Everything is material'. However, the only formula that occurs in $\forall x M x$ is $M x$, an open formula to which it makes no sense to ascribe truth or falsity. As we saw in Sect. 12.2, $M x$ corresponds to something like 'It is material'. How can we ascribe truth or falsity to $\forall x M x$ without assuming that $M x$ is true or false? More generally, the question is how can we define truth in an interpretation without assuming that the interpretation assigns truth values to open formulas.

Tarski has provided a clear answer to this question in his article *Pojęcie prawdy w językach nauk dedukcyjnych* (1933), which means "On the concept of truth in languages of deductive sciences". Tarski's idea, which is now adopted as part of the standard semantics of predicate logic, is that the truth conditions of closed formulas can be specified in terms of a notion other than truth, *satisfaction*, which is defined for all formulas relative to assignments of values to the variables.[1]

The notion of satisfaction can be illustrated by using again our example, $M x$. The reason why it makes no sense to assign a truth value to $M x$ is that x lacks denotation, so it cannot be asked whether the object denoted by x belongs to the extension of M. However, if one supposes that x denotes a specific object, then one can assign a truth value to $M x$ relative to that supposition. Just as 'It is material' is true relative to the supposition that 'it' denotes the Colisseum but false relative to the supposition that 'it' denotes the Holy Spirit (if it exists), $M x$ is true relative to the supposition that x denotes an object that belongs to the extension of M but false relative to the supposition that x denotes an object that does not belong to the extension of M. The satisfaction of a formula relative to an assignment of values to the variables amounts to its truth relative to the supposition that the variables denote

---

[1] This idea is developed in Tarski [64] and Tarski [63].

certain objects. To say that Mx is satisfied when a given object is assigned to x is to say that Mx is true relative to the supposition that x denotes that object.

Tarski's method enables us to define truth in terms of satisfaction, overcoming the complications generated by the symbolic machinery of quantification. Moreover, it enables us to define logical consequence in the same way. The next three sections set out a semantics for L_q based on this method. The semantics hinges on the following notion:

Definition 13.4 A *model* $\langle D, I \rangle$ is an ordered pair formed by a non-empty set D and a function I such that, for every individual constant a, $I(a) \in D$, and for every n-place predicate letter P, $I(P) \subseteq D^n$.

D is the *domain* of the model. Since there are no restrictions on D, beside the condition that $D \neq \emptyset$, D can include any kind and any number of objects. I is the *interpretation function*, which assigns to each individual constant an element of D, and to each n-place predicate letter an n-ary relation on D, that is, a set of n-tuples of elements of D.[2]

From now on we will adopt the following conventions. Given a model $\mathcal{M}$, the correspondent Latin letter M will indicate the domain of $\mathcal{M}$. In other terms, if $\mathcal{M} = \langle D, I \rangle$ then $M = D$. The square brackets with subscript $\mathcal{M}$, instead, will indicate the value of the interpretation function of $\mathcal{M}$. For example, if $\mathcal{M} = \langle D, I \rangle$ and a is an individual constant, then $[a]_{\mathcal{M}} = I(a)$.

13.3   Satisfaction

Models do not provide denotation for variables. In a model $\mathcal{M}$, the same variable can denote different objects. This is to say that different objects can be assigned to the variables in $\mathcal{M}$:

Definition 13.5 Given a model $\mathcal{M}$, an *assignment* σ is a function such that, for each variable x, $\sigma(x) \in M$.

That is, σ assigns to each variable x an element of M. Accordingly, we can define the denotation of a term t in $\mathcal{M}$ relative to σ, in symbols $[t]_{\mathcal{M},\sigma}$, as follows:

Definition 13.6

1 If t is an individual constant, $[t]_{\mathcal{M},\sigma} = [t]_{\mathcal{M}}$;
2 if t is a variable, $[t]_{\mathcal{M},\sigma} = \sigma(t)$.

---

[2]Tarski did not employ models so understood. The semantics he offered involves no relativization to domains, in that he took the domain for granted, following Frege, Russell, and Wittgenstein. However, nowadays it is standard to define models in this way.

Clause 1 says that the denotation of an individual constant a in $\mathcal{M}$ relative to σ is simply the object that a denotes in $\mathcal{M}$. Clause 2 says that the denotation of a variable x in $\mathcal{M}$ relative to σ is the object that σ assigns to x.

The *satisfaction of a formula by an assignment* σ *in a model* $\mathcal{M}$ is defined as follows:

Definition 13.7

1 σ satisfies $Pt_1 \ldots t_n$ iff $\langle [t_1]_{\mathcal{M},\sigma}, \ldots, [t_n]_{\mathcal{M},\sigma} \rangle \in [P]_{\mathcal{M}}$;
2 σ satisfies $\sim\alpha$ iff σ does not satisfy α;
3 σ satisfies $\alpha \supset \beta$ iff σ does not satisfy α or satisfies β;
4 σ satisfies $\forall x\alpha$ iff every x-variant of σ satisfies α.

Clause 1 defines satisfaction for atomic formulas. Causes 2 and 3 extend the definition to formulas containing $\sim$ and $\supset$. Clause 4 is the crucial one. To understand this clause, it must be taken into account that σ assigns values to all variables, while the only relevant variable in the case of $\forall x\alpha$ is x. That is, all that matters to the satisfaction of $\forall x\alpha$ is that α is satisfied for any value of x. This amounts to saying that α must be satisfied by every assignment that differs from σ at most for the value of x, that is, by every σ' such that $\sigma'(y) = \sigma(y)$ for every $y \neq x$. An x-*variant* of σ is precisely an assignment that differs from σ at most for the value of x.

To grasp Definition 13.7 it is useful to consider a couple of examples. Let $\mathcal{M}$ be a model whose domain is {Colisseum, Mole Antonelliana, Holy Spirit}, and where $[M]_{\mathcal{M}} = $ {Colisseum, Mole Antonelliana}. Let σ and σ' be such that $\sigma(x) = $ Colisseum and $\sigma'(x) = $ Holy Spirit. In $\mathcal{M}$, σ satisfies Mx, because the Colisseum belongs to $[M]_{\mathcal{M}}$, while σ' does not satisfy Mx, because the Holy Spirit does not belong to $[M]_{\mathcal{M}}$. Neither σ nor σ', instead, satisfies $\forall x Mx$, since for each of them there is an x-variant that does not satisfy Mx. Now let $\mathcal{M}$ be as before and suppose instead that $\sigma(x) = $ Colisseum and $\sigma'(x) = $ Mole Antonelliana. In this case both σ and σ' satisfy Mx. But again, neither of them satisfies $\forall x Mx$, since for each of them there is an x-variant that does not satisfy Mx.

13.4 Truth

A crucial fact about satisfaction is that, in every model, if two assignments σ and σ' agree on the values of the free variables in a formula α, then either both σ and σ' satisfy α or neither of them does. That is,

Theorem 13.1 *If σ and σ' are such that $\sigma(x) = \sigma'(x)$ for every x free in α, then σ satisfies α iff σ' satisfies α.*

Proof We reason by induction on the complexity of α, for an arbitrary model $\mathcal{M}$.

Basis. Let α be an atomic formula $Pt_1 \ldots t_n$. Suppose that $\sigma(x) = \sigma'(x)$ for every free x in $Pt_1 \ldots t_n$, that is, for every x in $Pt_1 \ldots t_n$. For each i such that $1 \leq i \leq n$, t_i is either an individual constant or a variable. In the first case

$[t_i]_{\mathcal{M},\sigma} = [t_i]_{\mathcal{M},\sigma'}$, for the value of t_i does not vary with assignments. In the second, $[t_i]_{\mathcal{M},\sigma} = [t_i]_{\mathcal{M},\sigma'}$, because by hypothesis σ and σ' assign the same values to every free variable. Since σ satisfies α iff $\langle[t_1]_{\mathcal{M},\sigma}, \ldots, [t_n]_{\mathcal{M},\sigma}\rangle \in [P]_{\mathcal{M}}$ and σ' satisfies α iff $\langle[t_1]_{\mathcal{M},\sigma'}, \ldots, [t_n]_{\mathcal{M},\sigma'}\rangle \in [P]_{\mathcal{M}}$, we get that σ satisfies $Pt_1 \ldots t_n$ iff σ' satisfies $Pt_1 \ldots t_n$.

Step. Assume that, for every formula of complexity less than or equal to n, if $\sigma(x) = \sigma'(x)$ for every free x, then the formula is satisfied by σ iff it is satisfied by σ'. Now assume that α has complexity $n+1$ and that $\sigma(x) = \sigma'(x)$ for every x free in α. Three cases are possible.

Case 1: α has the form $\sim\beta$. Since β has complexity n, by the induction hypothesis σ satisfies β iff σ' satisfies β. Consequently, σ satisfies $\sim\beta$ iff σ' satisfies $\sim\beta$.

Case 2: α has the form $\beta \supset \gamma$. Since β and γ have at most complexity n, by the induction hypothesis σ satisfies β iff σ' satisfies β, and σ satisfies γ iff σ' satisfies γ. So, if σ does not satisfy β or satisfies γ, the same goes for σ', and the other way round.

Case 3: α has the form $\forall x\beta$. In this case β is a formula of complexity n whose free variables are all the variables free in $\forall x\beta$ plus (at most) x. Suppose that σ does not satisfy $\forall x\beta$. Then there is an x-variant σ_* of σ that does not satisfy β. Let o be the object that σ_* assigns to x. Let σ'_* be the x-variant of σ' that assigns o to x. σ_* and σ'_* agree on the values of the free variables in β, for σ and σ' agree on the values of the free variables in $\forall x\beta$, and the only additional free variable that β can have is x, which denotes o both in σ_* and in σ'_*. By the induction hypothesis it follows that σ'_* does not satisfy β. Therefore, σ' does not satisfy $\forall x\beta$. By a similar reasoning, if one supposes that σ' does not satisfy $\forall x\beta$ one gets that σ does not satisfy $\forall x\beta$. □

From Theorem 13.1 we get that, in any model, either a closed formula is satisfied by all assignments or it is satisfied by none. Suppose that α is closed and consider two arbitrary assigments σ and σ'. Since it is not the case that some x in α is free, *a fortiori* it is not the case that some x in α is free and $\sigma(x) \neq \sigma'(x)$. This amounts to saying that $\sigma(x) = \sigma'(x)$ for every free x in α. By Theorem 13.1 it follows that σ satisfies α if and only if σ' satisfies α.

Since closed formulas have this feature, truth is definable in terms of satisfaction by all assignments, and falsity is definable in terms of satisfaction by no assignment:

Definition 13.8 $[\alpha]_{\mathcal{M}} = 1$ iff every assignment in $\mathcal{M}$ satisfies α.

Definition 13.9 $[\alpha]_{\mathcal{M}} = 0$ iff no assignment in $\mathcal{M}$ satisfies α.

Here $[\alpha]_{\mathcal{M}}$ indicates the truth value of α in $\mathcal{M}$. Definitions 13.8 and 13.9 imply that, for any closed formula α and for any $\mathcal{M}$, either $[\alpha]_{\mathcal{M}} = 1$ or $[\alpha]_{\mathcal{M}} = 0$. Thus, $\forall x Mx$ is false in a model $\mathcal{M}$ whose domain is {Colisseum, Mole Antonelliana, Holy Spirit}, and where $[M]_{\mathcal{M}} = $ {Colisseum, Mole Antonelliana}, for every assignment has some x-variant that does not satisfy Mx. Instead, $\forall x Mx$ is true in a model $\mathcal{M}'$ that differs from $\mathcal{M}$ only in that its domain does not include the Holy Spirit. In $\mathcal{M}'$ we get that, for every assignment σ, every x-variant of σ satisfies Mx. In any model,

$\forall x M x$ is either true or false, because either it is satisfied by all assignments or it is satisfied by none.

Note that Definitions 13.8 and 13.9 leave room for the possibility that an open formula is true, or false, in a model. For example, if $[M]_\mathcal{M}$ is the whole domain, Mx is satisfied by all assignments, while $\sim Mx$ is satisfied by none. As observed in Sect. 13.2, the ascription of truth or falsity to open formulas has no proper counterpart at the informal level. However, this should cause no worry, given that for any formula α in which a variable x is free, if α is satisfied by all assignments, the same goes for $\forall x\alpha$, and if α is satisfied by no assignment, the same goes for $\forall x\alpha$. So, whenever an open formula has a truth value, there is a correspondent closed formula that has the same truth value.

To conclude this section, here is a proof of a useful result that may be called *substitution lemma*:

Theorem 13.2 *Let α be a formula where a term t is substitutable for a variable x. If σ and σ' are assignments such that σ' differs from σ in that it assigns to x the object denoted by t in σ, then σ' satisfies α iff σ satisfies $(\alpha)^t_x$.*

Proof We reason by induction on the complexity of α, assuming that t is substitutable for x in α, and considering an arbitrary model $\mathcal{M}$.

Basis. Let α be an atomic formula $Pt_1 \ldots t_n$. For $1 \leq i \leq n$, let $t'_i = t$ if $t_i = x$, and $t'_i = t_i$ otherwise. Now take any t_i. If t_i is an individual constant, $[t'_i]_{\mathcal{M},\sigma} = [t_i]_{\mathcal{M},\sigma'}$ because $t'_i = t_i$ and the denotation of t_i is the same in σ and σ'. If $t_i = x$, then $t'_i = t$ and σ' assigns $[t]_{\mathcal{M},\sigma}$ to x, so $[t'_i]_{\mathcal{M},\sigma} = [t_i]_{\mathcal{M},\sigma'}$. If t_i is a different variable, then $t'_i = t_i$ and σ' assigns to t_i the same value assigned by σ, so $[t'_i]_{\mathcal{M},\sigma} = [t_i]_{\mathcal{M},\sigma'}$. Therefore, σ' satisfies $Pt_1 \ldots t_n$ iff σ satisfies $Pt'_1 \ldots t'_n$.

Step. Assume that the biconditional to be proved holds for every formula of complexity less than or equal to n and that α has complexity $n + 1$.

Case 1: α has the form $\sim\beta$. In this case $(\alpha)^t_x = \sim(\beta)^t_x$. σ satisfies $\sim(\beta)^t_x$ iff it does not satisfy $(\beta)^t_x$. By the induction hypothesis, σ does not satisfy $(\beta)^t_x$ iff σ' does not satisfy β. So it suffices to add that σ' does not satisfy β iff σ' satisfies $\sim\beta$.

Case 2: α has the form $\beta \supset \gamma$. In this case $(\alpha)^t_x = (\beta)^t_x \supset (\gamma)^t_x$. σ satisfies $(\beta)^t_x \supset (\gamma)^t_x$ iff either it does not satisfy $(\beta)^t_x$ or it satisfies $(\gamma)^t_x$. By the induction hypothesis, σ does not satisfy $(\beta)^t_x$ iff σ' does not satisfy β, and σ satisfies $(\gamma)^t_x$ iff σ' satisfies γ. So it suffices to add that σ' satisfies $\beta \supset \gamma$ iff either it does not satisfy β or it satisfies γ.

Case 3: α has the form $\forall y\beta$. In this case, either x is free in $\forall y\beta$ or it is not. Assume that x is free in $\forall y\beta$, so that $x \neq y$ and $(\forall y\beta)^t_x = \forall y(\beta)^t_x$. Suppose that σ' does not satisfy $\forall y\beta$. Then there is a y-variant σ'_* of σ' that does not satisfy β. Let o be the object that σ'_* assigns to y. Let σ_* be the y-variant of σ that assigns o to y. By the induction hypothesis, σ_* does not satisfy $(\beta)^t_x$. So σ does not satisfy $\forall y(\beta)^t_x$. By a similar reasoning, if we suppose that σ does not satisfy $\forall y(\beta)^t_x$, we get that σ' does not satisfy $\forall y\beta$. Now assume that x is not free in $\forall y\beta$ because it does not occur or it is bound. Then $(\forall y\beta)^t_x = \forall y\beta$. By Theorem 13.1 σ' satisfies $\forall y\beta$ iff σ satisfies $\forall y\beta$. $\qquad\square$

13.5   Logical Consequence

Logical consequence, like truth, is definable in terms of satisfaction:

Definition 13.10 $\Gamma \vDash \alpha$ iff, in every model, every assignment that satisfies the formulas in Γ satisfies α.

As in the case of L, we have that $\vDash \alpha$ if and only if $\emptyset \vDash \alpha$, and that $\emptyset \vDash \alpha$ if and only if $\Gamma \vDash \alpha$ for any Γ. Validity amounts to satisfaction by every assignment in every model, or equivalently, truth in every model.

Logical consequence so defined is not exactly a formal counterpart of entailment, because Definition 13.10 contemplates the possibility that Γ or α include open formulas, while entailment is restricted to sentences evaluable as true or false. But wherever Γ is a set of closed formulas and α is a closed formula, Definition 13.10 yields the result that is reasonable to expect, namely, that $\Gamma \vDash \alpha$ if and only if there is no model in which the formulas in Γ are true and α is false.

Something similar holds for satisfiability, logical equivalence, and contradiction, which are defined in terms of satisfaction as well.

Definition 13.11 A set of formulas Γ is *satisfiable* iff there is a model in which some assignment satisfies all the formulas in Γ.

Definition 13.12 Two formulas α and β are *logically equivalent*—that is, $\alpha \mathrel{\dashv\vDash} \beta$—iff, in every model and for every assignment, either α and β are both satisfied, or neither of them is satisfied.

Definition 13.13 Two formulas α and β are *contradictory* iff, in every model and for every assignment, one and only one of them is satisfied.

From Definition 13.11 it turns out that, when all the formulas in Γ are closed, Γ is satisfiable if and only if all the formulas in Γ are true in some model. Similarly, Definitions 13.12 and 13.13 can be rephrased in terms of truth and falsity when α and β are closed. Moreover, we can prove theorems analogous to Theorems 6.1–6.7 by rephrasing the proofs of those theorems in terms of satisfaction. This shows that L_q preserves the same properties of entailment that are preserved in L.

A basic fact about logical consequence is that it validates MP:

Theorem 13.3 $\alpha \supset \beta, \alpha \vDash \beta$

Proof Assume that an assignment σ satisfies $\alpha \supset \beta$ and α. Then, by clause 3 of Definition 13.7, σ satisfies β. □

Another fact, which specifically concerns quantification, is the following:

Theorem 13.4 $\vDash \forall x \alpha \supset (\alpha)_x^t$, *if t is substitutable for x in α.*

Proof Assume that σ satisfies $\forall x \alpha$. Then every x-variant of σ satisfies α. In particular, the x-variant σ' of σ which assigns to x the object denoted by t in σ satisfies α. By the substitution lemma (Theorem 13.2) it follows that σ satisfies $(\alpha)_x^t$. □

Theorem 13.4 expresses the principle of *Universal Instantiation*: if a condition holds for every object, then it holds for a particular object. Note that this theorem entails that $\vDash \forall x\alpha \supset \alpha$, given that any variable is trivially substitutable for itself.

A direct corollary of Theorems 13.3 and 13.4 is the following:

Theorem 13.5 $\forall x\alpha \vDash (\alpha)^t_x$ *if t is substitutable for x in* α.

Proof Assume that an assignment σ satisfies $\forall x\alpha$. By Theorem 13.4, σ satisfies $\forall x\alpha \supset (\alpha)^t_x$. By Theorem 13.3 it follows that σ satisfies $(\alpha)^t_x$. $\qquad\square$

The notion of logical consequence characterizes a set of valid forms expressible in L_q, that is, the set of ordered pairs Γ/α such that $\Gamma \vDash \alpha$. For example, consider the form $\forall x(Px \supset Qx)$, Pa/Qa, which is instantiated by the following argument:

(1) All philosophers are wise

(2) Socrates is a philosopher

(3) Socrates is wise

This form is proved valid by the fact that $\forall x(Px \supset Qx)$, $Pa \vDash Qa$. Suppose that σ satisfies $\forall x(Px \supset Qx)$ and Pa. Then, by Theorem 13.5, σ satisfies $Pa \supset Qa$ and Pa. It follows by Theorem 13.3 that σ satisfies Qa.

When $\vDash \alpha$, and α is closed, α represents a logical truth. We have seen that the logical truths expressible in L— tautologies—are sentences that are true in virtue of the meaning of the sentential connectives they contain. Tautologies also hold in L_q, in the sense that every formula of L_q that instantiates a tautological schema is valid. But some logical truths expressible in L_q are not tautologies. For example, 'Every red thing is red' is not a tautology, and is represented in L_q by the valid formula $\forall x(Px \supset Px)$. In general, every logical truth expressible in a propositional language is expressible in a predicate language, while the converse does not hold.

13.6 Undecidability

This last section draws attention to a crucial difference between propositional logic and predicate logic. As explained in Sect. 6.5, the semantics of a propositional language provides an effective method to tell whether a formula is a logical consequence of a set of formulas. A predicate language does not have this property. Although in some cases we can prove that logical consequence obtains, or that it does not obtain, there is no effective method that guarantees an answer in every case.

This undecidability result was established in 1936 by Alonzo Church.[3] Although a detailed exposition of its proof would take too far, it is important to get some familiarity with the notion of *recursiveness*, which underlies the overall line of reasoning. This notion, which primarily applies to numerical functions, is a precise counterpart of the notion of effective computability introduced in Sect. 6.5.

Recursive functions are functions from natural numbers to natural numbers defined in the following way: we start with an initial stock of basic functions that are clearly computable, we specify some operations that, when applied to computable functions, produce computable functions, and thus we delimit a class of functions obtainable from the initial stock by applying those operations a finite number of times. A couple of examples will help to grasp the core idea without bothering with the details of the definition. Take the factorial function, which is defined by the following equations:

1. $0! = S0$
2. $(Sy)! = y! \times Sy$

Clause 1 tells us that $y! = 1$ when $y = 0$, and clause 2 gives the value of the function for Sy in terms of its value for y. Now take the exponential function, which is defined as follows:

1. $x^0 = S0$
2. $x^{Sy} = (x^y \times x)$

Clause 1 tells us that $x^y = 1$ when $y = 0$, and clause 2—keeping x fixed—gives the value of the function for Sy in terms of its value for y. Since successor and multiplication are clearly computable, factorial and exponentiation turn out to be computable as well: the value of $y!$ and x^y for any y can be calculated in a finite number of steps by applying successor and multiplication. This definitional pattern characterizes recursive functions. More precisely, factorial and exponentiation belong to the class of *primitive recursive functions*, which constitute a subclass of recursive functions. Recursive functions, as distinct from primitive recursive functions, are called μ-*recursive*. But here we will simply talk about recursive functions without further qualifications.[4]

The proof of Church's undecidability result rests on the assumption that we can identify effective computability with recursiveness, that is, that the effectively computable functions are just the recursive functions. Given this assumption, which is known as *Church's thesis*, the decision problem about logical consequence— whether there is an effective method to tell whether a formula is a logical consequence of a set of formulas—is shown to be equivalent to a problem about

---

[3] Alonzo Church (1903–1995) was an American logician who studied and taught at Princeton University. He made major contributions to mathematical logic, theoretical computer science, and philosophy of language. His seminal works on undecidability are Church [5] and Church [6].

[4] Primitive recursion was originally defined in Gödel [20]. The broader notion of μ-recursion was later spelled out by Gödel, Herbrand, Church, and others.

recursive functions, such that if the former can be solved, then the same goes for the latter. Since it is provable that the latter problem cannot be solved, the same goes for the former.

Church's thesis is consistent with different accounts of effective computability. In particular, it accords with the characterization suggested by Alan Turing, who reached the undecidability result independently of Church.[5] Turing outlined an account of effective computability in terms of what can be computed by a suitably defined machine, the Turing machine. If we call *Turing's thesis* the assumption that the numerical functions that are effectively computable are just the Turing-computable functions, then Turing's thesis is equivalent to Church's thesis, because it is provable that a function is Turing-computable if and only if is recursive. This is why Church's thesis and Turing's thesis are often mentioned together under the label 'Church-Turing thesis'.[6]

Exercises

13.1 Is the alphabet of L_q denumerable?

13.2 Are these formulas of L_q?

(a) $\forall x \sim Px$
(b) $\forall x \sim Py$
(c) $\forall x \sim Pa$

13.3 Is the set of formulas of L_q decidable?

13.4 Explain why α is satisfied by all assignments in $\mathcal{M}$ if and only if $\forall x\alpha$ is satisfied by all assignments in $\mathcal{M}$.

13.5 Explain why $\forall x(Px \supset Px)$ is true in every model.

13.6 Prove what follows:

(a) $\forall x \forall y(\sim\forall z \sim Lxz \supset Lyx) \vDash \forall y(\sim\forall z \sim Laz \supset Lya)$
(b) $Lab \vDash \sim\forall z \sim Laz$
(c) $\forall y(\sim\forall z \sim Laz \supset Lya), \sim\forall z \sim Laz \vDash \forall y Lya$

---

[5]Alan Mathison Turing (1912–1954), British logician and mathematician, studied at the universities of Cambridge, King's College London, and Princeton, then worked as a cryptanalyst for the British Government. He made major contributions to the development of theoretical computer science, although his accomplishments were not fully recognized during his lifetime, partly because of his homosexuality, for which he was prosecuted, partly because his work as a cryptanalyst was proteced by state secret.

[6]Turing [65]. If you want to know more about recursiveness, Turing computability, and their equivalence, you may want to look at Boolos, Burgess, and Jeffrey [17], pp. 23–98.

13.7 Formalize in L_q the first argument presented in Sect. 11.1 and show that its conclusion is a logical consequence of its premise.

13.8 Prove by means of a counterexample that $\forall x \sim \forall y \sim Ryx \not\models \sim \forall x \sim \forall y Rxy$.

13.9 In Sect. 11.4 we saw that 'Every thing has a cause', at least on one plausible reading, does not entail 'There is a cause of every thing'. Show how this fact can be explained at the formal level.

13.10 Does the conclusion of this argument logically follow from its premises?

Everybody loves lovers; Romeo loves Juliet; therefore, everybody loves Juliet.[7]

---

[7]This example is drawn from Smith [61], p. 29.

Chapter 14
The System Q

14.1 Axioms and Inference Rule

This chapter sets out an axiomatic system in L_q called **Q**. The axioms of **Q** are all the formulas of L_q that instantiate the following schemas:

A1 $\alpha \supset (\beta \supset \alpha)$

A2 $(\alpha \supset (\beta \supset \gamma)) \supset ((\alpha \supset \beta) \supset (\alpha \supset \gamma))$

A3 $(\sim\alpha \supset \sim\beta) \supset (\beta \supset \alpha)$

A4 $\forall x \alpha \supset (\alpha)_x^t$, if t is substitutable for x in α.

A5 $\alpha \supset \forall x \alpha$, if x is not free in α.

A6 $\forall x (\alpha \supset \beta) \supset (\forall x \alpha \supset \forall x \beta)$

A7 $\forall x \alpha$, if α is an axiom.

A1–A3 are exactly as in **L** (Sect. 9.1). Instead, A4–A7 characterize **Q**, in that they specifically concern quantification. The unique rule of inference of **Q** is MP.[1]

A4 expresses the same principle expressed by Theorem 13.4, that is, Universal Instantiation. Here 'substitutable' is understood in the way explained in Sect. 13.1.

A5 is less intuitive than A4. On the one hand, it is easy to understand the restriction on α. If x could be free in α, the schema $\alpha \supset \forall x \alpha$ would produce formulas that we don't want to treat as axioms. For example, $Mx \supset \forall x Mx$ means something like 'If it is material, then everything is material'. On the other hand, the restriction on α makes the instances of A5 hardly translatable into natural language, although they clearly do not express false statements. An example is $Mc \supset \forall x Mc$: if the Colisseum is material, then for every object, the Colisseum is material.

A6 states a distributive property of $\forall$. To recognize the plausibility of this schema it suffices to consider the case in which x is free in α and β, as in $\forall x (Mx \supset \sim Sx) \supset$

---

[1] The label **Q** indicates that this system has axioms that concern quantification.

© The Author(s), under exclusive license to Springer Nature Switzerland AG 2021
A. Iacona, *LOGIC: Lecture Notes for Philosophy, Mathematics, and Computer Science*, Springer Undergraduate Texts in Philosophy,
https://doi.org/10.1007/978-3-030-64811-4_14

($\forall x\, Mx \supset \forall x{\sim}Sx$): if every material object is not spiritual, and every object is material, then every object is not spiritual.

Finally, A7 generates axioms from other axioms. The underlying idea is that if α deserves to be taken as an axiom, the addition of $\forall x$ cannot affect its status. This holds whether or not x is free in α. If x is free in α, we get that $\forall x\alpha$ is an axiom, which accords with the fact that the validity of α entails the validity of $\forall x\alpha$. If x is not free in α, the addition of $\forall x$ makes no difference, so it can do no harm.

As explained in Chapter 9, an axiomatic system differs from a natural deduction system in one important respect: in an axiomatic system it is harder to find derivations. So it might be asked why **Q** should be adopted instead of a natural deduction system. The reason is that an axiomatic system suits our purposes better than a natural deduction system. The aim of this chapter and of the next two is to outline some important syntactic and semantic properties of predicate logic, rather than deriving formulas from other formulas.

14.2   Derivability in Q

A derivation in **Q** is defined as follows for any formula α and any set of formulas Γ:

Definition 14.1   A *derivation of α from Γ* is a finite sequence of formulas that ends with α such that each of the formulas in the sequence instantiates A1-A7 or belongs to Γ or is obtained by means of MP from formulas that precede it.

A proof in **Q** is a derivation of α from Γ such that $\Gamma = \emptyset$. As in the case of **L**, we have that $\vdash \alpha$ if and only if $\emptyset \vdash \alpha$, and that $\vdash \alpha$ if and only if $\Gamma \vdash \alpha$ for every Γ.

Derivability, consistency, interderivability, and contradiction are understood as in Definitions 8.1–8.4, and it is easy to show that derivability in **Q** preserves the same fundamental properties that characterize **L**. In particular, the following theorems hold:

Theorem 14.1 $\alpha \vdash \alpha$

Proof Like the proof of Theorem 9.3.   □

Theorem 14.2 *If $\Gamma \vdash \alpha$ and $\Gamma \subseteq \Delta$, then $\Delta \vdash \alpha$.*

Proof Like the proof of Theorem 9.4.   □

Theorem 14.3 *If $\Gamma \vdash \alpha$ and $\Delta \cup \{\alpha\} \vdash \beta$, then $\Gamma \cup \Delta \vdash \beta$.*

Proof Like the proof of Theorem 9.5.   □

Theorem 14.4 *If $\alpha \in \Gamma$, then $\Gamma \vdash \alpha$.*

Proof Like the proof of Theorem 9.6.   □

Theorem 14.5 *If $\Gamma \vdash \alpha$ and $\Gamma \vdash \alpha \supset \beta$, then $\Gamma \vdash \beta$.*

Proof Like the proof of Theorem 9.7.   □

In what follows, Theorems 14.1–14.5 will be taken for granted without explicitly mentioning them.

14.3 Generalization Theorem

Another theorem, which is less obvious and therefore more interesting, is the *generalization theorem*:

Theorem 14.6 *If* $\Gamma \vdash \alpha$ *and no formula in* Γ *has x free, then* $\Gamma \vdash \forall x\alpha$.

Proof We reason by induction on the length of the derivation of α from Γ, assuming that no formula in Γ has x free.

Basis. Assume that there is a derivation of α from Γ of length 1. Two cases are possible.

Case 1: α is an axiom. In this case, by A7 $\forall x\alpha$ is also an axiom, so $\Gamma \vdash \forall x\alpha$.

Case 2: $\alpha \in \Gamma$. In this case, by hypothesis x is not free in α. Then, by A5, $\vdash \alpha \supset \forall x\alpha$, which entails that $\Gamma \vdash \alpha \supset \forall x\alpha$. Since $\Gamma \vdash \alpha$, we get that $\Gamma \vdash \forall x\alpha$.

Step. Assume that the conditional holds for every derivation of length less than or equal to n, and consider a derivation of α from Γ of length $n + 1$. The possible cases are three: α is an axiom, $\alpha \in \Gamma$, or α is obtained by MP. The first two cases are treated in the basis, so let us suppose that α is inferred from two formulas β and $\beta \supset \alpha$. Since β and $\beta \supset \alpha$ precede α in the derivation, by the induction hypothesis $\Gamma \vdash \forall x\beta$ and $\Gamma \vdash \forall x(\beta \supset \alpha)$. By A6, $\Gamma \vdash \forall x(\beta \supset \alpha) \supset (\forall x\beta \supset \forall x\alpha)$. Therefore, $\Gamma \vdash \forall x\alpha$. □

Note that the theorem includes the case in which $\Gamma = \emptyset$. In that case the condition that no formula in Γ has x free is vacuously satisfied, so we get that, if $\vdash \alpha$, then $\vdash \forall x\alpha$.

Theorem 14.6 expresses a principle—*Universal Generalization*—that is the inverse of Universal Instantiation: if one can derive a formula α that contains a free variable x without assuming anything specific about x, then one can also derive $\forall x\alpha$. Note that the restriction on Γ rules out undesired cases of the kind considered in connection with A5. For example, Theorem 14.6 does not make $\forall x Mx$ derivable from Mx, even though Mx is derivable from itself. Note also that the proof of Theorem 14.6 shows that A5 plays a significant role in **Q**. Despite its lack of intuitive appeal when considered in isolation, A5 justifies a plausible result.

14.4 Validity and Derivability

Derivability in **Q** is defined for any formula α and any set of formulas Γ, even though, as far as the formalization of arguments is concerned, the only interesting cases are those in which α is a closed formula and Γ is a set of closed formulas.

When α is a closed formula, Γ is a set of closed formulas, and $\Gamma \vdash \alpha$, then there is a set of valid arguments that have the form Γ/α. For example, $\forall x(Px \supset Qx), Pa \vdash Qa$.

(1)	$\forall x(Px \supset Qx)$	A
(2)	Pa	A
(3)	$\forall x(Px \supset Qx) \supset (Pa \supset Qa)$	A4
(4)	$Pa \supset Qa$	MP 1,3
(5)	Qa	MP 2,4

This accounts for the validity of the argument outlined in Sect. 13.5: if one assumes that all philosophers are wise and that Socrates is a philosopher, one can conclude that Socrates is wise. In general, the notion of derivability in **Q** characterizes a set of valid forms expressible in L_q, the set of ordered pairs Γ/α such that $\Gamma \vdash \alpha$.

The case of provability is similar. If α is a closed formula and $\vdash \alpha$, there is a set of logically true sentences that have the form α. An example of theorem of **Q** is $\forall x(Px \supset Px)$, which represents a logical truth, as we saw in Sect. 13.5: every red thing is red. To see that $\vdash \forall x(Px \supset Px)$ it suffices to recognize that $Px \supset Px$ is provable (Sect. 9.1), for the generalization theorem (Theorem 14.6) guarantees that if $\vdash \alpha$, then $\vdash \forall x \alpha$.

14.5   Deduction Theorem and Other Syntactic Results

Q shares with **L** the properties expressed by the theorems proved in Sects. 9.2 and 9.3. First of all, the deduction theorem holds for **Q**:

Theorem 14.7 *If* $\Gamma \cup \{\alpha\} \vdash \beta$, *then* $\Gamma \vdash \alpha \supset \beta$.

Proof Like the proof of theorem 9.8.   □

Note that the converse of the deduction theorem also holds:

Theorem 14.8 *If* $\Gamma \vdash \alpha \supset \beta$, *then* $\Gamma \cup \{\alpha\} \vdash \beta$.

Proof Assume that $\Gamma \vdash \alpha \supset \beta$. Then there is a derivation of β from $\Gamma \cup \{\alpha\}$ in which $\alpha \supset \beta$ is obtained from Γ and then β is obtained from $\alpha \supset \beta$ and α by means of MP.   □

The syntactic results proved in Sects. 9.2 and 9.3 hold as well. The theorems listed below are some examples:

Theorem 14.9 $\alpha \supset \beta, \beta \supset \gamma \vdash \alpha \supset \gamma$

Proof Like the proof of theorem 9.9.   □

Theorem 14.10 $\vdash \sim\sim\alpha \supset \alpha$

Proof Like the proof of theorem 9.12. □

Theorem 14.11 $\vdash (\alpha \supset \beta) \supset (\sim\beta \supset \sim\alpha)$

Proof Like the proof of theorem 9.16. □

Theorem 14.12 $\vdash \alpha \supset (\sim\beta \supset \sim(\alpha \supset \beta))$

Proof Like the proof of theorem 9.18. □

Theorem 14.13 $\vdash (\alpha \supset \beta) \supset ((\alpha \supset \sim\beta) \supset \sim\alpha)$

Proof Like the proof of theorem 9.22. □

Theorem 14.14 $\vdash (\sim\alpha \supset \beta) \supset ((\sim\alpha \supset \sim\beta) \supset \alpha)$

Proof Like the proof of theorem 9.23. □

Theorem 14.15 $\vdash \sim(\alpha \supset \beta) \supset \alpha$

Proof Like the proof of theorem 9.27. □

Theorem 14.16 $\vdash \sim(\alpha \supset \beta) \supset \sim\beta$

Proof Like the proof of theorem 9.28. □

14.6 Alphabetic Variants

One last theorem that we will consider concerns alphabetic variants:

Definition 14.2 An *alphabetic variant* of a formula α is a formula α' defined as follows.

1. If α is atomic, $\alpha' = \alpha$.
2. $(\sim\alpha)' = \sim\alpha'$
3. $(\alpha \supset \beta)' = \alpha' \supset \beta'$
4. $(\forall x\alpha)' = \forall y(\alpha')_x^y$, where y does not occur in α'.

In other words, α' differs from α only in that it replaces a bound variable which occurs in α with a different bound variable.

Theorem 14.17 *Given a formula α, a term t, and a variable x, there is an alphabetic variant α' of α such that $\alpha \dashv\vdash \alpha'$ and t is substitutable for x in α'.*

Proof Let α' be an alphabetic variant of α such that if $\alpha = \forall y\beta$, then $\alpha' = \forall z(\beta')_y^z$, where $z \neq x$ and $z \neq t$. Now it will be shown by induction on the complexity of α that the following conditions hold:

(a) $\alpha \dashv\vdash \alpha'$;

(b) t is substitutable for x in α'.

Basis. If α is atomic, then $\alpha' = \alpha$, so (a) holds because $\alpha \dashv\vdash \alpha$. Moreover, (b) holds because α' is atomic.

Step. Assume that (a) and (b) hold for every formula of complexity less than or equal to n, and that α has complexity $n + 1$. Three cases are possible.

Case 1: α has the form $\sim\beta$. In this case $\alpha' = \sim\beta'$. (a) holds for the following reason. By the induction hypothesis, $\beta' \vdash \beta$. From this and the deduction theorem (Theorem 14.7) we get that $\vdash \beta' \supset \beta$. By Theorem 14.11, $\vdash (\beta' \supset \beta) \supset (\sim\beta \supset \sim\beta')$. So, $\vdash \sim\beta \supset \sim\beta'$. By the converse of the deduction theorem (Theorem 14.8) we get that $\sim\beta \vdash \sim\beta'$. A similar reasoning shows that $\sim\beta' \vdash \sim\beta$. (b) holds because the induction hypothesis entails that t is substitutable for x in β'.

Case 2: α has the form $\beta \supset \gamma$. In this case $\alpha' = \beta' \supset \gamma'$. (a) holds for the following reason. By the induction hypothesis, $\beta \vdash \beta'$ and $\gamma' \vdash \gamma$, hence $\vdash \beta \supset \beta'$ and $\vdash \gamma' \supset \gamma$ by the deduction theorem (Theorem 14.7). If we apply Theorem 14.9 twice we get that $\beta' \supset \gamma' \vdash \beta \supset \gamma$. A similar reasoning shows that $\beta \supset \gamma \vdash \beta' \supset \gamma'$. (b) holds because the induction hypothesis entails that t is substitutable for x in β' and in γ'.

Case 3: α has the form $\forall y\beta$ and $\alpha' = \forall z(\beta')_y^z$, where $z \neq x$ and $z \neq t$. By the induction hypothesis, $\beta \vdash \beta'$, hence $\vdash \beta \supset \beta'$ by the deduction theorem (Theorem 14.7). By the generalization theorem (Theorem 14.6) it follows that $\vdash \forall y(\beta \supset \beta')$. Since $\vdash \forall y(\beta \supset \beta') \supset (\forall y\beta \supset \forall y\beta')$ by A6, we get that $\vdash \forall y\beta \supset \forall y\beta'$, hence that $\forall y\beta \vdash \forall y\beta'$ by the converse of the deduction theorem (Theorem 14.8). Moreover, $\vdash \forall y\beta' \supset (\beta')_y^z$ by A4, so $\forall y\beta' \vdash (\beta')_y^z$ for the same reason. By the generalization theorem (Theorem 14.6) it follows that $\forall y\beta' \vdash \forall z(\beta')_y^z$ (note that z does not occur in β' by definition). Since $\forall y\beta \vdash \forall y\beta'$ and $\forall y\beta' \vdash \forall z(\beta')_y^z$, it follows that $\forall y\beta \vdash \forall z(\beta')_y^z$. To prove the other direction of (a) we reason as follows. By A4, $\vdash \forall z(\beta')_y^z \supset ((\beta')_y^z)_z^y)$. But $((\beta')_y^z)_z^y = \beta'$, so $\vdash \forall z(\beta')_y^z \supset \beta'$. By the induction hypothesis, $\beta' \vdash \beta$, so we get $\vdash \beta' \supset \beta$ by the deduction theorem (Theorem 14.7). Theorem 14.9 then entails that $\vdash \forall z(\beta')_y^z \supset \beta$. Given the converse of the deduction theorem (Theorem 14.8), it follows that $\forall z(\beta')_y^z \vdash \beta$. By the generalization theorem (Theorem 14.6) we get that $\forall z(\beta')_y^z \vdash \forall y\beta$. Finally, (b) holds because t is substitutable for x in β' by the induction hypothesis and $z \neq t$. $\square$

Theorem 14.17 says that, for every formula α, there is a formula α' which differs from α only in the choice of bound variables and satisfies conditions (a) and (b). The utility of this theorem lies in the fact that the existence of alphabetic variants neutralizes a limit of A4. Consider the following formulas:

$\forall x \forall z R x z \supset \forall y R y y$
$\forall x \forall y R x y \supset \forall y R y y$

There is a clear sense in which these two formulas express the same truth: if a relation obtains between any two objects, then it obtains between any object and itself. However, they differ in one important respect. The first formula can be proved as follows. From A4 we get that $\vdash \forall x \forall z R x z \supset \forall z R y z$ and $\vdash \forall z R y z \supset R y y$. So $\vdash \forall x \forall z R x z \supset R y y$ by Theorem 14.9. From this and the converse of the deduction theorem (Theorem 14.8) we get that $\forall x \forall z R x z \vdash R y y$. By the generalization theorem (Theorem 14.6) it follows that $\forall x \forall z R x z \vdash \forall y R y y$. So, by the deduction theorem (Theorem 14.7), $\vdash \forall x \forall z R x z \supset \forall y R y y$. The second formula, instead, cannot be proved in the same way, because y is not substitutable for x in $\forall y R x y$, so A4 does not apply. This difference is due to the purely accidental fact that y occurs in the antecedent of the second formula. Theorem 14.17 fills this deductive lacuna. Since $\forall z R x z$ is an alphabetic variant of $\forall y R x y$, we have that $\forall y R x y \vdash \forall z R x z$, hence $\vdash \forall y R x y \supset \forall z R x z$. By the generalization theorem (Theorem 14.6) this entails that $\vdash \forall x (\forall y R x y \supset \forall z R x z)$. Given A6, it follows that $\vdash \forall x \forall y R x y \supset \forall x \forall z R x z$. From this and the provability of the first formula, given Theorem 14.9, we get that $\vdash \forall x \forall y R x y \supset \forall y R y y$. In substance, Theorem 14.17 entails that whenever the substitutability condition of A4 is not satisfied for purely accidental reasons, as in the case considered, we can find an alphabetic variant that leads to the desired result.

Exercises

14.1 Find a simpler expression that denotes the same formula:

(a) $(\alpha)^x_x$
(b) $((\alpha)^x_y)^y_x$

14.2 Consider the formula $((\alpha)^a_x)^y_a$, where a does not occur in α. Find a simpler expression that denotes the same formula.

14.3 Prove the following theorems:

Theorem 14.18 $\Gamma \cup \{\alpha\}$ *is inconsistent iff* $\Gamma \vdash {\sim}\alpha$

Theorem 14.19 $\Gamma \cup \{{\sim}\alpha\}$ *is inconsistent iff* $\Gamma \vdash \alpha$

14.4 Is **Q** effectively axiomatized?

14.5 Prove the following theorem:

Theorem 14.20 $\Gamma \vdash \alpha$ *iff there is a finite subset* Δ *of* Γ *such that* $\Delta \vdash \alpha$.

14.6 Prove that if $\beta_1, \ldots, \beta_n$ is a derivation of β_n from Γ such that the individual constant a does not occur in Γ, then, for a variable x that does not occur in $\beta_1, \ldots, \beta_n$, $(\beta_1)^x_a, \ldots, (\beta_n)^x_a$ is a derivation of $(\beta_n)^x_a$ from Γ.

14.7 Use the solution of Exercise 14.6 and the generalization theorem (Theorem 14.6) to prove that if $\Gamma \vdash \alpha$ and a is an individual constant that does not occur in Γ, then for some variable x that does not occur in α, there is a derivation of $\forall x (\alpha)_a^x$ from Γ in which a does not occur.

14.8 Use the solution of Exercise 14.7 and the generalization theorem (Theorem 14.6) to prove that if $\Gamma \vdash (\alpha)_x^a$, and a is an individual constant that occurs neither in Γ nor in α, then $\Gamma \vdash \forall x \alpha$.

14.9 Does Theorem 10.10 hold for **Q**?

14.10 For each of the following pairs of formulas, say whether the second formula is an alphabetic variant of the first:

(a) $\forall x \forall y (Px \supset Ry), \forall x \forall y (Px \supset Qy)$
(b) $\forall x \forall y (Px \supset Qy), \forall x \forall z (Px \supset Qz)$
(c) Pa, Pb

Chapter 15
Consistency, Soundness, Completeness

15.1 Consistency of Q

This chapter shows that **Q** is consistent, sound, and complete. The proof methods that will be employed to establish these results are the same that have been employed in Chapter 10 to prove the consistency, soundness, and completeness of **L**.

The proof of the consistency of **Q** hinges on the validity of its axioms. Let us start with A1-A3.

Theorem 15.1 $\vDash \alpha \supset (\beta \supset \alpha)$

Proof Since A1 is a tautological schema, every formula that instantiates A1 is satisfied by every assignment in every model. For every model and every assignment, four cases are possible: α and β are both satisfied, only α is satisfied, only β is satisfied, neither is satisfied. As is easy to verify, in each of these four cases $\alpha \supset (\beta \supset \alpha)$ is satisfied. □

Theorem 15.2 $\vDash (\alpha \supset (\beta \supset \gamma)) \supset ((\alpha \supset \beta) \supset (\alpha \supset \gamma))$

Proof The proof is analogous to that of Theorem 15.1. □

Theorem 15.3 $\vDash (\sim\alpha \supset \sim\beta) \supset (\beta \supset \alpha)$

Proof The proof is analogous to that of Theorems 15.1 and 15.2. □

Now it will be proved that A4-A7 are valid. The validity of A4 is already established by Theorem 13.4. So, we are left with A5-A7.

Theorem 15.4 $\vDash \alpha \supset \forall x \alpha$, *if x is not free in* α.

Proof Assume that σ satisfies α and that x is not free in α. Then, by Theorem 13.1, every x-variant of σ satisfies α. Therefore, σ satisfies $\forall x \alpha$. □

Theorem 15.5 $\vDash \forall x(\alpha \supset \beta) \supset (\forall x \alpha \supset \forall x \beta)$

© The Author(s), under exclusive license to Springer Nature Switzerland AG 2021
A. Iacona, *LOGIC: Lecture Notes for Philosophy, Mathematics, and Computer Science*, Springer Undergraduate Texts in Philosophy,
https://doi.org/10.1007/978-3-030-64811-4_15

Proof Assume that σ satisfies $\forall x(\alpha \supset \beta)$ and $\forall x\alpha$. Then every x-variant of σ satisfies $\alpha \supset \beta$ and α. By Theorem 13.3 it follows that every x-variant of σ satisfies β. Therefore, σ satisfies $\forall x\beta$.   □

Theorem 15.6 $\vDash \forall x\alpha$, *if α is an axiom.*

Proof Assume that α is valid *qua* axiom. Then $\vDash \forall x\alpha$.   □

Theorems 15.1–15.6 justify the conclusion that all the theorems of **Q** are valid, which in turn entails that **Q** is consistent.

Theorem 15.7 *If* $\vdash \alpha$ *in* **Q***, then* $\vDash \alpha$.

Proof Assume that $\vdash \alpha$. Then there is a proof of α where each formula is valid, either because it instantiates A1-A7, or because it is obtained from two formulas that precede it by means of MP, which preserves validity given Theorem 13.3. Therefore, $\vDash \alpha$.   □

Theorem 15.8 *In* **Q** *there is no α such that* $\vdash \alpha$ *and* $\vdash {\sim}\alpha$.

Proof Suppose that $\vdash \alpha$. By Theorem 15.7 it follows that $\vDash \alpha$. But then $\nvDash {\sim}\alpha$. So, by Theorem 15.7 we get that $\nvdash {\sim}\alpha$.   □

15.2   Soundness of Q

The definitions of soundness and completeness adopted here are the same that hold for **L**, that is, Definitions 10.2 and 10.3. As in the case of **L**, soundness and completeness can be phrased in terms of satisfiability and consistency, in accordance with the following theorems:

Theorem 15.9 **Q** *is sound iff every satisfiable set of formulas of* **Q** *is consistent.*

Proof Like the proof of theorem 10.6, replacing 'interpretation' with 'assignment' and using Theorem 14.19 instead of Theorem 9.30.   □

Theorem 15.10 **Q** *is complete iff every consistent set of formulas of* **Q** *is satisfiable.*

Proof Like the proof of theorem 10.7, replacing 'interpretation' with 'assignment' and using Theorem 14.19 instead of Theorem 9.30.   □

The soundness of **Q** is proved on the basis of Theorem 15.7.

Theorem 15.11 *If* $\Gamma \vdash \alpha$ *in* **Q***, then* $\Gamma \vDash \alpha$.

Proof Assume that $\Gamma \vdash \alpha$. Then, by Theorem 14.20, there is a finite subset Δ of Γ such that $\Delta \vdash \alpha$. Either $\Delta = \emptyset$ or $\Delta \neq \emptyset$. If $\Delta = \emptyset$, then $\vdash \alpha$. By Theorem 15.7, it follows that $\vDash \alpha$, and so that $\Gamma \vDash \alpha$. If $\Delta \neq \emptyset$, then $\Delta = \{\beta_1, \ldots, \beta_n\}$ for some n, and $\beta_1, \ldots, \beta_n \vdash \alpha$. If we apply the deduction theorem (Theorem 14.7) n times we get that $\vdash \beta_1 \supset (\ldots (\beta_n \supset \alpha))$. By Theorem 15.7, $\vDash \beta_1 \supset (\ldots (\beta_n \supset \alpha))$. So there is no model in which an assignment satisfies $\beta_1, \ldots, \beta_n$ but does not satisfy α. This means that $\Delta \vDash \alpha$. It follows that $\Gamma \vDash \alpha$. □

15.3 Completeness of **Q**

The completeness of **Q** will be proved in two steps. First it will be shown that, if a set of formulas of **Q** is consistent, there is a theory that includes it as a subset and enjoys certain properties. Then it will be proved that a theory with those properties is satisfiable, so the same goes for the initial set. This justifies the conclusion that every consistent set of formulas of **Q** is satisfiable.

As in the case of **L**, the first part of the proof hinges on Theorem 10.10, which entails that every consistent set of formulas of **Q** is a subset of a consistent and negation-complete theory. However, there is a complication. In this case, consistency and negation-completeness do not suffice to prove satisfiability. What we need is a theory that, beside being consistent and negation-complete, has a third property: for every formula α and variable x, there is an individual constant a— called *Henkin witness*—such that $\vdash \sim\forall x\alpha \supset \sim(\alpha)_x^a$. To say that a theory has Henkin witnesses is to say that whenever a universal formula does not hold, then some specific instance of it does not hold. To complete the first part of the proof we need the following theorem:

Theorem 15.12 *If Γ is a consistent set of formulas of **Q**, then there is a consistent and negation-complete theory T in a richer language L, such that $\Gamma \subseteq T$ and T has Henkin witnesses.*

Proof Let Γ be a consistent set of formulas of **Q**. Assume that a denumerable set of individual constants is added to the language of **Q** to obtain an augmented language L. Let $\langle\langle\alpha_1, x_1\rangle, \langle\alpha_2, x_2, \rangle, \langle\alpha_3, x_3\rangle \ldots\rangle$ be an enumeration of the ordered pairs formed by a formula of L and a variable. Let β_1 be $\sim\forall x_1\alpha_1 \supset \sim(\alpha_1)_{x_1}^{a_1}$, where a_1 is the first additional individual constant which does not occur in α_1, and, for $n > 1$, let β_n be $\sim\forall x_n\alpha_n \supset \sim(\alpha_n)_{x_n}^{a_n}$, where a_n is the first additional individual constant which does not occur in α_n or in $\beta_1, \ldots, \beta_{n-1}$. Finally, let Γ_∞ be the set obtained by adding all these formulas to Γ.

The following reasoning shows that Γ_∞ is consistent. Suppose that a contradiction is derivable in Γ_∞. Then, since a finite number of new formulas suffices to derive that contradiction, and Γ is consistent by hypothesis, there must be a set $\Gamma\cup\{\beta_1, \ldots, \beta_n\}$ which is the smallest inconsistent subset of Γ_∞. By Theorem 14.18, $\Gamma\cup\{\beta_1, \ldots \beta_{n-1}\} \vdash \sim\beta_n$. Since $\sim\beta_n$ is $\sim(\sim\forall x_n\alpha_n \supset \sim(\alpha_n)_{x_n}^{a_n})$, by Theorems 14.15 and 14.16 we obtain:

(a) $\Gamma \cup \{\beta_1, \ldots \beta_{n-1}\} \vdash \sim\forall x_n\alpha_n$
(b) $\Gamma \cup \{\beta_1, \ldots \beta_{n-1}\} \vdash \sim\sim(\alpha_n)_{x_n}^{a_n}$

By Theorem 14.10, (b) entails that $\Gamma \cup \{\beta_1, \ldots \beta_{n-1}\} \vdash (\alpha_n)_{x_n}^{a_n}$. It follows that $\Gamma \cup \{\beta_1, \ldots \beta_{n-1}\} \vdash \forall x_n\alpha_n$ (see Exercise 14.8). Given (a), this means that $\Gamma \cup$

$\{\beta_1, \ldots \beta_{n-1}\}$ is inconsistent, which contradicts the supposition that $\Gamma \cup \{\beta_1, \ldots \beta_n\}$ is the smallest inconsistent subset of Γ_∞.

Since Γ_∞ is consistent, by Theorem 10.10 there is a consistent and negation-complete theory T such that $\Gamma_\infty \subseteq T$. T is an extension of Γ, given that $\Gamma \subseteq \Gamma_\infty$. So it suffices to prove that, for every formula α and variable x, there is an individual constant a such that $T \vdash \sim\forall x\alpha \supset \sim(\alpha)_x^a$. Let $\langle \alpha_n, x_n \rangle$ be any pair in the enumeration $\langle\langle \alpha_1, x_1 \rangle, \langle \alpha_2, x_2, \rangle, \langle \alpha_3, x_3 \rangle \ldots \rangle$. Γ_∞ includes β_n, that is, $\sim\forall x_n\alpha_n \supset \sim(\alpha_n)_{x_n}^{a_n}$. Since $\Gamma_\infty \subseteq T$, also T includes β_n.   □

Now we are ready for the second part of the proof, the justification of the step that leads to the final result: every theory that enjoys the three properties required by Theorem 15.12 is satisfiable.

Theorem 15.13 *If T is a consistent and negation-complete theory that has Henkin witnesses, then T is satisfiable.*

Proof Let T be a theory with the three properties required. Let $\mathcal{M}$ be a model defined as follows:

(i) the domain of $\mathcal{M}$ is the set of terms of L_q;
(ii) the interpretation function of $\mathcal{M}$ assigns to every individual constant the constant itself, and to every n-place predicate letter P a relation R such that $\langle t_1, \ldots, t_n \rangle \in R$ iff $T \vdash Pt_1 \ldots t_n$.

Let σ be an assignment in which each variable of L_q denotes the variable itself. Now it will be shown by induction that, for any formula α, σ satisfies α iff $T \vdash \alpha$.

Basis. Assume that α is an atomic formula $Pt_1 \ldots t_n$. Then σ satisfies α iff $\langle t_1, \ldots, t_n \rangle \in R$, where R is the relation assigned to P by the interpretation function. By (ii), $\langle t_1, \ldots, t_n \rangle \in R$ iff $T \vdash Pt_1 \ldots t_n$.

Step. Assume that the biconditional to be proved holds for any formula of complexity less than or equal to n, and consider a formula α of complexity $n + 1$.

Case 1: α has the form $\sim\beta$. Suppose that σ satisfies $\sim\beta$. Then σ does not satisfy β. By the induction hypothesis it follows that $T \nvdash \beta$. Since T is negation-complete, $T \vdash \sim\beta$. Now suppose that $T \vdash \sim\beta$. Then $T \nvdash \beta$ by the consistency of T. By the induction hypothesis it follows that σ does not satisfy β. So, σ satisfies $\sim\beta$.

Case 2: α has the form $\beta \supset \gamma$. Suppose that σ does not satisfy $\beta \supset \gamma$. Then σ satisfies β and does not satisfy γ. By the induction hypothesis it follows that $T \vdash \beta$ and $T \nvdash \gamma$, which entails that $T \vdash \sim\gamma$, given that T is negation-complete. Since T $\vdash \beta \supset (\sim\gamma \supset \sim(\beta \supset \gamma))$ by Theorem 14.12, we get that $T \vdash \sim(\beta \supset \gamma)$. Since T is consistent, $T \nvdash \beta \supset \gamma$. Now suppose that $T \nvdash \beta \supset \gamma$. Then $T \vdash \sim(\beta \supset \gamma)$, given that T is negation-complete. By Theorems 14.15 and 14.16, $T \vdash \sim(\beta \supset \gamma) \supset \beta$ and $T \vdash \sim(\beta \supset \gamma) \supset \sim\gamma$. It follows that $T \vdash \beta$ and $T \vdash \sim\gamma$. Since T is consistent, $T \nvdash \gamma$. By the induction hypothesis it follows that σ satisfies β and does not satisfy γ, which means that σ does not satisfy $\beta \supset \gamma$.

Case 3: α has the form $\forall x\beta$. Suppose that σ does not satisfy $\forall x\beta$. Then there is an x-variant σ' of σ that does not satisfy β. So there is an alphabetic variant β' of β such that σ' does not satisfy β'. Let t be the term denoted by x in σ'. Then, by the substitution lemma (Theorem 13.2), σ does not satisfy $(\beta')_x^t$. By the induction hypothesis it follows that $T \nvdash (\beta')_x^t$. But then $T \nvdash \forall x\beta'$, because $T \vdash \forall x\beta' \supset (\beta')_x^t$ by A4, and T is deductively closed: if $\forall x\beta'$ were provable in T, the same would go for $(\beta')_x^t$. Since β' is an alphabetic variant of β, by Theorem 14.17 $\forall x\beta \dashv\vdash \forall x\beta'$, so $T \nvdash \forall x\beta$. Now suppose that σ satisfies $\forall x\beta$. Then every x-variant of σ satisfies β, in particular the x-variant in which x denotes the individual constant a. By the substitution lemma (Theorem 13.2) it follows that σ satisfies $(\beta)_x^a$. By the induction hypothesis we get that $T \vdash (\beta)_x^a$. Since T is consistent, $T \nvdash \sim(\beta)_x^a$. This entails that $T \nvdash \sim\forall x\beta$, for $T \vdash \sim\forall x\beta \supset \sim(\beta)_x^a$, so if $\sim\forall x\beta$ were provable in T, $\sim(\beta)_x^a$ would also be provable in T. Since T is negation-complete, we get that $T \vdash \forall x\beta$. $\square$

The model constructed in this proof is a *canonical model* for T. Its domain is formed by symbols of the language of T itself, and its interpretation function is defined in such a way as to obtain the desired result. Note that in case 3 the assumption that $T \vdash \sim\forall x\beta \supset \sim(\beta)_x^a$ is necessary to prove the left-to-right direction of the biconditional. This shows why consistency and negation-completeness do not suffice to prove satisfiability.

Theorem 15.14 *If $\Gamma \vDash \alpha$, then $\Gamma \vdash \alpha$ in* **Q**

Proof Assume that Γ is a consistent set of formulas of **Q**. By Theorem 15.12, there is a consistent and negation-complete theory T such that $\Gamma \subseteq T$ and T has Henkin witnesses. By Theorem 15.13, T is satisfiable. So, Γ is satisfiable as well. By Theorem 15.10, this is to say that if $\Gamma \vDash \alpha$, then $\Gamma \vdash \alpha$ in **Q**. $\square$

15.4 Compactness Theorem

One important corollary of the soundness and completeness theorems (Theorems 15.11 and 15.14) is the *compactness theorem*:

Theorem 15.15 *If every finite subset of a set of formulas Γ is satisfiable, then Γ is satisfiable.*

Proof Assume that Γ is unsatisfiable. Since the completeness theorem (Theorem 15.14) entails that every consistent set of formulas is satisfiable, it follows that Γ is inconsistent. This means that $\Gamma \vdash \alpha$ and $\Gamma \vdash \sim\alpha$ for some α. So, there is a finite subset Δ of Γ such that $\Delta \vdash \alpha$ and $\Delta \vdash \sim\alpha$ (Theorem 14.20). Since the soundness theorem (Theorem 15.11) entails that every satisfiable set of formulas is consistent, it follows that Δ is unsatisfiable. Therefore, some finite subset of Γ is unsatisfiable. $\square$

15.5   Final Remarks

Let us close this chapter with some remarks about the significance of the completeness and soundness theorems (Theorems 15.11 and 15.14). As we have seen, the notions of logical consequence and derivability that characterize L_q and Q are distinct formal counterparts of the pretheoretical notion of entailment. Each of these two notions may be regarded as intuitively adequate in some sense. On the one hand, the notion of logical consequence draws its intuitive appeal from the fact that it involves some sort of truth preservation. On the other, the notion of derivability is intuitively acceptable insofar as a derivation formally represents a sequence of inferential steps each of which is clearly legitimate.

In both cases, of course, there are significant differences. Although logical consequence involves some sort of truth preservation, like entailment, it is not the same sort of truth preservation: one thing is to preserve truth across models, another thing is to preserve truth across possible states of affairs. Consider again our example:

(1)   All philosophers are wise
(2)   Socrates is a philosopher
(3)   Socrates is wise

The legitimacy of the inference from (1) and (2) to (3) seems to lie in the fact that every imaginable situation in which every philosopher is wise and Socrates is a philosopher is a situation in which Socrates is wise. But the definition of logical consequence entails a quantification on interpretations. This can hardly be regarded as part of the pretheoretical understanding of entailment. When we judge the argument above as valid, we do *not* think that it is valid because, no matter what 'Socrates, 'philosopher' and 'wise' mean, (3) is true if (1) and (2) are true.[1]

Similarly, there are important respects in which derivability does not resemble entailment. The most striking difference is that entailment has to do with truth, as noted above, while derivability is defined without making any reference to semantic notions. For example, the intuitive legitimacy of a basic rule of inference such as MP—which occurs as part of the definition of derivation in Q—can hardly be recognized without taking into account that MP necessarily preserves truth.

These differences should not surprise. There is no reason to expect that a formal notion designed for theoretical purposes resembles in all respects the pretheoretical notion from which it originates. Nonetheless, each of the two notions is intuitively credible to some extent, and it is reasonable to assume that this credibility plays some role in the justification of the notion itself.

As long as this assumption is granted, the completeness and soundness theorems (Theorems 15.11 and 15.14) show an interesting fact, namely, that any consideration about the intuitive credibility of the notion of logical consequence indirectly applies

---

[1] Etchemendy [10] emphasizes this point.

to the notion of derivability, and that any consideration about the intuitive credibility
of the notion of derivability indirectly applies to the notion of logical consequence.
Since logical consequence and derivability are extensionally equivalent, in that they
characterize the same class of valid forms, any justificatory property that can be
ascribed to one of the two notions can be ascribed to the other as well.

Exercises

15.1 In the proof of theorem 15.12 it is assumed that a denumerable set of
individual constants is added to the language of Γ. Explain why the proof can take
for granted that this addition preserves the consistency of Γ.

15.2 In the proof of theorem 15.13, case 3, it is assumed that if σ' does not satisfy
β, and β' is an alphabetic variant of β, then σ' does not satisfy β'. Justify this
assumption.

15.3 In the proof of theorem 15.13, case 3, the right-to-left direction of the
biconditional is proved indirectly through β', which is an alphabetic variant of β. Is
this detour necessary?

15.4 Is the domain of the model adopted in the proof of theorem 15.13 a countable
set?

15.5 Is **Q** negation-complete?

15.6 Let T be the set of theorems of **Q**. Is T maximally consistent?

15.7 Let T be the set of valid formulas of **Q**. Is T maximally consistent?

15.8 Prove the following theorem:

Theorem 15.16 *If $\Gamma \vDash \alpha$, there is a finite subset Δ of Γ such that $\Delta \vDash \alpha$.*

15.9 Prove by means of Theorem 15.16 that if a set of formulas Γ is unsatisfiable,
then some finite subset of Γ is unsatisfiable.

15.10 Prove that the compactness theorem (Theorem 15.15) is equivalent to
Theorem 15.16.

Chapter 16
Undecidability and Related Results

16.1 Undecidability of Q

This chapter dwells on some facts about **Q** that concern decidability and related notions. Let us start with the following theorem, which directly follows from the soundness and completeness of **Q**:

Theorem 16.1 *The set of theorems of* **Q** *is undecidable.*

Proof The set of valid formulas of **Q** is undecidable (Sect. 13.6). Since **Q** is sound and complete, the set of theorems of **Q** is identical to the set of valid formulas of **Q**. So it is undecidable. □

Theorem 16.1 implies that **Q** is undecidable in the following sense:

Definition 16.1 A system S is *decidable* iff the set of the theorems of S is decidable.

It is important to note that the undecidability of **Q** is compatible with the fact that **Q** is effectively axiomatized. More generally, a system can be undecidable even if it is effectively axiomatized: effective axiomatization does not entail decidability.

As we shall see in the next two sections, effective axiomatization entails a weaker property, *effective enumerability*:

Definition 16.2 A set Γ is *effectively enumerable* iff there is an effective method to list, in some order, the members of Γ.

Finite sets trivially satisfy this condition. If Γ is finite, one can list all its elements. If Γ = ∅, effective enumerability is assumed by convention. An infinite set can be effectively enumerable as well. In this case the procedure can never finish. But for any specified element of Γ, it must eventually appear on the list.

© The Author(s), under exclusive license to Springer Nature Switzerland AG 2021
A. Iacona, *LOGIC: Lecture Notes for Philosophy, Mathematics, and Computer Science*, Springer Undergraduate Texts in Philosophy,
https://doi.org/10.1007/978-3-030-64811-4_16

Decidability and effective enumerability are related because decidability entails effective enumerability. If Γ is decidable, its elements can be listed in the following way: take any object x and check whether $x \in \Gamma$. If $x \in \Gamma$, put x as the first item in the list, otherwise leave x out. Then, take another object, repeat the procedure, and so on. This way, every element of Γ will eventually appear in the list. Effective enumerability, instead, does not entail decidability: a set can be effectively enumerable without being decidable.

16.2 Gödel Numbering

The effective enumerability of the theorems of $\mathbf{Q}$ can be proved by means of a method introduced by Gödel—the *arithmetization of syntax*—which applies to any effectively axiomatized system. The following definition holds for any language L:

Definition 16.3 A *Gödel numbering of* L is an assignment of numbers—called *Gödel numbers*—to the symbols, formulas, and sequences of formulas of L in such a way that there is a one-to-one correspondence between the Gödel numbers on the one hand and the symbols, formulas, and sequences of formulas on the other, and there is an effective method, given a symbol, formula, or sequence of formulas, for finding its Gödel number, and an effective method, given a number, for finding whether it is a Gödel number and if so which symbol, formula, or sequence of formulas it is the Gödel number of.

There are many ways of assigning numbers to the expressions of L in accordance with this definition. Here is one. Let us fix a basic code by associating an odd number to each symbol of L:

s_0	s_1	s_2	s_3	s_4	s_5	$\cdots$
1	3	5	7	9	11	$\cdots$

Our numbering scheme for the expressions of L is given in terms of this basic code as follows. Let the expression e be a sequence of n symbols, and let $c_1, \ldots, c_n$ be the basic code numbers of these symbols. The Gödel number of e is calculated by using the basic code number c_i of each symbol as an exponent for the i-th prime number π_i, for $1 \leq i \leq n$, and then multiplying the results, that is, $2^{c_1} \times 3^{c_2} \times 5^{c_3} \cdots \times \pi_n^{c_n}$. For example, the Gödel number of the simple expression s_2 is 2^5, the Gödel number of the complex expression $s_1 s_2$ is $2^3 \times 3^5$, and so on. Since these numbers are uniquely decomposable into prime factors by the fundamental theorem of arithmetic (Sect. 1.3), there is a unique decoding of them. Finally, derivations are coded as follows. Given a sequence of formulas $\alpha_1, \ldots \alpha_n$, we first code each α_i by a regular Gödel number g_i to yield a sequence of numbers $g_1, \ldots, g_n$. We then encode this sequence of regular Gödel numbers using a single super Gödel number by repeating the trick of multiplying powers of primes to get $2^{g_1} \times 3^{g_2} \times 5^{g_3} \times \cdots \times \pi_n^{g_n}$.

16.3 Effective Enumerability of the Theorems of Q

The method just described can be used to prove the following theorem:

Theorem 16.2 *If a system S is effectively axiomatized, the set of theorems of S is effectively enumerable.*

Proof Let L be the language of S. Consider a Gödel numbering of L. Given this numbering, the finite sequences of formulas of L can be listed in the order of the corresponding Gödel numbers. So, the set of finite sequences of formulas of L is effectively enumerable. Let $\langle s_1, s_2, s_3 \ldots \rangle$ be an enumeration of such sequences. Since there is an effective method for telling whether or not something is a proof in S, we can obtain an enumeration of the theorems of S as follows. First we test s_1 to see whether it is a proof. If it is a proof, we set down the last formula of s_1 as the first term of a sequence of formulas. Then we test s_2. If it is a proof, we set down the last formula of s_2 as the next term in the sequence (or as the first term, if s_1 was not a proof), and so on.   □

Theorem 16.2 shows the connection between effective axiomatization and effective enumerability. Even though effective axiomatization does not entail decidability, as noted in Sect. 16.1, it entails effective enumerability. This is why the following theorem holds:

Theorem 16.3 *The set of theorems of* **Q** *is effectively enumerable.*

Proof **Q** is effectively axiomatized. Therefore, by Theorem 16.2, the set of theorems of **Q** is effectively enumerable.   □

A direct corollary of Theorem 16.2 concerns the set of valid formulas of **Q**. We know that this set is undecidable. But undecidability does not rule out effective enumerability, and now we are in a position to say what follows:

Theorem 16.4 *The set of valid formulas of* **Q** *is effectively enumerable.*

Proof By Theorem 16.3, the set of theorems of **Q** is effectively enumerable. Since **Q** is sound and complete, the set of valid formulas of **Q** is identical to that set, so it is effectively enumerable.   □

16.4 A Further Corollary

What about the set of *non*-valid formulas of **Q**? Is it effectively enumerable? The answer to this question is provided by a theorem due to Post, which establishes a relation between a set of natural numbers A and its *relative complement* with respect to a superset B, that is, between A and the set of elements of B which are not in A.[1]

---

[1] Post [52].

Theorem 16.5 *For any two sets of natural numbers A and B such that $A \subseteq B$, A is decidable iff both A and its relative complement with respect to B are effectively enumerable.*

Proof Let $\overline{A}$ be the relative complement of A with respect to B. Assume that A is decidable. If $A = \emptyset$, then A is effectively enumerable by convention, and $\overline{A}$ is effectively enumerable as well, for $\overline{A} = B$. The case in which $\overline{A} = \emptyset$ is similar. If $A \neq \emptyset$, let $\langle a_0, a_1, a_2, \dots \rangle$ be an effective enumeration of B. Since A is decidable, one can go through this enumeration and tell, for each of its elements, whether or not it belongs to A, so as to provide an effective enumeration of A and an effective enumeration of $\overline{A}$. Now assume that A and $\overline{A}$ are effectively enumerable. If A is finite, then it is decidable. If $\overline{A}$ is finite, A is decidable as well, for any effective method for deciding whether a number belongs to $\overline{A}$ is also a method for deciding whether it belongs to A. So we are left with the case in which A and $\overline{A}$ are both infinite. Let $\langle a_0, a_1, a_2, \dots \rangle$ and $\langle b_0, b_1, b_2, \dots \rangle$ be effective enumerations of A and $\overline{A}$ respectively. Then, for any n, consider in order $a_0, b_0, a_1, b_1, \dots$, keeping track of whether they are in A or in $\overline{A}$. Sooner or later n will turn up in this list, and one will know whether n is in A. So A is decidable.   □

What holds for natural numbers holds for the formulas of a language, given that formulas can be associated with natural numbers.

Theorem 16.6 *For any set of formulas Γ of a language L, Γ is decidable iff both Γ and its relative complement with respect to L are effectively enumerable.*

Proof Let $\overline{\Gamma}$ be the set of formulas of L that do not belong to Γ. Consider a Gödel numbering of L. Then there are two sets A and $\overline{A}$ of natural numbers formed by the Gödel numbers assigned to the formulas in Γ and $\overline{\Gamma}$. By Theorem 16.5, A is decidable iff A and $\overline{A}$ are effectively enumerable. So the same goes for Γ and $\overline{\Gamma}$.   □

Theorem 16.6, combined with Theorem 16.4, entails that the set of non-valid formulas of **Q** is not effectively enumerable:

Theorem 16.7 *The set of non-valid formulas of **Q** is not effectively enumerable.*

Proof By Theorem 16.4 the set of valid formulas of **Q** is effectively enumerable. If the set of non-valid formulas of **Q** were effectively enumerable as well, from Theorem 16.6 it would follow that the set of valid formulas of **Q** is decidable. Since it is not, the set of non-valid formulas of **Q** is not effectively enumerable.   □

16.5   Recursive Axiomatization and Decidability

The results presented in the foregoing sections can be rephrased by adopting the notion of recursiveness, which is a precise counterpart of the notion of effective computability. As we have seen, this notion chararacterizes a definite class of numerical functions. Since numerical properties and relations are definable in terms of their characteristic functions, as explained in Sect. 6.5, we can say that a numerical property or relation is *recursively decidable* when its characteristic function is recursive. The same goes for any syntactic property or relation, given that syntactic properties and relations can be reduced to numerical properties and relations through arithmetization. On the assumption that a function is recursive just in case it is effectively computable—Church's thesis—decidability can be identified with recursive decidability.

In Sect. 16.1 we saw that effective axiomatization does not entail decidability. The same point can be phrased in terms of recursiveness by adopting the following definitions:

Definition 16.4 A system S is *recursively axiomatized* iff the properties of being a formula of S, an axiom of S, or a derivation in S are recursively decidable.

Definition 16.5 A system S is *recursively decidable* iff the set of theorems of S is recursively decidable.

The point is that a system can be recursively undecidable even if it is recursively axiomatized.

Similar reformulations can be provided for the theorems concerning effective enumerability. To say that a set is *recursively enumerable* is to say that there is a recursive function that enumerates its elements. Accordingly, Theorem 16.2 can be rephrased as follows: if a system S is recursively axiomatized, then the set of theorems of S is recursively enumerable.

Exercises

16.1 Can we obtain a Gödel numbering of a language L by using a basic code in which each symbol of L corresponds to an even number?

s_0	s_1	s_2	s_3	s_4	s_5	...
0	2	4	6	8	10	...

16.2 Is the set of valid formulas of **L** effectively enumerable?

16.3 Is the set of non-valid formulas of **L** effectively enumerable?

16.4 Is **Q** recursively axiomatized?

16.5 Is **Q** recursively decidable?

16.6 Is the set of theorems of **Q** recursively enumerable?

16.7 Is the set of valid formulas of **Q** recursively enumerable?

16.8 Explain why the following holds, given Theorem 16.2: if a system S is effectively axiomatized and negation-complete, then S is decidable.

16.9 Explain why the conditional stated in Exercise 16.8 holds no matter whether or not S is consistent.

16.10 Explain why every recursively axiomatized and negation-complete system is recursively decidable.

Chapter 17
First-Order Logic

17.1 First-Order Languages and Systems

So far we have focused on L_q. But there are many predicate languages, for the alphabet of L_q can be enlarged or restricted in various ways. One can add to L_q further individual constants, further predicate letters, further variables, the connectives $\wedge$, $\vee$, $\exists$, or the symbol $=$. Moreover, one can add to L_q function symbols that, when combined with individual constants or variables, form complex terms which denote operations on the domain. For example, if s denotes the successor function in a model whose domain is a set of numbers, sx will denote the successor of the number assigned to x. Just as some symbols can be added to L_q, others can be removed: one can reduce the predicate letters, and reduce or eliminate the individual constants.

Any language obtained from L_q by means of zero, one, or more modifications of the kind considered is a *first-order language*. This label indicates that the only variables of the language are individual variables that refer to objects. Higher order languages—second-order, third-order, and so on—include predicate variables that refer to properties, other variables that refer to properties of properties, and so on.

Although a first-order language can be obtained by adding any number of symbols to L_q, here we will assume that the new symbols are at most countably many. This assumption implies that the result of the addition is a denumerable set, for the alphabet of L_q is denumerable, and the union of a denumerable set and a countable set is denumerable (see Exercises 3.10 and 13.1). So, we will restrict consideration to first-order languages with a denumerable alphabet.

The expression 'first-order' can also be applied to systems. For any first-order language L, a system in L is a *first-order system*. Thus, **Q** is a first-order system, and the same goes for any other system in L_q, or in a variant of L_q. In particular, any system that is deductively equivalent to **Q** is a first-order system. The term 'first-order logic' is generally used to indicate any such system.

© The Author(s), under exclusive license to Springer Nature Switzerland AG 2021 153
A. Iacona, *LOGIC: Lecture Notes for Philosophy, Mathematics, and Computer Science*, Springer Undergraduate Texts in Philosophy,
https://doi.org/10.1007/978-3-030-64811-4_17

17.2   First-Order Logic with Identity

An example of first-order language is the language obtained by adding $=$ to L_q. Let us call L_{qi} this variant. An appropriate interpretation of L_{qi}, that is, an interpretation that respects the intended meaning of $=$, is a model in which $=$ denotes the relation of identity, so its extension includes all and only the ordered pairs of objects of the domain whose first member is identical to the second. A model of this kind is called *normal*.

Let Q_i be the system in L_{qi} obtained by adding the following axioms to Q:

A8 $\forall x x = x$
A9 $\forall x \forall y (x = y \supset (\alpha \supset \alpha'))$, if α' differs from α at most in that y replaces x in some free occurrence.

A8 says that everything is identical to itself, which may be regarded as a self-evident truth. A9 expresses the principle known as *Indiscernibility of Identicals*: if x is identical to y, then whatever is predicable of x is also predicable of y. In the formulation of A9, the notation α' is adopted instead of $(\alpha)_x^y$, because the latter implies substitution in α of all the free occurrences of x with y, which is not what A9 requires.

As explained in Sect. 2.1, identity is an equivalence relation: it is reflexive, symmetric, and transitive. Q_i preserves this basic fact about identity. A8 directly states reflexivity. Moreover, given A8 and A9, symmetry and transitivity are provable:

$$\forall x \forall y (x = y \supset y = x)$$
$$\forall x \forall y \forall z (x = y \supset (y = z \supset x = z))$$

The term 'first-order logic with identity' is generally used to indicate any system in L_{qi}, or in a variant of L_{qi}, which is deductively equivalent to Q_i.

Q_i is consistent, sound, and complete. This can be shown through the same methods that have been employed in Chapter 15 to establish the consistency, soundness, and completeness of Q.

Theorem 17.1 *In Q_i there is no α such that $\vdash \alpha$ and $\vdash \sim\alpha$.*

Proof The proofs of theorems 15.1–15.6 can easily be adapted to show that every formula of Q_i that instantiates A1–A7 is satisfied by all assignments in every normal model. Clearly, the same goes for every formula of Q that instantiates A8. Now consider A9. Suppose that $x = y$ is satisfied by an assignment σ in a normal model. Then σ assigns the same object to x and y. So, if σ satisfies α, and α' differs from α at most in that y replaces x in some free occurrence, then σ satisfies α'. That is, σ satisfies $x = y \supset (\alpha \supset \alpha')$. Thus, every assignment satisfies $\forall y (x = y \supset (\alpha \supset \alpha'))$, and the same goes for $\forall x \forall y (x = y \supset (\alpha \supset \alpha'))$. Since the axioms of Q_i are satisfied by all assignments in every normal model, and MP preserves satisfaction, every theorem of Q_i is satisfied by all assigments in every normal model. The consistency of Q_i follows from this for the reason explained in the proof of theorem 15.8.   □

Theorem 17.2 *If* $\Gamma \vdash \alpha$ *in* Q_i, *then* $\Gamma \vDash \alpha$.

Proof As explained in the proof of theorem 17.1, every theorem of Q_i is satisfied by all assigments in every normal model. The soundness of Q_i follows from this by a reasoning analogous to that employed in the proof of theorem 15.11.   □

Theorem 17.3 *If* $\Gamma \vDash \alpha$, *then* $\Gamma \vdash \alpha$ *in* Q_i.

Proof As in the case of Q, the proof has two parts. First it is shown that, for every consistent set Γ of formulas of Q_i, there is a consistent and negation-complete theory T such that $\Gamma \subseteq T$ and T has Henkin witnesses. Then it is shown that T is satisfiable. Since Q_i is exactly like Q as far as Theorem 15.12 is concerned, the first part remains unchanged. Instead, the second needs a refinement. A canonical model for T cannot be constructed by using the set of terms of L_{qi} as a domain and considering an assignment in which every variable denotes itself. The reason is that two distinct terms t and t' may be such that $T \vdash t = t'$, in which case it turns out that the formula $t = t'$ is not satisfied by the chosen assignment even though it belongs to T. What is needed to prove the desired result is that t and t' have the same denotation iff $T \vdash t = t'$. This is obtained if the domain is a set whose elements are sets of terms of L_{qi} obtained by grouping the terms of L_{qi} on the basis of the following condition: t and t' belong to the same set iff $T \vdash t = t'$. The relation thus defined is an equivalence relation, since $=$ is reflexive, symmetric, and transitive, as noted above. Let $\mathcal{M}$ be the model used in the proof of theorem 15.13. Let $\mathcal{M}'$ be a model whose domain is the set of equivalence classes so defined, and the interpretation function of $\mathcal{M}'$ is such that, for every n-place predicate letter P, $\langle [t_1], \ldots [t_n] \rangle \in [P]_{\mathcal{M}'}$ iff $\langle t_1, \ldots, t_n \rangle \in [P]_{\mathcal{M}}$. Then it can be shown by induction that there is an assignment that satisfies α iff $T \vdash \alpha$. The details of the proof are boring, and you can live without them. But at least it should be clear that $\mathcal{M}'$ rules out that distinct terms can denote distinct objects when their identity is provable in T.   □

17.3   First-Order Theory

Given a system S and a set Γ of formulas of S, let $S+\Gamma$ be the system obtained by adding those formulas to S as axioms. In this case every theorem of S is a theorem of $S+\Gamma$, for every proof in S is a proof in $S+\Gamma$. That is, if T is the set of theorems of S, and T' is the set of theorems of $S+\Gamma$, then T' is an extension of T.

The importance of first-order logic lies not only in the results that can be obtained within a first-order system, but also in those that can be obtained by combining a first-order system with a set of axioms which concern some specific subject, that is, a set of *proper axioms*. The following definition holds for any set of formulas that can be proved by extending a first-order system in this way:

Definition 17.1 A *first-order theory* is a deductively closed set of formulas of a first-order language.

In particular, any set of formulas that can be proved by extending a first-order system in such a way that the resulting system is recursively axiomatized is *recursively axiomatized first-order theory*. From now on we will restrict consideration to theories of this kind, and we will refer to them by using the same name of the system by means of which they are obtained. For example, the name $\mathbf{Q_i}$ will denote both the system presented in Sect. 17.2 and the set of its theorems.

A key notion that is used to describe first-order theories at the semantic level is the notion of *model*, understood as follows:

Definition 17.2 A *model of a theory T* is an interpretation of the language of T that makes true every formula in T.

To say that a first-order theory *has* a model is to say that there is at least one interpretation of its language that makes true all its formulas. The same definition holds for any set of formulas.

Note that having a model is not quite the same thing as being satisfiable. The latter property is weaker than the former, as it requires satisfaction by at least one assignment in at least one interpretation. For example, the set $\{Mx, \sim My\}$ is satisfiable, but does not have a model. So, if we add Mx and $\sim My$ to a first-order system as proper axioms, we get a satisfiable theory that has no model. However, the difference between being satisfiable and having a model does not really matter insofar as proper axioms are closed formulas, for in that case we get that whenever a theorem is satisfied by some assignment in a given interpretation, the theorem is true in that interpretation.

Usually, the set of models of a first-order theory is individuated on the basis of an *intended model*, that is, an interpretation of its language that intuitively provides the correct reading of its proper axioms. The intended model may be understood either as a paradigmatic interpretation, or as a set of distinct but relevantly similar interpretations. In any case, every interpretation that is sufficiently similar to the intended model will make true the proper axioms of the theory. More generally, any first-order theory can be associated with a set of interpretations of its language, which is fixed by its proper axioms.

17.4   The Language of Basic Arithmetic

Let $\mathsf{L_a}$ be a language obtained from $\mathsf{L_{qi}}$ by removing the predicate letters and adding the connectives $\wedge, \vee, \exists$, the individual constant 0, and the function symbols $s, +, \times$. To simplify the notation, $+$ and $\times$ will occur between the respective terms, writing $x + y$ or $x \times y$ instead of $+xy$ or $\times xy$, and the standard numerals $1, 2, 3 \ldots$ will abbreviate the complex terms $s0, ss0, sss0 \ldots$. Moreover, for every n, $\overline{n}$ will refer to the numeral that denotes n.

L_a is designed to talk about numbers. Its intended interpretation is a normal model whose domain is $\mathbb{N}$, and whose interpretation function is such that the individual constant 0 denotes the number 0, and the symbols $s, +, \times$ denote respectively the functions successor, addition, and multiplication.

Although L_a is relatively simple, it is able to express a considerably wide class of numerical properties and relations. A couple of examples will help to illustrate. Consider the property of being prime. A number n has this property when it is greater than 1 and its only factors are 1 and itself. That is, n is prime if and only if $n \neq 1$ and, of any two numbers that multiply to give n, one of them is 1. Therefore, the property of being prime can be expressed as follows:

$$x \neq 1 \wedge \forall y \forall z (y \times z = x \supset (y = 1 \vee z = 1))$$

For every n, the formula obtained from this formula by replacing x with $\bar{n}$ is true in the intended interpretation of L_a if and only if n is prime. More generally,

Definition 17.3 A formula α with a free variable x *expresses* a numerical property P in a language L iff, for every n, if n has P, then $(\alpha)_x^{\bar{n}}$ is true in the intended interpretation of L, and if n does not have P, then $\sim(\alpha)_x^{\bar{n}}$ is true in the intended interpretation of L.

A similar definition holds for numerical relations. For example, the relation less-than-or-equal-to can be expressed in L_a as follows:

$$\exists z(z + x = y)$$

For every m, n, the formula obtained from this formula by replacing x and y with $\bar{m}$ and $\bar{n}$ is true in the intended interpretation of L_a if and only if $m \leq n$. More generally,

Definition 17.4 A formula α with two free variables x and y *expresses* a numerical relation R in a language L iff, for every m, n, if R obtains between m and n, then $(\alpha)_{x,y}^{\bar{m},\bar{n}}$ is true in the intended interpretation of L, and if R does not obtain between m and n, then $\sim(\alpha)_{x,y}^{\bar{m},\bar{n}}$ is true in the intended interpretation of L.

Here $(\alpha)_{x,y}^{\bar{m},\bar{n}}$ is the formula obtained from α by replacing x with $\bar{m}$ and y with $\bar{n}$.

As we saw in Sect. 6.5, every numerical property or relation is definable in terms of its characteristic function. Thus, a language can express a numerical property or relation if and only if it can express its characteristic function. This means that Definitions 17.3 and 17.4 can be rephrased in terms of the following definition:

Definition 17.5 A formula α with two free variables x and y *expresses* a function F in a language L iff, for any m, n, if $F(n) = m$, then $(\alpha)_{x,y}^{\bar{m},\bar{n}}$ is true in the intended interpretation of L, and if $F(n) \neq m$, then $\sim(\alpha)_{x,y}^{\bar{m},\bar{n}}$ is true in the intended interpretation of L.

A remarkable fact about L_a, which will not be proved here, is that L_a can express every recursive function, namely, for every recursive function F, there is a formula of L_a that expresses F. Since recursively decidable numerical properties and relations are definable in terms of recursive functions, this means that L_a can express every recursively decidable numerical property or relation.[1]

17.5 Peano Arithmetic

Now we will consider a theory in L_a that is based on an axiomatization of arithmetic initially suggested by Richard Dedekind and then developed by Peano in *Arithmetices principia, nova methodo exposita* (1889).[2] This theory, called *Peano Arithmetic* or **PA**, is obtained by adding the following axioms to A1-A9:

PA1 $\forall x s x \neq 0$
PA2 $\forall x \forall y (s x = s y \supset x = y)$
PA3 $\forall x (x + 0 = x)$
PA4 $\forall x \forall y (x + s y = s(x + y))$
PA5 $\forall x (x \times 0 = 0)$
PA6 $\forall x \forall y (x \times s y = x + (x \times y))$
PA7 $((\alpha)_x^0 \wedge \forall x (\alpha \supset (\alpha)_x^{sx})) \supset \forall y (\alpha)_x^y$, for every α in which x is free.

It is easy to see that PA1–PA7 are true in the intended interpretation of L_a. PA1 says that there is no number of which 0 is successor. PA2 guarantees that distinct numbers have distinct successors. PA3 and PA4 define addition. PA5 and PA6 define multiplication. Finally, PA7 expresses the Induction Principle. **PA** is not the only axiomatization of arithmetic, for other axioms could be adopted instead of PA1–PA7, thereby obtaining different results. But at least it may be regarded as a paradigmatic axiomatization of arithmetic.

In order to get a rough idea of the deductive power of **PA**, we must take into account the following definitions, which may regarded as syntactic analogues of Definitions 17.3 and 17.4:

Definition 17.6 A formula α with a free variable x *represents* a numerical property P in a system S iff, for every n, if n has P, then $(\alpha)_x^{\bar{n}}$ is a theorem of S, and if n does not have P, then $\sim(\alpha)_x^{\bar{n}}$ is a theorem of S.

---

[1] The proof of this fact goes back to Gödel [20].
[2] Peano [47]. Julius Wilhelm Richard Dedekind (1831–1916) was a German mathematician who made important contributions to the foundations of the arithmetic of the real and the natural numbers.

Definition 17.7 A formula α with two free variables x and y *represents* a relation R in a system S iff, for any m, n, if R obtains between m and n, then $(\alpha)_{x,y}^{\overline{m},\overline{n}}$ is a theorem of S, and if R does not obtain between m and n, then $\sim(\alpha)_{x,y}^{\overline{m},\overline{n}}$ is a theorem of S.

For example, the first of the two formulas considered in Sect. 17.4 represents the property of being prime in a system S just in case, for every n, if n is prime, this formula is a theorem of S, and if n is not prime then its negation is a theorem of S. Similarly, the second formula represents the relation less-then-or-equal-to in a system S just in case, for every m, n, if $m \leq n$, this formula is a theorem of S, otherwise its negation is a theorem of S.

As in the case of Definitions 17.3 and 17.4, Definitions 17.6 and 17.7 can be rephrased as follows, given that numerical properties and relations can be defined in terms of their characteristic functions:

Definition 17.8 A formula α with two free variables x and y *represents* a function F in a system S iff, for any m, n, if $F(n) = m$, then $(\alpha)_{x,y}^{\overline{m},\overline{n}}$ is a theorem of S, and if $F(n) \neq m$, then $\sim(\alpha)_{x,y}^{\overline{m},\overline{n}}$ is a theorem of S.

Representing is not the same thing as expressing. Whether a property, a relation, or a function can be expressed in a system S depends on the richness of the language of S. Instead, whether a property, a relation, or a function can be represented in S depends on the deductive power of S.

A remarkable fact about **PA**, which is distinct from the fact about L_a stated in Sect. 17.4, is that **PA** can represent every recursive function: for every recursive function F, there is a formula that represents F in **PA**. Since recursive functions characterize recursively decidable properties and relations, this means that all recursively decidable numerical properties and relations are representable in **PA**. The adequacy of **PA** as a theory of arithmetic can be measured in terms of this capacity.[3]

In general, a theory of arithmetic is *recursively adequate* when it can represent all recursively decidable numerical properties and relations. The idea that guides this way of talking is that we ideally want our formal machinery to be able to track any mechanical calculation that we can perform informally. For example, we are able to determine whether a number has the property of being prime, or whether two numbers stand in the less-than-or-equal-to relation. So, any formal system that diminishes our ability to determine such properties or relations would miss something important.

---

[3] Again, the proof of this fact goes back to Gödel [20].

Exercises

17.1 Formalize in L_{qi} the following sentences:

(a) Only Alf can win this race
(b) Nobody is Napoleon
(c) Those who love themselves do not love other people

17.2 Explain why $\{Mx, \sim My\}$ has no model.

17.3 Explain why, if T is the theory formed by the theorems of $S + \Gamma$ and all the formulas in Γ are true in the intended model of T, then T is consistent.

17.4 Explain why the following formulas are provable in Q_i:

$$\forall x \forall y (x = y \supset y = x)$$
$$\forall x \forall y \forall z (x = y \supset (y = z \supset x = z))$$

17.5 Is L_a recursively decidable?

17.6 Is the set of axioms of **PA** recursively decidable?

17.7 Is the set of derivations of **PA** recursively decidable?

17.8 Is **PA** recursively axiomatized?

17.9 Is **PA** consistent?

17.10 Can the axioms of **PA** be true in a model with a finite domain?

Chapter 18
Theories and Models

18.1 Cardinality

This chapter presents some general results that hinge on the notion of *cardinality*. To explain what cardinality is, let us start with finite sets. If A is finite, the size of A is expressed by a natural number: for some n, A has exactly n elements. For example, $\{2, 1, 3\}$ has exactly 3 elements. If natural numbers are identified with sets, this thought can be phrased in a rigorous way. Assume that $0 = \emptyset$ and that for every $n > 0$, $n = \{0, \dots, n - 1\}$. The *cardinal number* of A is definable as the number n such that there is a one-to-one correspondence between A and n. Thus, the cardinal number of $\{2, 1, 3\}$ is 3 because there is a one-to-one correspondence between $\{2, 1, 3\}$ and $\{0, 1, 2\}$.

Now let us turn to infinite sets. If A is infinite, the size of A cannot be expressed by means of a natural number, for by definition there is no n such that A contains exactly n elements. But an important analogy remains: the size of A can be measured in terms of one-to-one correspondence with some set. The notion of *transfinite number* introduced by Georg Cantor is intended to capture this idea. The transfinite number of $\mathbb{N}$, called $\aleph_0$, is the cardinal number of every set that corresponds one-to-one to $\mathbb{N}$, that is, every denumerable set. Cantor has shown that $\aleph_0$ is the smallest transfinite number, and that, for every transfinite number $\aleph_n$, there is a greater transfinite number $\aleph_{n+1}$. An example of transfinite number greater than $\aleph_0$ is the "cardinal of the continuum", which expresses the cardinality of $\mathbb{R}$.[1]

---

[1] Georg Ferdinand Ludwig Philipp Cantor (1845–1918), a German mathematician, developed the theory of transfinite numbers, spelling out its fundamental concepts and proving its most important theorems. Although today set theory is widely accepted as a fundamental part of mathematics, this was not always the case, and Cantor had to argue for his view. Some theologians criticized the theory of transfinite numbers because they saw it as a challenge to the absolute infinity of God. Cantor contended that we can conceive God as the Absolute Infinite, a number which is bigger than

© The Author(s), under exclusive license to Springer Nature Switzerland AG 2021
A. Iacona, *LOGIC: Lecture Notes for Philosophy, Mathematics, and Computer Science*, Springer Undergraduate Texts in Philosophy,
https://doi.org/10.1007/978-3-030-64811-4_18

Cardinal numbers provide a scale of measurement for sets. The cardinality of A, indicated as $|A|$, is expressed by the cardinal number—natural or transfinite—associated with A. In what follows, we will assume that $|A| = |B|$ if and only if there is a one-to-one correspondence between A and B, that $|A| \leq |B|$ if and only if there is a one-to-one function that maps A into B, and that $|A| < |B|$ if and only if there is a one-to-one function that maps A into B but there is no one-to-one correspondence between A and B. For example, $\mathbb{N}$ and the set of even numbers have the same cardinality, in spite of the fact that $\mathbb{N}$ contains odd numbers in addition to even numbers. Instead, $\mathbb{R}$ is greater than $\mathbb{N}$, because its cardinality is greater than $\aleph_0$.

The notion of cardinality is employed to express properties of first-order theories that somehow depend on the size of the domain of their models. Since the domain of a model $\mathcal{M}$ is a set M, one can talk about the cardinality of $\mathcal{M}$ by referring to the cardinality of M. In other terms, the cardinality of $\mathcal{M}$ is $|M|$. Thus, $\mathcal{M}$ is called finite, denumerable, countable, and so on, depending on whether M is finite, denumerable, countable, and so on.

18.2 Löwenheim-Skolem Theorems

One result that deserves attention is the following theorem:

Theorem 18.1 *If a set of formulas Γ is satisfiable, then Γ is satisfiable in a countable model.*

Proof Assume that Γ is satisfiable. Then, by the soundness theorem (Theorem 15.11), Γ is consistent. From this follows that Γ is satisfiable in a countable model. If the language of Γ does not contain the symbol $=$, the proof of theorem 15.13 shows that a denumerable model satisfies a theory that includes Γ (see Exercise 15.5). If the language of Γ contains the symbol $=$, then a theory that includes Γ is satisfiable in a normal model that is either finite or denumerable, that is, a normal model whose domain is a set of equivalence classes of terms of the language of Γ (see proof of theorem 17.3). $\qquad\square$

Theorem 18.1 entails that if a first-order theory T is satisfiable, then T is satisfiable in a countable model. When the formulas in T are closed, this amounts to saying that if T has a model, then it has a countable model. Note that the proof rests on the assumption that the language of Γ is denumerable, namely, that it has denumerably many symbols. More generally, Theorem 18.1 holds for any countable language.

---

any conceivable or inconceivable quantity. In fact, he believed that God himself communicated to him the theory of transfinite numbers.

The same goes for the following corollary:

Theorem 18.2 *If a set of formulas Γ is satisfiable in a model of cardinality κ such that $\kappa > \aleph_0$, then Γ is satisfiable in a model of cardinality λ such that $\lambda \leq \aleph_0$.*

Proof Assume that Γ is satisfiable in a model of cardinality κ such that $\kappa > \aleph_0$. Since Γ is satisfiable, by Theorem 18.1 it is satisfiable in a model of cardinality λ such that $\lambda \leq \aleph_0$.   □

If we imagine transfinite cardinals as ordered along a ladder that starts from $\aleph_0$ and goes up as the cardinality increases, Theorem 18.2 says something about "downward" preservation of satisfaction: if a set of formulas is satisfied at any point of the ladder, then it is satisfied at its lowest point, namely, $\aleph_0$.

A complementary result, which yields the "upward" direction, is the following:

Theorem 18.3 *If a set of formulas Γ is satisfiable in an infinite model of cardinality λ, then for every κ such that $\lambda \leq \kappa$, Γ is satisfiable in a model of cardinality κ.*

Proof Let $\mathcal{M}$ be a model of cardinality λ in which Γ is satisfiable. Let $\mathcal{M}'$ be a model of cardinality κ such that $M' = M \cup \overline{M}$ and $\lambda \leq \kappa$. Let $\mathcal{M}'$ agree with $\mathcal{M}$ on the values of the individual constants. Finally, let it be granted that, for some arbitrarily chosen element c of M, every element of $\overline{M}$ behaves like c. That is, for every n-place predicate letter P and every n-tuple $\langle e_1, \ldots, e_n \rangle$ of elements of M', $\langle e_1, \ldots, e_n \rangle \in [P]_{\mathcal{M}'}$ iff $\langle e'_1, \ldots, e'_n \rangle \in [P]_{\mathcal{M}}$, where $e'_i = e_i$ if $e_i \in M$ and $e'_i = c$ if $e_i \in \overline{M}$. Given this stipulation, it can be shown by induction that, for any formula α, if α is satisfied by some assignment in $\mathcal{M}$, then α is satisfied by some assignment in $\mathcal{M}'$. The details of the reasoning depend on the language adopted, but it is easy to see that, for any assignment in $\mathcal{M}$ that satisfies α, if $e'_1, e'_2, e'_3 \ldots$ are the objects denoted by $x, y, z \ldots$, then there is an assignment in $\mathcal{M}'$ that satisfies α according to which $x, y, z \ldots$ denote $e_1, e_2, e_3 \ldots$. Therefore, Γ is satisfiable in $\mathcal{M}'$.   □

Theorem 18.3 entails that if a first-order theory T is satisfiable in an infinite model of cardinality λ, then for every κ such that $\lambda \leq \kappa$, T is satisfiable in a model of cardinality κ. When the formulas in T are closed, we get that, if T has an infinite model of cardinality λ, then for every κ such that $\lambda \leq \kappa$, T has a model of cardinality κ.

A direct corollary of theorem 18.3 is the following:

Theorem 18.4 *If a set of formulas Γ is satisfiable in a model of cardinality $\aleph_0$, then for every κ such that $\aleph_0 \leq \kappa$, Γ is satisfiable in a model of cardinality κ.*

Proof From Theorem 18.3, by taking $\lambda = \aleph_0$.   □

The four results just outlined are generally associated to the names of Leopold Löwenheim and Thoralf Skolem, who proved the first two. Often, the label 'Löwenheim-Skolem theorem' is used to refer specifically to Theorem 18.1, or to Theorem 18.2. At other times it is used to refer to the conjunction of theorems 18.2 and 18.4, or Theorems 18.1–18.4. In the latter case a distinction is drawn between 'downward Löwenheim-Skolem theorem' and 'upward Löwenheim-Skolem theorem'. But there is no widespread agreement on the terminology.[2]

Theorems 18.1–18.4 show that any first-order theory that admits infinite models has a limited descriptive capacity, in that it is unable to provide a complete description of its intended model. On the one hand, if the intended model has any cardinality κ, for $\kappa > \aleph_0$, the description provided by the theory is incomplete in the sense that its theorems can be made true by a model of cardinality less than κ. For example, a geometrical theory whose intended domain is the set of points in space, which has a cardinality greater than $\aleph_0$, can be made true by a set of cardinality $\aleph_0$. On the other, if the intended model has any cardinality κ, for $\kappa \geq \aleph_0$, the description provided by the theory is incomplete in the sense that its theorems are made true by a model of cardinality greater than κ. For example, an arithmetical theory whose intended domain is the set of natural numbers, which has cardinality $\aleph_0$, can be made true by a model of cardinality greater than $\aleph_0$.

Of course, not every first-order theory admits infinite models. A first-order theory may include formulas that impose a maximum finite cardinality to its models. But no minimally interesting first-order theory involves such restrictions. For example, **PA** admits only infinite models (see Exercise 17.10), and the same goes for other interesting first-order theories.

18.3 Isomorphism

The implications of the results considered in Sect. 18.2 may be elaborated in terms of some further notions that are widely employed to describe the semantic properties of first-order theories. The following definitions apply to any pair of models $\mathcal{M}$ and $\mathcal{M}'$:

Definition 18.1 A *homomorphism* of $\mathcal{M}$ into $\mathcal{M}'$ is a function h that maps M into M' such that

1 for each individual constant a, $h([a]_{\mathcal{M}}) = [a]_{\mathcal{M}'}$;
2 for each n-place predicate letter P and every n-tuple $\langle e_1, \ldots, e_n \rangle$ of elements of M, $\langle e_1, \ldots, e_n \rangle \in [P]_{\mathcal{M}}$ iff $\langle h(e_1), \ldots, h(e_n) \rangle \in [P]_{\mathcal{M}'}$;

Definition 18.2 An *isomorphism* of $\mathcal{M}$ into $\mathcal{M}'$ is a function h such that h is a homomorphism of $\mathcal{M}$ into $\mathcal{M}'$ and h is one-to-one.

Definition 18.3 $\mathcal{M}$ and $\mathcal{M}'$ are *isomorphic* iff there is an isomorphism of $\mathcal{M}$ onto $\mathcal{M}'$, that is, an isomorphism that maps M onto M'.

---

[2]Leopold Löwenheim (1878–1957), a German mathematician, proved a first result in Löwenheim [43]. Albert Thoralf Skolem (1887–1863), a Norwegian mathematician, provided a simplified version of Löwenheim's result in Skolem [59]. These results were first outlined in their full generality in Maltsev [46]. The upward result is attributed to Tarski. Surely it cannot be ascribed to Skolem, who did not believe in the existence of nondenumerable sets.

Note that Definition 18.1 does not contemplate function symbols. If the language contains such symbols, the following condition must be added: for each n-place function symbol f and each n-tuple $\langle e_1, \ldots, e_n \rangle$ of elements of M, $h[f]_{\mathcal{M}}(e_1, \ldots, e_n) = [f]_{\mathcal{M}'}(h(e_1), \ldots, h(e_n))$.

Some examples may help. Suppose that we have only three individual constants, a, b, c, and one one-place predicate letter P. Let $\mathcal{M}$ be as follows:

$M = \{$Colisseum, Mole Antonelliana, Holy Spirit$\}$
$[a]_{\mathcal{M}} = $ Colisseum
$[b]_{\mathcal{M}} = $ Mole Antonelliana
$[c]_{\mathcal{M}} = $ Holy Spirit
$[P]_{\mathcal{M}} = \{$Colisseum, Mole Antonelliana$\}$.

Let $\mathcal{M}'$ be as follows:

$M' = \{1, 2, 3, 4\}$
$[a]_{\mathcal{M}'} = 2$
$[b]_{\mathcal{M}'} = 2$
$[c]_{\mathcal{M}'} = 1$
$[P]_{\mathcal{M}'} = \{2, 4\}$.

Let h be a function that maps M into M' such that h(Colisseum) $= 2$, h(Mole Antonelliana) $= 2$, and h(Holy Spirit) $= 1$. h is a homomorphism of $\mathcal{M}$ into $\mathcal{M}'$, because $h([a]_{\mathcal{M}}) = [a]_{\mathcal{M}'}$, $h([b]_{\mathcal{M}}) = [b]_{\mathcal{M}'}$, $h([c]_{\mathcal{M}}) = [c]_{\mathcal{M}'}$, and for every element e of M, $e \in [P]_{\mathcal{M}}$ if and only if $h(e) \in [P]_{\mathcal{M}'}$.

Now suppose that $\mathcal{M}$ is as before, but that $\mathcal{M}'$ is as follows:

$M' = \{1, 2, 3, 4\}$
$[a]_{\mathcal{M}'} = 2$
$[b]_{\mathcal{M}'} = 4$
$[c]_{\mathcal{M}'} = 1$
$[P]_{\mathcal{M}'} = \{2, 4\}$.

Let h be such that h(Colisseum) $= 2$, h(Mole Antonelliana) $= 4$, and h(Holy Spirit) $= 1$. In this case h is a homomorphism of $\mathcal{M}$ into $\mathcal{M}'$ and is one-to-one, so it is an isomorphism of $\mathcal{M}$ into $\mathcal{M}'$.

Finally, suppose that $\mathcal{M}$ is as before, but that $\mathcal{M}'$ is as follows:

$M' = \{1, 2, 4\}$
$[a]_{\mathcal{M}'} = 2$
$[b]_{\mathcal{M}'} = 4$
$[c]_{\mathcal{M}'} = 1$
$[P]_{\mathcal{M}'} = \{2, 4\}$.

Again, let h be such that h(Colisseum) $= 2$, h(Mole Antonelliana) $= 4$, and h(Holy Spirit) $= 1$. In this case h is an isomorphism which maps M onto M', so $\mathcal{M}$ and $\mathcal{M}'$ are isomorphic.

As the last example illustrates, the intuition that underlies Definition 18.3 is that two models can have the same form, although they differ in their matter. In $\mathcal{M}$ the individual constants a, b, c name two monuments and one divine entity, while in $\mathcal{M}'$ they name three numbers. Similarly, in $\mathcal{M}$ the predicate letter P is read as 'material', while in $\mathcal{M}'$ is read as 'even'. But $\mathcal{M}$ and $\mathcal{M}'$ have something in common, namely, in both models the objects denoted by a and b belong to the extension of P, while the object denoted by c does not.

18.4   Isomorphic Models of a Theory

A basic theorem about isomorphic models is the following:

Theorem 18.5 *If h is an isomorphism of $\mathcal{M}$ onto $\mathcal{M}'$, σ is an assignment in $\mathcal{M}$, and σ' is an assignment in $\mathcal{M}'$ such that for every variable x, $[x]_{\mathcal{M}',\sigma'} = h([x]_{\mathcal{M},\sigma})$, then, for any formula α, σ satisfies α in $\mathcal{M}$ iff σ' satisfies α in $\mathcal{M}'$.*

Proof We reason by induction on the complexity of α, assuming that σ and σ' satisfy the condition required.

Basis. Let α be an atomic formula $Pt_1 \ldots t_n$. In this case, $[t_i]_{\mathcal{M}',\sigma'} = h([t_i]_{\mathcal{M},\sigma})$ for any $1 \leq i \leq n$. If $e_1, \ldots, e_n$ are the elements of M denoted by $t_1, \ldots, t_n$ in σ, and $h(e_1), \ldots, h(e_n)$ are the elements of M' denoted by $t_1, \ldots, t_n$ in σ', by Definition 18.1 $\langle e_1, \ldots, e_n \rangle \in [P]_{\mathcal{M}}$ iff $\langle h(e_1), \ldots, h(e_n) \rangle \in [P]_{\mathcal{M}'}$. Therefore, σ satisfies $Pt_1 \ldots t_n$ in $\mathcal{M}$ iff σ' satisfies $Pt_1 \ldots t_n$ in $\mathcal{M}'$.

Step. Assume that every formula of complexity less than or equal to n is satisfied by σ in $\mathcal{M}$ iff it is satisfied by σ' in $\mathcal{M}'$, and that α has complexity $n + 1$. Three cases are possible.

Case 1: α has the form $\sim\beta$. In this case, σ satisfies $\sim\beta$ in $\mathcal{M}$ iff it does not satisfy β in $\mathcal{M}$. By the induction hypothesis, σ does not satisfy β in $\mathcal{M}$ iff σ' does not satisfy β in $\mathcal{M}'$. So it suffices to add that σ' does not satisfy β in $\mathcal{M}'$ iff it satisfies $\sim\beta$ in $\mathcal{M}'$.

Case 2: α has the form $\beta \supset \gamma$. In this case, σ satisfies $\beta \supset \gamma$ in $\mathcal{M}$ iff either it does not satisfy β in $\mathcal{M}$ or it satisfies γ in $\mathcal{M}$. By the induction hypothesis σ does not satisfy β in $\mathcal{M}$ iff σ' does not satisfy β in $\mathcal{M}'$, and σ satisfies γ in $\mathcal{M}$ iff σ' satisfies γ in $\mathcal{M}'$. So it suffices to add that σ' satisfies $\beta \supset \gamma$ in $\mathcal{M}'$ iff either it does not satisfy β in $\mathcal{M}'$ or it satisfies γ in $\mathcal{M}'$.

Case 3: α has the form $\forall x\beta$. Suppose that σ does not satisfy $\forall x\beta$ in $\mathcal{M}$. Then there is an x-variant σ_* of σ that does not satisfy β. Let σ'_* be an assignment in $\mathcal{M}'$ according to which each variable denotes the value that h assigns to the object denoted by the same variable in $\sigma*$. By the induction hypothesis σ'_* does not satisfy β in $\mathcal{M}'$. Since σ'_* is an x-variant of σ', being exactly like σ' as far as the values of the variables other than x are concerned, it follows that σ' does not satisfy $\forall x\beta$ in $\mathcal{M}'$. A similar reasoning shows that if σ' does not satisfy $\forall x\beta$ in $\mathcal{M}'$, then σ does not satisfy $\forall x\beta$ in $\mathcal{M}$. $\square$

From Theorem 18.5 we obtain the following theorems:

Theorem 18.6 *For any formula α, if $\mathcal{M}$ and $\mathcal{M}'$ are isomorphic, then $[\alpha]_{\mathcal{M}} = 1$ iff $[\alpha]_{\mathcal{M}'} = 1$.*

Proof Let h be an isomorphism of $\mathcal{M}$ onto $\mathcal{M}'$. Suppose that it is not the case that $[\alpha]_{\mathcal{M}} = 1$, namely, that in $\mathcal{M}$ there is at least one assignment σ that does not satisfy α. Then in $\mathcal{M}'$ there is at least one assignment σ' that does not satisfy α: if σ' is such that $[x]_{\mathcal{M}',\sigma'} = h([x]_{\mathcal{M},\sigma})$ for every x, by Theorem 18.5 σ' does not satisfy α. So, if $[\alpha]_{\mathcal{M}'} = 1$, then $[\alpha]_{\mathcal{M}} = 1$. The converse conditional is obtained in similar way.   □

Theorem 18.7 *For any first-order theory T, if $\mathcal{M}$ and $\mathcal{M}'$ are isomorphic, then $\mathcal{M}$ is a model of T iff $\mathcal{M}'$ is a model of T.*

Proof Assume that $\mathcal{M}$ and $\mathcal{M}'$ are isomorphic. For every α in T, Theorem 18.6 entails that α is true in $\mathcal{M}$ iff is true in $\mathcal{M}'$.   □

A remarkable fact that emerges from Theorem 18.7 is that, given any model $\mathcal{M}$ of a theory T, it can always be shown that there is another model of T. It suffices to take a set M' such that $|M'| = |M|$ and define $\mathcal{M}'$ in such a way that there is an isomorphism of $\mathcal{M}$ onto $\mathcal{M}'$. By Theorem 18.7 it then follows that $\mathcal{M}'$ is a model of T. This fact, just as the results considered in Sect. 18.2, suggests that a first-order theory has a limited descriptive capacity, and may foster general reflections on the indeterminacy of language.

Willard V. O. Quine appealed to the plurality of models of first-order theories to argue for what he called "inscrutability of reference". According to Quine, it is wrong to think that an expression of natural language, like 'cat', determinately refers to objects of a certain kind, cats. For even though there are true sentences in which the expression occurs, such as 'Cats have four legs', the truth of these sentences does not univocally fix its reference. The plurality of the models of first-order theories seems to give substance to this thesis, in that it suggests that any description leaves indeterminate what exactly it is about: no matter how rich and detailed it may be, there will always be distinct interpretations that make it true.[3]

18.5 Categoricity

A last notion that is employed to describe the semantic properties of first-order theories is the notion of *categoricity*, which may be defined in at least two ways.

---

[3] Willard Van Orman Quine (1908–2000), an American philosopher, is widely considered one of the dominant figures in analytic philosophy in the second half of the twentieth century. He produced original and important works in several areas, including logic, ontology, epistemology, and the philosophy of language. He presents his arguments about the inscrutability of reference in Quine [54], among other works.

The first definition provides an absolute criterion of categoricity, as it involves unrestricted quantification over models:

Definition 18.4 A first-order theory is *categorical* iff all its models are isomorphic.

The condition imposed by Definition 18.4 is rather strong. As we saw in Sect. 18.2, any minimally interesting first-order theory admits infinite models. But any first-order theory that admits infinite models has models of different cardinality. On the one hand, if it has models of cardinality greater than $\aleph_0$, by Theorem 18.2 it also has models of cardinality $\aleph_0$. On the other, if it has models of cardinality $\aleph_0$, by Theorem 18.3 it also has models of cardinality greater than $\aleph_0$. Since two models cannot be isomorphic if they differ in cardinality, any minimally interesting first-order theory is non-categorical according to Definition 18.4.

The second definition imposes a weaker condition, as it provides a relative criterion of categoricity:

Definition 18.5 A first-order theory is κ-*categorical* iff all its models of cardinality κ are isomorphic.

In this case the quantification is restricted to models of cardinality κ. The difference between Definitions 18.4 and 18.5 turns out clear if one thinks that a theory can be categorical relative to a given cardinality even if it admits models of different cardinality.

The two definitions just outlined can be used to illustrate a significant fact about **PA**. We have seen that the intended model of **PA** is a normal model whose domain is $\mathbb{N}$ and where the individual constant 0 denotes the number 0 and the symbols $s, +, \times$ denote respectively the functions successor, addition, and multiplication. A *standard model* of **PA** is a model that is isomorphic to its intended model, that is, a model that verifies PA1-PA7 in a denumerable domain formed by elements each of which is obtained from a first element by applying a finite number of times the successor operation. The fact, however, is that some models of **PA** are *non-standard*, in that they are not isomorphic to its intended model.

There are at least two ways to show that **PA** has non-standard models. One is to show that **PA** has models of cardinality greater than $\aleph_0$:

Theorem 18.8 **PA** *has non-denumerable non-standard models.*

Proof **PA** has a model of cardinality $\aleph_0$, namely, its intended model. By Theorem 18.3, this entails that **PA** has models of cardinality greater than $\aleph_0$. Since such models are not isomorphic to the intended model, they are non-denumerable non-standard models. □

Theorem 18.8 entails that **PA** is non-categorical in the first sense. This, however, does not rule out that **PA** is κ-categorical for some κ. To prove non-categoricity in the second sense it must be shown that **PA** is not categorical relative to a given cardinality. In particular, since the intended model of **PA** has cardinality $\aleph_0$, it must shown that **PA** is not $\aleph_0$-categorical. The following theorem states precisely this fact.

Theorem 18.9 **PA** *has denumerable non-standard models.*

Proof Let $\mathcal{M}$ be the intended model of **PA**. Let an individual constant a be added to the language of **PA**. Let **PA**$'$ be a theory obtained by adding to **PA** an infinite list of formulas $a \neq 0$, $a \neq 1$, $a \neq 2,\ldots$, one for each numeral. Now consider any finite subset Γ of **PA**$'$. Γ includes at most a finite number of new formulas. So, an interpretation that assigns to a a number that is not denoted by any of the numerals that occur in the new formulas in Γ but for the rest is exactly like $\mathcal{M}$ is a model of Γ. For example, if Γ includes $\{a \neq 0, a \neq 1, a \neq 2\}$, an interpretation that assigns 3 to a is a model of Γ. Since any finite subset of **PA**$'$ has a model, by the compactness theorem (Theorem 15.15) **PA**$'$ has a model. So by the Löwenheim-Skolem theorem (Theorem 18.1) it has a countable model. If we add to this that **PA**$'$ does not admit finite models (see Exercise 17.10), we get that **PA**$'$ has a denumerable model. More precisely, **PA**$'$ has a denumerable normal model. Let $\mathcal{M}'$ be such model. Since **PA**$'$ is an extension of **PA**, $\mathcal{M}'$ is a model of **PA**. However, $\mathcal{M}$ and $\mathcal{M}'$ are not isomorphic. For suppose they are. Then there is an isomorphism h of $\mathcal{M}$ onto $\mathcal{M}'$. Let $e_0, e_1, e_2 \ldots$ be the elements of M' that h assigns to $0, 1, 2 \ldots$, the elements of M. h must be such that every numeral denotes in $\mathcal{M}'$ the object that h assigns to its denotation in $\mathcal{M}$. But then no denotation can consistently be assigned to a in $\mathcal{M}'$. On the one hand, a cannot denote some e_i, because the additional formulas of **PA**$'$, which are true in $\mathcal{M}'$, rule out that a denotes the same object denoted by a numeral. On the other, a cannot denote a different object, because h is a one-to-one function that maps M onto M', so in M' there is no object other than $e_0, e_1, e_2 \ldots$.   □

A final note. Although the last two theorems concern **PA**, their proofs do not depend on specific features of **PA**. This means that similar theorems are provable for other arithmetical theories. The implications of the compactness theorem (Theorem 15.15) and the Löwenheim-Skolem theorem (Theorem 18.1) with respect to non-standard models hold for arithmetic in general.

Exercises

18.1 Is it true that if $A \subseteq B$ and $A \neq B$, then $|A| < |B|$?

18.2 Explain why if $|A| < |B|$ for every finite A, then B is infinite.

18.3 Are there first-order theories that admit models of cardinality 0?

18.4 Are there first-order theories that admit models of cardinality 1?

18.5 Are there first-order theories that do not admit models of cardinality 1?

18.6 Let T be an extension of $\mathbf{Q_i}$ which includes the formula $\forall x \forall y x = y$. Explain why T does not admit infinite models.

18.7 Suppose, as in Sect. 18.3, that we have only three individual constants a, b, c, and one one-place predicate letter P. Let $\mathcal{M}$ and $\mathcal{M}'$ be as follows:

$M = \{$Colisseum, Mole Antonelliana, Holy Spirit$\}$
$[a]_{\mathcal{M}} =$ Colisseum
$[b]_{\mathcal{M}} =$ Mole Antonelliana
$[c]_{\mathcal{M}} =$ Holy Spirit
$[P]_{\mathcal{M}} = \{$Colisseum, Mole Antonelliana$\}$.

$M' = \{$Paris, Rome, Turin$\}$
$[a]_{\mathcal{M}'} =$ Rome
$[b]_{\mathcal{M}'} =$ Turin
$[c]_{\mathcal{M}'} =$ Paris
$[P]_{\mathcal{M}'} = \{$Rome, Turin$\}$

Are $\mathcal{M}$ and $\mathcal{M}'$ isomorphic?

18.8 Let T be a maximally consistent extension of $\mathbf{Q_i}$ which includes the formula $\forall x \forall y x = y$. Explain why any two models of T are isomorphic.

18.9 Explain why the theory considered in Exercise 18.8 is categorical the sense of Definition 18.4.

18.10 Explain why the theory considered in Exercise 18.8 is 1-categorical in the sense of Definition 18.5.

Chapter 19
Gödel's Incompleteness Theorems

19.1 Overview

In his famous article *On formally undecidable propositions of Principia Mathematica and related systems I* (1931), Gödel established two results that marked a point of no return in the history of logic. These results, known as *first incompleteness theorem* and *second incompleteness theorem*, deserve attention both for the ingenious reasoning that justifies them and for the significance of their implications.[1]

Let us start with some clarifications about the title of Gödel's article. First, 'formally undecidable propositions' is to be read as 'formulas which are not provable and whose negation is not provable'. So, formal undecidability is definable in terms of negation-completeness: to say that some formulas are formally undecidable in a system S is to say that S is negation-incomplete, that is, it is not the case that, for every α, either $\vdash \alpha$ or $\vdash \sim\alpha$ in S. This is why Gödel's theorems are called "incompleteness" theorems.

Second, *Principia Mathematica* (mentioned in Sect. 3.4) is the treatise by means of which Russell and Whitehead wanted to show that the truths of arithmetic can be deduced by a restricted set of logical axioms and definitions. Gödel's article is about *Principia Mathematica* "and related systems" because the results it establishes apply to a wide class of systems that includes the one defined in *Principia Mathematica*. More precisely, they apply to any recursively axiomatized and recursively adequate system in the language of basic arithmetic. Since **PA** satisfies these conditions, and is simpler than the system defined in *Principia Mathematica*, we will use **PA** to illustrate Gödel's results.

Finally, the 'I' in the title indicates that Gödel's article was intended to be the first part of a longer work. Part II was expected to provide the proof of the second

---

[1]Gödel [20].

A. Iacona, *LOGIC: Lecture Notes for Philosophy, Mathematics, and Computer Science*, Springer Undergraduate Texts in Philosophy,
https://doi.org/10.1007/978-3-030-64811-4_19

incompleteness theorem, which is only very briefly indicated in part I. But part II was never written, although it is quite clear how the second theorem can be obtained. Here we will focus on the first theorem, which says that a system of the kind described cannot be negation-complete.

Why is negation-completeness so important? Suppose that our project is to pin down the truths of basic arithmetic by means of a system S. It is plausible to assume that any question that can be framed in the language of S—for example, whether 3 is prime, or whether 3 is greater than 2—has a definite answer, which is grounded in the intended model of S. This is to say that any assertion that can be made in the language of S is either true or false. So we may expect that it is possible to lay down a set of axioms that settle every truth of basic arithmetic, in the sense that every such truth is derivable from them. We would ideally like to lay down the axioms of S in such a way that a formula α is provable in S if α is true in the intended model of S, and similarly that $\sim\alpha$ is provable in S if α is false in the intended model of S.

This project, which goes back to Frege, was regarded as a promising line of investigation at the time of Gödel's article. It was pursued by Russell and Whitehead as part of their "logicist" program, but also by other prominent logicians and mathematicians who had different ideas, most notably by Hilbert. The first incompleteness theorem sabotages the whole project, for it shows that there cannot be a system of the kind desired: any recursively axiomatized and recursively adequate system in the language of basic arithmetic will be negation-incomplete.

In what follows, we will consider two versions of the first incompleteness theorem: one is semantic, the other is syntactic. The two versions are basically equivalent, although Gödel privileged the second in his article. At that time, for various reasons, logicians regarded the idea of truth with some suspicion. So it was very important for Gödel to show that his theorem could be obtained without invoking semantic notions.[2]

19.2   The Arithmetization of Syntax

The proof of the first incompeteness theorem crucially depends on the arithmetization of syntax. Let us start with a Gödel numbering of L_a based on the following code:

$\sim$	$\supset$	$\forall$	$=$	(	)	0	s	$+$	$\times$	x	y	z	$\ldots$
1	3	5	7	9	11	13	15	17	19	21	23	25	$\ldots$

---

[2]The next sections are based on Smith [60], which provides a thorough presentation of Gödel's theorems.

The numbering scheme is like that considered in Sect. 16.2. If the expression e is a sequence of n symbols, and $c_1, \ldots, c_n$ are the basic code numbers of these symbols, the Gödel number of e is calculated by using the basic code number c_i of each symbol as an exponent for the i-th prime number π_i, for $1 \leq i \leq n$, and then multiplying the results, that is, $2^{c_1} \times 3^{c_2} \times 5^{c_3} \times \cdots \times \pi_n^{c_n}$. Sequences of formulas are coded accordingly. Given a sequence of formulas $\alpha_1, \ldots, \alpha_n$, we first code each α_i by a regular Gödel number g_i to yield a sequence of numbers $g_1, \ldots, g_n$. We then encode this sequence of regular Gödel numbers using a single super Gödel number by multiplying powers of primes to get $2^{g_1} \times 3^{g_2} \times 5^{g_3} \times \cdots \times \pi_n^{g_n}$.

For any expression e of $\mathsf{L_a}$, the notation $\ulcorner e \urcorner$ will be used to denote the Gödel number of e. For example, $ss0$ is a term of $\mathsf{L_a}$. Given our coding scheme, the Gödel number of $ss0$ is $2^{15} \times 3^{15} \times 5^{13}$. Therefore, $\ulcorner ss0 \urcorner$ denotes the number $2^{15} \times 3^{15} \times 5^{13}$. In a way, $\ulcorner e \urcorner$ can be thought of as referring to e via our coding scheme. Similarly, the expression $\ulcorner U \urcorner$, where U abbreviates a formula of $\mathsf{L_a}$, will indicate the Gödel number for the unabbreviated original formula that we call U.

The corner quotes, beside enabling us to refer to the Gödel numbers of the expressions of $\mathsf{L_a}$, enable us to talk about the terms of L that refer to such numbers. Another convention we will adopt is the following: $\overline{\ulcorner e \urcorner}$ stands for $\mathsf{L_a}$'s numeral for the Gödel number of e. For example, $\overline{\ulcorner ss0 \urcorner}$ stands for the numeral of $\mathsf{L_a}$ that denotes the number $2^{15} \times 3^{15} \times 5^{13}$, which is a long term $sss\ldots.s0$. In other words, simple corner quotes are used in the metalanguage to talk about numbers, while overlined corner quotes are abbreviations of expressions of the object language.

The Gödel numbering considered enables us to define numerical properties that correspond to the basic syntactic categories of $\mathsf{L_a}$: we can stipulate that n has the property T if and only if n is the Gödel number of a term, that n has the property F if and only if n is the Gödel number of a formula, that n has the property C if and only if n is the Gödel number of a closed formula, and so on. T, F, C, and similar properties can be checked in a purely mechanical way. For example, to check whether n has the property T it suffices to decode n, which is a mechanical procedure that requires a finite number of steps, and ask whether the resulting expression is a term, which is also a mechanical procedure that requires a finite number of steps. Although these are nothing but informal remarks, it is provable that T, F, C, and similar properties are recursively decidable, namely, that they can be associated with recursive functions in the way explained in Sect. 13.6.

Once these numerical properties are defined, a numerical relation Prf can be defined as follows:

Definition 19.1 Prf obtains between m and n iff m is the Gödel number of a proof in **PA** of the formula with Gödel number n.

To determine whether Prf obtains between m and n it suffices to proceed as follows. First decode m. Second, ask whether the result is a sequence of formulas. Third, if it is a sequence of formulas, ask whether each formula in the sequence is an axiom or a consequence of previous formulas. Finally, if the latter condition is satisfied, ask whether the last formula of the sequence has Gödel number n. Again, these are just informal remarks, but it is provable that Prf is recursively decidable.

19.3 The Gödel Sentence

The next step is to define a numerical relation that is slightly more complex than *Prf*. This increase of complexity is due to an operation called *diagonalization*:

Definition 19.2 The *diagonalization of a formula* α with one free variable is the formula $(\alpha)^{\ulcorner \alpha \urcorner}$ obtained from α by substituting the free variable with the numeral for the Gödel number of α.

The same thing could be said in a somewhat clumsier way by using our standard notation for substitution: if α is a formula with one free variable x, the diagonalization of α is $(\alpha)_x^{\ulcorner \alpha \urcorner}$. Here, however, we will omit the variable to keep it as simple as possible.

Why is this operation called diagonalization? Imagine an enumeration of the formulas of $\mathsf{L_a}$ with one free variable, $\alpha_{n_0}, \alpha_{n_1}, \alpha_{n_2} \ldots$, where each formula in the enumeration is indexed by its own Gödel number. Suppose that we produce a square array as follows:

$$(\alpha_{n_0})^{\overline{n_0}} \quad (\alpha_{n_0})^{\overline{n_1}} \quad (\alpha_{n_0})^{\overline{n_2}} \quad \ldots$$
$$(\alpha_{n_1})^{\overline{n_0}} \quad (\alpha_{n_1})^{\overline{n_1}} \quad (\alpha_{n_1})^{\overline{n_2}} \quad \ldots$$
$$(\alpha_{n_2})^{\overline{n_0}} \quad (\alpha_{n_2})^{\overline{n_1}} \quad (\alpha_{n_2})^{\overline{n_2}} \quad \ldots$$

In this array, the formulas of the form $(\alpha_{n_n})^{\overline{n_n}}$ lie down the diagonal. Since n_n is the Gödel number of α_{n_n}, we have that $(\alpha_{n_n})^{\overline{n_n}} = (\alpha_{n_n})^{\ulcorner \alpha_{n_n} \urcorner}$. This is the sense in which $(\alpha)^{\ulcorner \alpha \urcorner}$ is the diagonalization of α.

Given Definition 19.2, a numerical relation *Gdl* can be defined as follows:

Definition 19.3 *Gdl* obtains between m and n iff m is the Gödel number of a proof in **PA** of the diagonalization of the formula with Gödel number n.

Gdl differs from *Prf* only in that it involves diagonalization. Since *Prf* is recursively decidable, and diagonalization is a purely mechanical operation on the formulas of $\mathsf{L_a}$, *Gdl* is recursively decidable as well. Therefore, there is a formula α_{Gdl} with two free variables x and y that expresses *Gdl* in $\mathsf{L_a}$. That is, if m and n stand in the relation *Gdl*, then $(\alpha_{Gdl})_{x,y}^{\overline{m},\overline{n}}$ is true, while if m and n do not stand in the relation *Gdl*, then $\sim(\alpha_{Gdl})_{x,y}^{\overline{m},\overline{n}}$ is true. Similarly, there is a formula α_{Gdl} with two free variables x and y that represents *Gdl* in **PA**. That is, if m and n stand in the relation *Gdl*, then $\mathbf{PA} \vdash (\alpha_{Gdl})_{x,y}^{\overline{m},\overline{n}}$, while if m and n do not stand in the relation *Gdl*, then $\mathbf{PA} \vdash \sim(\alpha_{Gdl})_{x,y}^{\overline{m},\overline{n}}$.

Let U be the formula defined as follows:

Definition 19.4 $U = \forall x \sim \alpha_{Gdl}$

Unlike α_{Gdl}, U has only one free variable, namely, y. Informally speaking, U says that no number is the Gödel number of a proof in **PA** of the diagonalization of the formula with Gödel number y, which means that the diagonalization of the formula with Gödel number y is unprovable in **PA**.

Now let the diagonalization of U be defined follows:

Definition 19.5 $G = (U)^{\overline{\ulcorner U \urcorner}} = (\forall x {\sim} \alpha_{Gdl})^{\overline{\ulcorner U \urcorner}}$

The formula G is a *Gödel sentence*, that is, it is a closed formula that enjoys the remarkable property of being true if and only if it is unprovable in **PA**. To see why, consider what it takes for G to be true. G is true if and only if no number is the Gödel number of a proof in **PA** of the diagonalization of the formula with Gödel number $\ulcorner U \urcorner$. Since the formula with Gödel number $\ulcorner U \urcorner$ is U, and its diagonalization is G, the truth of G requires that no number is the Gödel number of a proof in **PA** of G itself, which means that G is unprovable in **PA**.

There is a straightforward sense in which G states its own unprovability. Of course, when unpacked, G is just a formula which contains quantifiers, connectives, the identity symbol, and so on. Its intended interpretation is the intended model of **PA**. So G talks about numbers, not about proofs or formulas. However, G can be described as indirectly stating its own unprovability, for given our coding scheme, we can recognize that G is true when no number is the Gödel number of a proof of G. In other words, given that scheme, we can see that G is constructed in such a way as to make it true just when it is unprovable.

19.4   First Incompleteness Theorem: Semantic Version

Now we are ready for the proof of the first incompleteness theorem. Let us start with the semantic version, phrased in terms of **PA**:

Theorem 19.1   *If* **PA** *is sound, then there is a true formula G such that* **PA** $\nvdash$ *G and* **PA** $\nvdash {\sim}G$.

Proof   Assume that **PA** is sound. Then **PA** $\nvdash G$, for if G were provable, then, by the soundness of **PA**, G would be true, and we know that G is true iff it is unprovable. So G is true precisely because it is unprovable, and consequently ${\sim}G$ is false. By the soundness of **PA** it follows that **PA** $\nvdash {\sim}G$.   □

This proof can easily be generalized. If T is a recursively axiomatized theory in the language of basic arithmetic—L_a or a suitable variant—then we can define a Gödel sentence in T. Therefore, we can prove what follows:

Theorem 19.2   *If T is sound, then there is a true formula G in the language of T such that* $T \nvdash G$ *and* $T \nvdash {\sim}G$.

Proof   Like the proof of theorem 19.1, by replacing **PA** with T.   □

Three remarks will help to gain a better understanding of Theorem 19.2. First, if any sound recursively axiomatized theory of arithmetic is negation-incomplete, then there is no recursively axiomatized theory of arithmetic whose theorems are all and only the truths expressible in the language of basic arithmetics. This shows that it is impossible to pin down the truths of basic arithmetic by means of a deductive apparatus of the kind considered. In other words, arithmetical truth is not reducible to provability in some single axiom system.

Second, Theorem 19.2 shows not only that any sound recursively axiomatized theory of arithmetic is negation-incomplete, but also that any such theory is incompletable, so to say. Let it be granted that T is negation-incomplete because $T \nvdash G$ and $T \nvdash \sim G$ for some G. This gap cannot be repaired by simply adding G as a new axiom. Consider the augmented theory $T' = T \cup \{G\}$. T' is exactly like T as far as the features required by Theorem 19.2 are concerned. So the theorem entails that there is a true formula G' such that $T' \nvdash G'$ and $T' \nvdash \sim G'$. And since T' is an extension of T, we have that $T \nvdash G'$ and $T \nvdash \sim G'$. In other words, repairing the gap in T by adding G as a new axiom leaves some other formulas that are undecidable in T still undecidable in the augmented theory. Thus, no matter how many new axioms you add to T, you will end up with a negation-incomplete theory.

The third remark, which is related to the second, is that Theorem 19.2 does *not* show that there are truths of basic arithmetic which are not provable in any sound recursively axiomatized theory. If G is such that $T \nvdash G$ and $T \nvdash \sim G$, this does not rule out that G or $\sim G$ is provable in some other sound recursively axiomatized theory. As we have just seen, $T \cup \{G\}$ is a sound recursively axiomatized theory in which G is trivially provable, even though there will be a different sentence G' which is not provable in $T \cup \{G\}$. From the fact that any theory includes some formally undecidable sentences it does not follow that some sentences are formally undecidable in any theory.

19.5   First Incompleteness Theorem: Syntactic Version

The syntactic version of the first incompleteness theorem requires a further definition:

Definition 19.6 A theory T is *ω-consistent* iff there is no formula α with a free variable x such that $T \vdash (\alpha)_x^{\overline{n}}$ for every n but $T \vdash \sim \forall x \alpha$.

T is *ω-inconsistent* when it is not ω-consistent, that is, when there is a formula α with a free variable x such that $T \vdash (\alpha)_x^{\overline{n}}$ for every n but $T \vdash \sim \forall x \alpha$. ω-inconsistency resembles plain inconsistency in two respects: it is a purely syntactic property, and is definitely undesirable. Suppose that we have a theory T in which $(\alpha)_x^{\overline{n}}$ is provable for every n. Then it would be ideal if $\forall x \alpha$ were also provable in T. After all, the intended model of a theory of arithmetic is an interpretation in which if $(\alpha)_x^{\overline{n}}$ is true for every n, then $\forall x \alpha$ is true as well. To say that T is ω-inconsistent, instead, is to say that we can prove the negation of what we would like to prove. This is a very bad thing, which evidently prevents T from being acceptable. Therefore, ω-consistency is a minimal requirement for any respectable theory of arithmetic.

Note that ω-consistency is directly related to the idea that the axioms of our theory are true in its intended model. Consider **PA**. The axioms of **PA** are true in its intended model, so the same goes for its theorems. Now suppose that **PA** $\vdash (\alpha)_x^{\overline{n}}$ for every n. Then, for every n, $(\alpha)_x^{\overline{n}}$ is true in the intended model of **PA**, that is, every natural number satisfies α. So $\forall x \alpha$ is true in the indended model of **PA**, which means that $\sim\forall x \alpha$ is false in that model. It follows that **PA** $\nvdash \sim\forall x \alpha$, hence that **PA** is ω-consistent. More generally, if a theory of arithmetic T is ω-inconsistent, then the axioms that generate T cannot be all true in the intended model of T. Given that we do not want such a thing, our theory must be ω-consistent.

Note also that ω-consistency entails plain consistency. The reason is that T's being ω-consistent is a matter of its not containing a certain combination of formulas, which entails that T does not contain every formula. An inconsistent theory, instead, is a theory that contains every formula (see Exercises 10.1 and 10.2).

Now we are ready for the syntactic version of the first incompleteness theorem. As in the case of the semantic version, we will prove the theorem for **PA**, then generalize the result.

Theorem 19.3 *If* **PA** *is ω-consistent, then there is a formula G such that* **PA** $\nvdash G$, *and* **PA** $\nvdash \sim G$.

Proof First it will be shown that, if **PA** is ω-consistent, then **PA** $\nvdash G$. Assume that **PA** is ω-consistent. Then it is consistent. Now suppose that there is a proof of G in **PA**, hence a Gödel number m that codes it. Since G is the diagonalization of U, the relation Gdl obtains between m and $\ulcorner U \urcorner$. This entails that there is a formula α_{Gdl} with two free variables x and y such that **PA** $\vdash (\alpha_{Gdl})_{x,y}^{\overline{m},\overline{\ulcorner U \urcorner}}$. But $G = (\forall x \sim \alpha_{Gdl})^{\overline{\ulcorner U \urcorner}}$, so if G is a theorem, the same goes for its instances. In particular, **PA** $\vdash \sim(\alpha_{Gdl})_{x,y}^{\overline{m},\overline{\ulcorner U \urcorner}}$, which makes **PA** inconsistent, contrary to the initial hypothesis. Therefore, **PA** $\nvdash G$.

Now it will be shown that, if **PA** is ω-consistent, then **PA** $\nvdash \sim G$. Assume that **PA** is ω-consistent. Then, given what has been proved, **PA** $\nvdash G$. It follows that no m is the Gödel number of a proof of G. Since G is the diagonalization of U, for each m, the relation Gdl does not obtain between m and $\ulcorner U \urcorner$. So, for each m, **PA** $\vdash \sim(\alpha_{Gdl})_{x,y}^{\overline{m},\overline{\ulcorner U \urcorner}}$. Now suppose that **PA** $\vdash \sim G$. This means that **PA** $\vdash \sim(\forall x \sim \alpha_{Gdl})^{\overline{\ulcorner U \urcorner}}$, so it entail that **PA** is ω-inconsistent, contrary to the initial assumption. Therefore, **PA** $\nvdash \sim G$.   □

Since **PA** is ω-consistent, as noted above, Theorem 19.3 shows that **PA** is negation-incomplete.

The proof of theorem 19.3 can be generalized. If T is a recursively axiomatized and recursively adequate theory in the language of basic arithmetic, then a Gödel sentence can be defined in T. Therefore, we can prove what follows:

Theorem 19.4 *If T is ω-consistent, then there is a formula G such that* $T \nvdash G$ *and* $T \nvdash \sim G$.

Proof Like the proof of theorem 19.3, by replacing **PA** with T.   □

Theorem 19.4 is the result that people usually have in mind when they talk about the first incompleteness theorem—or simply "Gödel's theorem"—without qualifications. Note that now the distinction between the semantic version and the syntactic version is clear: while in Theorem 19.2 the antecedent of the conditional requires the soundness of T, in Theorem 19.4 the antecedent of the conditional requires the ω-consistency of T.

19.6   Second Incompleteness Theorem

The second incompleteness theorem is closely related to the first. Roughly speaking, this theorem says that if a recursively axiomatized and recursively adequate theory that contains enough arithmetic is consistent, then it cannot prove its own consistency.

As it emerges from Sect. 19.2, a recursively axiomatized and recursively adequate theory T whose language includes the language of basic arithmetic has the resources to express and represent provability in T. More specifically, some formula α_{Prf} with two free variables x and y represents the relation Prf that obtains between two numbers m and n when m is the Gödel number of a proof in T of the formula whose Gödel number is n. Accordingly, a formula P with one free variable y can be defined as follows:

$$P = \exists x \alpha_{Prf}$$

Informally speaking, P says that the formula with Gödel number y is provable in T. Let $\perp$ indicate absurdity, and assume that T proves $\perp$ if and only if T is inconsistent. Then $\sim P^{\ulcorner \perp \urcorner}$—abbreviated as Con_T—is a closed formula of the language of T that says that T is consistent. The second incompleteness theorem can be phrased as follows:

Theorem 19.5 *For any theory T which contains enough arithmetic, if T is consistent, then $T \nvdash Con_T$.*

The line of reasoning that leads to Theorem 19.5 is the following. The proof of the first half of Theorem 19.4 shows that, if T is consistent, then $T \nvdash G$. This is expressed in the language of T as $Con_T \supset \sim P^{\ulcorner G \urcorner}$. Moreover, if T contains enough arithmetic, it is itself able to replicate the reasoning for the first incompleteness theorem. In other words, if T is strong enough, we have that $T \vdash Con_T \supset \sim P^{\ulcorner G \urcorner}$. This is called "formalized first theorem". The formalized first theorem, combined with the fact that the equivalence between G and $\sim P^{\ulcorner G \urcorner}$ is provable in T, yields that if $T \vdash Con_T$, then $T \vdash G$. Since we know, again from the proof of the first half of Theorem 19.4, that if $T \vdash G$, then T is inconsistent, we get that if $T \vdash Con_T$, then T is inconsistent. Therefore, if T is consistent, then $T \nvdash Con_T$.

In his article, Gödel just stated a version of Theorem 19.5, relying on the thought that a strong enough theory must be able to prove the formalized first theorem. He did not spell out the details. The hard work of taking a strong enough theory and showing that it proves the formalized first theorem was first done for a particular case by Hilbert and Paul Bernays in their *Grundlagen der Mathematik* (1939). The details of their proof are—the story goes—due to Bernays, who had discussed it with Gödel during a transatlantic voyage.[3]

Exercises

19.1 Can a system be complete without being negation-complete?

19.2 Is Q_i negation-complete?

19.3 Is **PA** complete?

19.4 Gödel's first incompleteness theorem bears bad news for **PA** because negation-completeness is a desideratum for a theory of arithmetic. But why is negation-completeness *not* a desideratum for Q_i?

19.5 What property of **PA** makes it provable that *Prf* is recursively decidable?

19.6 Why is it provable that *Gdl* is recursively decidable?

19.7 Does the proof of theorem 19.1 depend on the assumption that **PA** is recursively adequate?

19.8 Does the proof of theorem 19.3 depend on the assumption that **PA** is recursively adequate?

19.9 Are there models of **PA** in which the sentence G is false?

19.10 Explain why the solution of Exercise 19.9 entails that there are non-standard models of **PA**.

---

[3]Hilbert and Bernays [25]. Paul Isaac Bernays (1888–1977), assistant and close collaborator of Hilbert, was a Swiss mathematician who made major contributions to axiomatic set theory and the philosophy of mathematics.

Chapter 20
Rudiments of Modal Logic

20.1 Modal Operators

This last chapter aims to provide a concise presentation of modal logic, the logic of necessity and possibility. A modal language is a language that contains, in addition to the symbols of a propositional or predicate language, the modal operators $\square$ and $\lozenge$, which mean respectively 'it is necessary that' and 'it is possible that'. A system in a modal language—a system of modal logic—extends a system of propositional logic or predicate logic by means of axioms and inference rules that specifically concern modality.

The interpretation of $\square$ and $\lozenge$ hinges on the notion of *possible world*, which can be traced back to Leibniz's *Theodicy* (1710) and is widely employed in some areas of contemporary philosophy. A possible world—or simply, a world—is understood as a complete scenario that constitutes a way things might be. For example, my chair might not be red, which means that there are worlds in which my chair is not red. Here 'complete' implies that no detail is left out, that is, the scenario is as specific as it can be. Thus, any world in which my chair is not red is a world in which my chair has some particular colour.[1]

Assuming that there is a plurality of worlds, and that every sentence is true or false relative to each of them, the meaning of $\square$ and $\lozenge$ is defined in terms of quantification on worlds: $\square\alpha$ is true if and only if α is true in all worlds, while $\lozenge\alpha$ is true if and only if α is true in some world. This reading of 'it is necessary that' and 'it is possible that', originally suggested by Rudolf Carnap in *Meaning and Necessity* (1947), is the core hypothesis that underlies the semantics of modal languages.[2]

---

[1] Leibniz [38].

[2] Paul Rudolf Carnap (1891–1970) was a German philosopher who studied in Jena (where he learned from Frege), then spent a considerable part of his academic career in the United States, in Chicago, Princeton, and Los Angeles. He is best known as one of the founders of logical positivism,

A. Iacona, *LOGIC: Lecture Notes for Philosophy, Mathematics, and Computer Science*, Springer Undergraduate Texts in Philosophy, https://doi.org/10.1007/978-3-030-64811-4_20

To illustrate, consider the sentences 'It is necessary that $2 + 2 = 4$' and 'It is necessary that it is raining'. As noted in Sect. 4.5, these two sentences seem to have different truth values. This can be explained as follows: the first sentence is true because in all worlds $2 + 2 = 4$, while the second is false because it is not the case that in all worlds it is raining. Now consider 'It is possible that it is raining' and 'It is possible that $2 + 2 = 5$'. Again, these two sentences seem to have different truth values. This can be explained as follows: the first sentence is true because in some worlds it is raining, while the second is false because there is no world in which $2 + 2 = 5$.

On this account of necessity and possibility, $\Box$ and $\Diamond$ are interdefinable, just like $\forall$ and $\exists$. To say that $\Box\alpha$ is true is to say that there are no worlds in which α is false, so that $\sim\Diamond\sim\alpha$ is true. Similarly, to say that $\Diamond\alpha$ is true is to say that it is not the case that α is false in all worlds, so that $\sim\Box\sim\alpha$ is true.

20.2   A Modal Propositional Language

Let us begin with a modal propositional language called $\mathsf{L_m}$. The alphabet of $\mathsf{L_m}$ is the following:

$p, q, r, \ldots$
$\sim, \supset, \Box$
$(,)$

The formulas of $\mathsf{L_m}$ are defined as follows:

Definition 20.1

1 $p, q, r \ldots$ are formulas;
2 if α is a formula, $\sim\alpha$ is a formula;
3 if α and β are formulas, $(\alpha \supset \beta)$ is a formula;
4 if α is a formula, $\Box\alpha$ is a formula.

The connectives $\wedge, \vee, \Diamond$ are definable in terms of $\sim, \supset, \Box$.

The semantics of L_m is based on the analysis of $\Box$ and $\Diamond$ outlined in the previous section, in the formal framework developed by Saul Kripke.[3]

An interpretation of $\mathsf{L_m}$ is a model defined as follows:

---

and a leading contributor to formal semantics and inductive logic. His analysis of modal operators is outlined in Carnap [4].

[3] Saul Aaron Kripke (1940), American logician and philosopher, is one of the most powerful and influential thinkers in contemporary analytic philosophy. He began his work on the semantics of modal logic while he was still a high-school student in Omaha, Nebraska. In his groundbreaking paper Kripke [34] he proved a completeness result for modal logic.

Definition 20.2 A *model* is an ordered triple $\langle W, R, V \rangle$, where W is a non-empty set, R is a relation on W, and V is a function such that, for every atomic formula α and every $w \in W$, $V(\alpha, w) \in \{1, 0\}$.

W is a set of worlds. R is the relation of *accessibility*. Informally speaking, to say that w' is accessible from w is to say that w' is a possible scenario relative to w. V is a valuation function that assigns values to formulas relative to worlds. W and R constitute the *frame* of the model, that is, they fix how many worlds there are, and which worlds are accessible from which. We say that $\langle W, R, V \rangle$ *is based* on $\langle W, R \rangle$. So, whenever two models differ only in the valuation function, they are based on the same frame.

The truth of a formula α in a world w in a model $\mathcal{M} = \langle W, R, V \rangle$ is defined as follows, assuming that $[\alpha]_{\mathcal{M}, w}$ indicates the value of α in w in $\mathcal{M}$:

Definition 20.3

1 If α is atomic, $[\alpha]_{\mathcal{M}, w} = 1$ iff $V(\alpha, w) = 1$;
2 $[\sim\alpha]_{\mathcal{M}, w} = 1$ iff $[\alpha]_{\mathcal{M}, w} = 0$;
3 $[\alpha \supset \beta]_{\mathcal{M}, w} = 1$ iff $[\alpha]_{\mathcal{M}, w} = 0$ or $[\beta]_{\mathcal{M}, w} = 1$;
4 $[\Box\alpha]_{\mathcal{M}, w} = 1$ iff, for every w' such that $\langle w, w' \rangle \in R$, $[\alpha]_{\mathcal{M}, w'} = 1$.

Clause 1 is trivial: if α is atomic, its value in w is nothing but the value that V assigns to it relative to w. Clause 2 and 3 stipulate that $\sim$ and $\supset$ behave in the usual truth-functional way. Clause 4 specifies the meaning of $\Box$ in terms of a quantification on worlds: $\Box\alpha$ is true in w just in case α is true in every w' accessible from w.

Validity is defined accordingly, relative to a model, relative to a frame, and relative to a class of frames:

Definition 20.4 α is *valid in a model* $\mathcal{M}$ iff $[\alpha]_{\mathcal{M}, w} = 1$ for every w.

Definition 20.5 α is *valid on a frame* $\mathcal{F}$ iff α is valid in every model based on $\mathcal{F}$.

Definition 20.6 α is *valid with respect to a class of frames* C—or C-*valid*—iff α is valid on every frame in C.

To illustrate how $\mathsf{L_m}$ may be employed to formalize natural language, consider the sentence 'If Alf is a bachelor, he must be unmarried'. This sentence contains the expression 'must', which indicates a necessary connection between being bachelor and being unmarried. So, it is formalized in $\mathsf{L_m}$ as $\Box(p \supset q)$, where p stands for 'Alf is a bachelor' and q stands for 'Alf is unmarried'.

Note that no adequate formalization of 'If Alf is a bachelor, he must be unmarried' can be given in a propositional language. In a propositional language, this sentence is formalized as $p \supset q$, where q stands either for 'Alf is unmarried' or for 'Necessarily, Alf is unmarried'. But neither option is satisfactory. In the first case we miss the modal force conveyed by the sentence: what is said is not simply that it is not the case that Alf is a bachelor without being unmarried, but rather that it *cannot* be the case. In the second we locate necessity in the wrong place, that is, in the consequent. What is said is not that, if Alf is a bachelor, then he is necessarily unmarried, because if Alf is actually a bachelor, the truth of the sentence would make it impossible for him to be married.

The example just considered shows that formalization in a modal language enables us to dissipate an ambiguity that may prompt fallacious inferences, the ambiguity between $\Box(p \supset q)$ and $p \supset \Box q$. One thing is to say that a conditional is necessary, another thing is to say that its consequent is necessary if its antecedent holds. This is the traditional distinction between *necessitas consequentiae* and *necessitas consequentis*, that is, between necessity of the consequence and necessity of the consequent. $\Box(p \supset q)$ and $p \supset \Box q$ are not equivalent, because the former does not entail the latter. Consider a model $\mathcal{M}$ with two worlds w and w' such that w' is accessible from w and the following holds: $[p]_{\mathcal{M},w} = 1$, $[p]_{\mathcal{M},w'} = 0$, $[q]_{\mathcal{M},w} = 1$, $[q]_{\mathcal{M},w'} = 0$. In this case, as is easy to verify, $[\Box(p \supset q)]_{\mathcal{M},w} = 1$, but $[p \supset \Box q]_{\mathcal{M},w} = 0$.

20.3   The System K

The key question that one must confront when one constructs a system in a modal language is which formulas of the language deserve the status of theorems in virtue of being logical truths. This question, initially addressed by Clarence Irving Lewis, admits different answers, because $\Box$ may be understood in different ways. As Lewis recognized, different interpretations of $\Box$ motivate different systems of modal logic, each of which determines a definite set of theorems.[4]

This section and the next outline five systems of modal propositional logic, which are all extensions of **L**. For each of them, it will be explained how the interpretation of $\Box$ associated with the system constrains the relation of accessibility. More precisely, we will focus on three properties of this relation: reflexivity, symmetry, and transitivity. A model, or a frame, can be reflexive or non-reflexive, symmetric or non-symmetric, transitive or non-transitive, depending on whether its accessibility relation has the corresponding property.

The first system is called **K**. The axioms of **K** are the formulas of $\mathsf{L_m}$ that instantiate A1-A3 (see Sect. 9.1) and the following schema:

K $\Box(\alpha \supset \beta) \supset (\Box\alpha \supset \Box\beta)$

---

[4]Clarence Irving Lewis (1883–1964) was an American logician who studied and taught at Harvard University. His seminal works on modal logic stem from his reflections on conditionals, and more specifically from his dissatisfaction with the material account of conditionals adopted in *Principia Mathematica*, see Lewis [40], Lewis [41], Lewis and Langford [42].

If a conditional is necessary and its antecedent is necessary, then its consequent is also necessary.[5]

The inference rules of **K** are MP and *Necessitation*:

N If $\vdash \alpha$, then $\vdash \Box\alpha$.

N says that the necessitation of a theorem is itself a theorem. Since theorems represent logical truths, this means that the necessitation of a logical truth is itself a logical truth. It is easy to see that MP and N preserve validity, that is, if they are applied to formulas that are valid in a model, the resulting formulas are also valid in that model.

K provides a minimal deductive basis that is shared by a family of systems known as *normal modal logics*. From now on, the symbol $\vdash$ will be used to indicate derivability in **K**, assuming that a derivation in **K** is defined in the usual way, and we will restrict consideration to proofs in **K**, that is, finite sequences of formulas such that each formula is an axiom or is obtained from other formulas by means of MP or N.

One basic deductive property of **K** is that whenever we can prove a theorem of the form $\alpha \supset \beta$, we can also prove $\Box\alpha \supset \Box\beta$.

Theorem 20.1 *If* $\vdash \alpha \supset \beta$*, then* $\vdash \Box\alpha \supset \Box\beta$.

Proof Assume that $\vdash \alpha \supset \beta$. Then, by N it follows that $\vdash \Box(\alpha \supset \beta)$. Since $\vdash \Box(\alpha \supset \beta) \supset (\Box\alpha \supset \Box\beta)$ by K, we obtain that $\vdash \Box\alpha \supset \Box\beta$. $\Box$

Here is an example of how this rule can be used:

Theorem 20.2 $\vdash \Box(\alpha \supset \beta) \supset (\Diamond\alpha \supset \Diamond\beta)$

Proof

(1)	$\vdash (\alpha \supset \beta) \supset (\sim\beta \supset \sim\alpha)$	T 9.16
(2)	$\vdash \Box(\alpha \supset \beta) \supset \Box(\sim\beta \supset \sim\alpha)$	T 20.1 1
(3)	$\vdash \Box(\sim\beta \supset \sim\alpha) \supset (\Box\sim\beta \supset \Box\sim\alpha)$	K
(4)	$\vdash \Box(\alpha \supset \beta) \supset (\Box\sim\beta \supset \Box\sim\alpha)$	T 9.9 2,3
(5)	$\vdash (\Box\sim\beta \supset \Box\sim\alpha) \supset (\sim\Box\sim\alpha \supset \sim\Box\sim\beta)$	T 9.16
(6)	$\vdash \Box(\alpha \supset \beta) \supset (\sim\Box\sim\alpha \supset \sim\Box\sim\beta)$	T 9.9 4,5
(7)	$\vdash \Box(\alpha \supset \beta) \supset (\Diamond\alpha \supset \Diamond\beta)$	$\Box/\Diamond$ 6

$\Box$

This proof mentions Theorems 9.16 and 9.9 because the latter are provable in **K** for the same reasons for which they are provable in **L**, namely, that A1-A3 and MP hold in **K**. The notation $\Box/\Diamond$ indicates that (7) is obtained from (6) in virtue of the interdefinability of $\Box$ and $\Diamond$. The same conventions will be adopted in the proofs that follows.

---

[5]This system is named **K** in honour of Kripke. The label comes from Lemmon and Scott [8].

A derived rule that can be adopted in **K** is SE: whenever one has a proof of $\gamma \equiv \gamma'$, one can replace γ by γ' in any formula. To see that SE holds in **K** it suffices to go back to the proof set out in Sect. 9.4, and add that whenever α is $\Box\beta$ and α' is $\Box\beta'$, we have that $\vdash \alpha \equiv \alpha'$ because Theorem 20.1 entails that if $\vdash \beta \equiv \beta'$, then $\vdash \Box\beta \equiv \Box\beta'$. Here are some equivalence results that can easily be established by using SE.

Theorem 20.3 $\vdash (\Box\alpha \supset \alpha) \equiv (\sim\alpha \supset \Diamond\sim\alpha)$

Proof The left-to-right direction is proved as follows:

(1) $\vdash (\Box\alpha \supset \alpha) \supset (\sim\alpha \supset \sim\Box\alpha)$ T 9.16

(2) $\vdash (\Box\alpha \supset \alpha) \supset (\sim\alpha \supset \sim\Box\sim\sim\alpha)$ SE 1

(3) $\vdash (\Box\alpha \supset \alpha) \supset (\sim\alpha \supset \Diamond\sim\alpha)$ $\Box/\Diamond$ 2.

The proof of the right-to-left direction uses exactly the same principles.   □

Theorem 20.4 $\vdash (\alpha \supset \Box\Diamond\alpha) \equiv (\Diamond\Box\sim\alpha \supset \sim\alpha)$

Proof The left-to-right direction is proved as follows:

(1) $\vdash (\alpha \supset \Box\Diamond\alpha) \supset (\sim\Box\Diamond\alpha \supset \sim\alpha)$ T 9.16

(2) $\vdash (\alpha \supset \Box\Diamond\alpha) \supset (\sim\Box\sim\sim\Diamond\sim\sim\alpha \supset \sim\alpha)$ SE 1

(3) $\vdash (\alpha \supset \Box\Diamond\alpha) \supset (\Diamond\Box\sim\alpha \supset \sim\alpha)$ $\Box/\Diamond$ 2

The proof of the right-to-left direction is similar but uses Theorem 9.17 instead of Theorem 9.16.   □

Theorem 20.5 $\vdash (\Box\alpha \supset \Box\Box\alpha) \equiv (\Diamond\Diamond\sim\alpha \supset \Diamond\sim\alpha)$

Proof The left-to-right direction is proved as follows:

(1) $\vdash (\Box\alpha \supset \Box\Box\alpha) \supset (\sim\Box\Box\alpha \supset \sim\Box\alpha)$ T 9.16

(2) $\vdash (\Box\alpha \supset \Box\Box\alpha) \supset (\sim\Box\sim\sim\Box\sim\sim\alpha \supset \sim\Box\sim\sim\alpha)$ SE 1

(3) $\vdash (\Box\alpha \supset \Box\Box\alpha) \supset (\Diamond\Diamond\sim\alpha \supset \Diamond\sim\alpha)$ $\Box/\Diamond$ 2

The proof of the right-to-left direction uses exactly the same principles.   □

Theorem 20.6 $\vdash (\Diamond\alpha \supset \Box\Diamond\alpha) \equiv (\Diamond\Box\sim\alpha \supset \Box\sim\alpha)$

Proof The left-to-right direction is proved as follows:

(1) $\vdash (\Diamond\alpha \supset \Box\Diamond\alpha) \supset (\sim\Box\Diamond\alpha \supset \sim\Diamond\alpha)$ T 9.16

(2) $\vdash (\Diamond\alpha \supset \Box\Diamond\alpha) \supset (\sim\Box\sim\sim\Diamond\sim\sim\alpha \supset \sim\Diamond\sim\sim\alpha)$ SE1

(3) $\vdash (\Diamond\alpha \supset \Box\Diamond\alpha) \supset (\Diamond\Box\sim\alpha \supset \Box\sim\alpha)$ $\Box/\Diamond$

The proof of the right-to-left direction uses exactly the same principles.   □

At the semantic level, **K** imposes no restriction on frames, for K is valid on every frame. Suppose that $[\Box\alpha \supset \Box\beta]_{\mathcal{M},w} = 0$ for some $\mathcal{M}$, w. Then $[\Box\alpha]_{\mathcal{M},w} = 1$ and $[\Box\beta]_{\mathcal{M},w} = 0$. This means that there is a w' accessible from w such that $[\alpha]_{\mathcal{M},w'} = 1$ and $[\beta]_{\mathcal{M},w'} = 0$, so that $[\Box(\alpha \supset \beta)]_{\mathcal{M},w} = 0$. Since MP and N preserve validity, every theorem of **K** is valid on every frame.

20.4 The Systems **T**, **B**, **S4**, **S5**

The second system, **T**, is obtained by adding to **K** the following axiom schema, which is sometimes called *Axiom of necessity*:

T $\Box\alpha \supset \alpha$

The principle expressed by T straightforwardly follows from the idea that necessity amounts to truth in all worlds: if it is necessary that things are a certain way, then things are that way.[6]

A provably equivalent principle, which holds in **T**, is the following: if things are a certain way, then it is possible that they are that way.

Theorem 20.7 T $\vdash \alpha \supset \Diamond\alpha$

Proof

(1) **T** $\vdash \Box\sim\alpha \supset \sim\alpha$ T
(2) **T** $\vdash \sim\sim\alpha \supset \Diamond\sim\sim\alpha$ T 20.3 1
(3) **T** $\vdash \alpha \supset \Diamond\alpha$ SE 2

$\Box$

At the semantic level, the restriction on frames imposed by **T** is that accessibility is reflexive, for T holds in all reflexive frames. If $\mathcal{M}$ is reflexive, there is no w such that $[\Box\alpha]_{\mathcal{M},w} = 1$ but $[\alpha]_{\mathcal{M},w} = 0$, for the worlds that are accessible from w include w itself. Conversely, T does not hold in non-reflexive frames, because there are non-reflexive models that falsify T. Suppose that $\mathcal{M}$ is a model where $[\alpha]_{\mathcal{M},w} = 0$ but $[\alpha]_{\mathcal{M},w'} = 1$ for every w' accessible from w. In this case $[\Box\alpha]_{\mathcal{M},w} = 1$ but $[\alpha]_{\mathcal{M},w} = 0$, so we have a counterexample to T.

The three remaining systems are extensions of **T** that combine T with further principles concerning iterated modalities, that is, sequences of modal operators in formulas. The system **B** is obtained by adding to **T** the following axiom schema:

B $\alpha \supset \Box\Diamond\alpha$

If things are a certain way, necessarily it is possible that things are that way.[7]

A provably equivalent principle, which holds in **B**, is the following: if it is possible that things are necessarily a certain way, then things are that way.

---

[6]The label **T** comes from Feys [12], where the system is called t.

[7]This system, just as its characteristic axiom schema, is named after Brouwer, the founder of intuitionism (see Sect. 1.5), even though it was never used by Brouwer. See Hughes and Cresswell [27], p. 70, for an explanation.

Theorem 20.8 B $\vdash \Diamond\Box\alpha \supset \alpha$

Proof

(1) **B** $\vdash \sim\alpha \supset \Box\Diamond\sim\alpha$ B
(2) **B** $\vdash \Diamond\Box\sim\sim\alpha \supset \sim\sim\alpha$ T 20.4 1
(3) **B** $\vdash \Diamond\Box\alpha \supset \alpha$ SE 2

$\Box$

At the semantic level, the restriction on frames imposed by **B** is that accessibility is reflexive and symmetric. As we have seen, T holds in all reflexive frames. Instead, B holds in all symmetric frames. If $\mathcal{M}$ is symmetric, there is no w such that $[\alpha]_{\mathcal{M},w} = 1$ but $[\Box\Diamond\alpha]_{\mathcal{M},w} = 0$. To see this it suffices to think that the falsity of $\Box\Diamond\alpha$ in w would require the falsity of $\Diamond\alpha$ in some w' accessible from w, but then α could not be true in w, being w accessible from w'. Conversely, B does not hold in non-symmetric frames, for there are non-symmetric models that falsify B. Suppose that $\mathcal{M}$ is a model with exactly two worlds w and w' such that w' is accessible from w while w is not accessible from w'. If $[\alpha]_{\mathcal{M},w} = 1$ and $[\alpha]_{\mathcal{M},w'} = 0$, we get that $[\Diamond\alpha]_{\mathcal{M},w'} = 0$, so that $[\alpha]_{\mathcal{M},w} = 1$ and $[\Box\Diamond\alpha]_{\mathcal{M},w} = 0$.

The fourth system, **S4**, is an extension of **T** that differs from **B**: although **B** and **S4** are both extensions of **T**, neither of them is an extension of the other. Instead of adding B to **T**, **S4** is obtained by adding the following axiom schema to **T**:

S4 $\Box\alpha \supset \Box\Box\alpha$

If it is necessary that things are a certain way, necessarily it is necessary that things are that way.[8]

A provably equivalent principle, which holds in **S4**, is the following: if it is possible that it is possible that things are a certain way, then it is possible that things are that way.

Theorem 20.9 S4 $\vdash \Diamond\Diamond\alpha \supset \Diamond\alpha$

Proof

(1) **S4** $\vdash \Box\sim\alpha \supset \Box\Box\sim\alpha$ S4
(2) **S4** $\vdash \Diamond\Diamond\sim\sim\alpha \supset \Diamond\sim\sim\alpha$ T 20.5 1
(3) **S4** $\vdash \Diamond\Diamond\alpha \supset \Diamond\alpha$ SE 2

$\Box$

Given S4 and Theorem 20.9, **S4** includes two important reduction laws for iterated modalities:

Theorem 20.10 S4 $\vdash \Box\Box\alpha \equiv \Box\alpha$

Proof From T and S4. $\Box$

---

[8]The label **S4** derives from Lewis and Langford [42], where a system deductively equivalent to this is fourth in a series of modal systems.

Theorem 20.11 S4 $\vdash \Diamond\Diamond\alpha \equiv \Diamond\alpha$

Proof From Theorems 20.7 and 20.9.   □

Theorems 20.10 and 20.11 entail that any sequence of adjacent occurrences of the same modal operator can be reduced to a single occurrence of that operator.

At the semantic level, the restriction on frames imposed by **S4** is that accessibility is reflexive and transitive. While T holds in all reflexive frames, S4 holds in all transitive frames. If $\mathcal{M}$ is transitive, there is no w such that $[\Box\alpha]_{\mathcal{M},w} = 1$ but $[\Box\Box\alpha]_{\mathcal{M},w} = 0$. To see this it suffices to think that the falsity of $\Box\Box\alpha$ in w would require the falsity of $\Box\alpha$ in some w' accessible from w, and that the latter would in turn require the falsity of α in some w'' accessible from w', but then $\Box\alpha$ could not be true in w, being w'' accessible from w. Conversely, S4 does not hold in non-transitive frames, for there are non-transitive models that falsify S4. Suppose that $\mathcal{M}$ is a model with exactly three worlds w, w', w'' such that w' is accessible from w and w'' is accessible from w' but w'' is not accessible from w. If $[\alpha]_{\mathcal{M},w'} = 1$ and $[\alpha]_{\mathcal{M},w''} = 0$, we get that $[\Box\alpha]_{\mathcal{M},w} = 1$ and $[\Box\alpha]_{\mathcal{M},w'} = 0$, so that $[\Box\alpha]_{\mathcal{M},w} = 1$ but $[\Box\Box\alpha]_{\mathcal{M},w} = 0$.

The fifth and last system is **S5**. This system is an extension of **T** as well, since it is obtained by adding to **T** the following axiom schema:

S5 $\Diamond\alpha \supset \Box\Diamond\alpha$

If it is possible that things are a certain way, then it is necessarily possible that things are that way.[9]

A provably equivalent principle, which holds in **S5**, is the following: if it is possible that things are necessarily a certain way, then things are necessarily that way.

Theorem 20.12 S5 $\vdash \Diamond\Box\alpha \supset \Box\alpha$

Proof

(1) **S5** $\vdash \Diamond\sim\alpha \supset \Box\Diamond\sim\alpha$ S5

(2) **S5** $\vdash \Diamond\Box\sim\sim\alpha \supset \Box\sim\sim\alpha$ T 20.6 1

(3) **S5** $\vdash \Diamond\Box\alpha \supset \Box\alpha$ SE 2

□

S5 is the strongest system among those considered. While **B** and **S4** are alternative extensions of **T**, so that some theorems of **B** are not provable in **S4** and some theorems of **S4** are not provable in **B**, **S5** is an extension of both, because B and S4 are both provable in **S5**.

---

[9] As in the case of **S4**, the name of this system derives from Lewis and Langford [42].

Theorem 20.13 S5 $\vdash \alpha \supset \Box\Diamond\alpha$

Proof

(1) **S5** $\vdash \Diamond\Box\sim\alpha \supset \Box\sim\alpha$ T 20.12
(2) **S5** $\vdash \Box\sim\alpha \supset \sim\alpha$ T
(3) **S5** $\vdash \Diamond\Box\sim\alpha \supset \sim\alpha$ T 9.9 1,2
(4) **S5** $\vdash \sim\Box\sim\Box\sim\alpha \supset \sim\alpha$ $\Box/\Diamond$ 3
(5) **S5** $\vdash \alpha \supset \Box\sim\Box\sim\alpha$ SE 4
(6) **S5** $\vdash \alpha \supset \Box\Diamond\alpha$ $\Box/\Diamond$ 5

$\Box$

Theorem 20.14 S5 $\vdash \Box\alpha \supset \Box\Box\alpha$

Proof

(1) **S5** $\vdash \Diamond\Box\alpha \supset \Box\alpha$ T 20.12
(2) **S5** $\vdash \Box\Diamond\Box\alpha \supset \Box\Box\alpha$ T 20.1 1
(3) **S5** $\vdash \Box\alpha \supset \Box\Diamond\Box\alpha$ T 20.13
(4) **S5** $\vdash \Box\alpha \supset \Box\Box\alpha$ T 9.9 3,2

$\Box$

S5 includes, in addition to the two reduction laws that hold in **S4**—Theorems 20.10 and 20.11—two further reduction laws:

Theorem 20.15 S5 $\vdash \Box\Diamond\alpha \equiv \Diamond\alpha$

Proof From T and S5. $\Box$

Theorem 20.16 S5 $\vdash \Diamond\Box\alpha \equiv \Box\alpha$

Proof From Theorems 20.7 and 20.12. $\Box$

These four reduction laws make it possible to simplify iterated modalities by deleting the first of any pair of adjacent modal operators. So they guarantee that any sequence of adjacent modal operators can be reduced to a single modal operator.

At the semantic level, the restriction on frames imposed by **S5** is that accessibility is reflexive, symmetric, and transitive. This turns out clear if one thinks that reflexivity is required by T, and that symmetry and transitivity are required by B and S4, which are provable on the basis of S5.

The systems considered so far provide different ways of determining a definite set of logical truths expressible in L_m. Of course, this leaves room for philosophical reflections on the "correct" interpretation of $\Box$. Some claims about necessity are widely shared. For example, it is generally assumed as metaphysically plausible that accessibility is reflexive, so that T must hold. However, other claims are more controversial. For example, there is no widespread agreement on the assumption that accessibility is transitive, which implies that S4 or S5 must hold. In any case, the philosophical questions concerning the adequacy of the systems of modal logic are beyond the purposes of this chapter.

20.5   A Modal Predicate Language

Just as a modal propositional language is obtained by adding modal operators to a propositional language, a modal predicate language is obtained by adding modal operators to a predicate language. Let L_{qm} be a language with the following alphabet:

$P, Q, R, \ldots$
$a, b, c, \ldots$
$\sim, \supset, \forall, \square$
$x, y, z, \ldots$
$(,)$

The formation rules of L_{qm} are the following:

Definition 20.7

1 If P is a n-place predicate letter and $t_1, \ldots, t_n$ are terms, $Pt_1 \ldots t_n$ is a formula;
2 if α is a formula, $\sim\alpha$ is a formula;
3 if α and β are formulas, $(\alpha \supset \beta)$ is a formula;
4 if α is a formula and x is a variable, $\forall x\alpha$ is a formula;
5 if α is a formula, $\square\alpha$ is a formula.

The connectives $\wedge, \vee, \exists, \Diamond$ are definable in terms of $\sim, \supset, \forall, \square$.
The simplest way to interpret L_{qm} is to define a model as follows:

Definition 20.8   A *model* is an ordered quadruple $\langle W, R, D, I \rangle$, where W is a non-empty set, R is a relation on W, D is a non-empty set, and I is a function such that, for every individual constant a, $I(a) \in D$, and for every n-place predicate letter P, $I(P)$ is a function that assigns to every element of W a set of n-tuples of elements of D.

W and R are exactly as in Definition 20.2. This implies that a model of L_m and a model of L_{qm} can have the same set of worlds W and the same relation of accessibility R, in which case they are based on the same frame $\langle W, R \rangle$. D is the domain of the model. I is the interpretation function. To understand I it suffices to think that an interpretation of L_{qm} must assign to every predicate letter an extension in every world. For example, if my chair is red in our world but green in another world, it belongs to the set of red things in our world but not in that world.

Assuming that the notions of assignment and denotation of a term in an assignment are like in L_q, we can define the satisfaction of a formula α by an assignment σ in a world w in a model $\mathcal{M}$:

Definition 20.9

1 σ satisfies $Pt_1 \ldots t_n$ in w iff $\langle [t_1]_{\mathcal{M},\sigma}, \ldots, [t_n]_{\mathcal{M},\sigma} \rangle \in [P]_{\mathcal{M},w}$;
2 σ satisfies $\sim\alpha$ in w iff σ does not satisfy α in w;
3 σ satisfies $\alpha \supset \beta$ in w iff σ does not satisfy α in w or it satisfies β in w;
4 σ satisfies $\forall x\alpha$ in w iff every x-variant of σ satisfies α in w;
5 σ satisfies $\square\alpha$ in w iff, for every w' such that $\langle w, w' \rangle \in R$, σ satisfies α in w'.

In clause 1, $[P]_{\mathcal{M},w}$ indicates the extension of P in w in $\mathcal{M}$, that is, the set of n-tuples that I assigns to P relative to w. Clauses 2–4 are analogous to those of $\mathsf{L_q}$, with the only difference that satisfaction is relative to w. Finally, clause 5 says that the satisfaction of $\Box\alpha$ in w depends on the satisfaction of α in the worlds accessible from w.

Truth and falsity are defined in terms of satisfaction, as in $\mathsf{L_q}$:

Definition 20.10 $[\alpha]_{\mathcal{M},w} = 1$ iff α is satisfied by every assignment in w.

Definition 20.11 $[\alpha]_{\mathcal{M},w} = 0$ iff α is satisfied by no assignment in w.

Finally, validity is understood in accordance with Definitions 20.4–20.6.

The metaphysical implications of the semantics just outlined have been widely debated. In particular, the idea that the same individuals exist in all possible worlds raises quite thorny philosophical questions. Consider the following schema, known as *Barcan formula*:[10]

BF $\forall x\Box\alpha \supset \Box\forall x\alpha$

Any formula that instantiates BF, such as $\forall x\Box Fx \supset \Box\forall x Fx$, is valid in this semantics. Suppose that $[\Box\forall x Fx]_{\mathcal{M},w} = 0$ for some $\mathcal{M}$ and w. Then there is a w' accessible from w such that $[\forall x Fx]_{\mathcal{M},w'} = 0$, so some assignment does not satisfy Fx in w'. It follows that some assignment does not satisfy $\Box Fx$ in w, so that $[\forall x\Box Fx]_{\mathcal{M},w} = 0$. However, it is not obvious that BF expresses a logical truth. Suppose that all the objects that actually exist are material, so that non-material objects such as ghosts do not exist. Suppose also that the property of being material is essential to the objects that actually exist, so that those objects are necessarily material. Apparently, in the scenario described it is still possible that there are non-material objects such as ghosts. Yet BF implies the contrary: if everything is necessarily material, then necessarily everything is material. The example becomes even more vivid if we consider the formula $\Diamond\exists x Fx \supset \exists x\Diamond Fx$, which is equivalent to $\forall x\Box\sim Fx \supset \Box\forall x\sim Fx$: to say that it is possible that spiritual objects exist is not the same thing as to say that some of the existing objects could be spiritual, or so it appears.

The crux of the matter is the fixed domain. If one is inclined to think that in the scenario considered it is possible that there are spiritual objects, it is because one takes for granted that there might be spiritual objects other than the objects that are actually material. This is why the most natural alternative to the semantics outlined is to define models in such a way that each world has its own domain, so that existence becomes world-relative. In other terms, in addition to a set of worlds W and a domain D, the model will include a function F that assigns a subset of D to each element of W. Satisfaction and truth can thus be defined in such a way

---

[10]This schema is named after Ruth Barcan Marcus (1921–2012), an American logician and philosopher best known for her seminal work in modal logic. Barcan [2] presents the first fully formal system of quantified modal logic.

that the evaluation of a formula in a world depends exclusively on the objects that belong to the subset of D that F assigns to that world.[11]

Independently of which semantics is adopted, L_{qm} has a greater expressive capacity than L_m. This is due to the fact that L_{qm} allows different combinations of modal operators and quantifiers. Consider the distinction between *de dicto* and *de re* modal statements, which may be illustraded by means of the sentence 'Some rich could be poor'. On one reading, this sentence says that it is possible that there is an x such that x is both rich and poor. On another reading, it says that there is an x such that x is rich and it is possible that x is poor. The first reading is *de dicto*, because it ascribes a modal property—possible truth—to a sentence, 'Some rich are poor'. The second reading is *de re*, because it ascribes a modal property—possible poorness—to an object. The two readings can be represented as $\Diamond \exists x (Rx \wedge Px)$ and $\exists x (Rx \wedge \Diamond Px)$. Note that in L_m the only kind of formulas containing $\Diamond$ are those of the form $\Diamond \alpha$, so 'Some rich could be poor' can be formalized only as $\Diamond p$, where p stands for 'Some rich are poor'.

20.6   Systems of Modal Predicate Logic

As explained in Sect. 20.3, a system of modal propositional logic is obtained by adding to a system of propositional logic a set of modal axioms and N. A system of modal predicate logic is obtained in a similar way. Given a system S of modal propositional logic, Sq is a system of modal predicate logic whose axioms are formulas obtained by substitution from the theorems of S or instances of A4–A7, and whose inference rules are MP and N.

An example of system of modal predicate logic is $S5_q$, the system whose axioms are the formulas of L_{qm} obtained by substitution from the theorems of **S5** and the formulas of L_{qm} that instantiate A4-A7, and whose inference rules are MP and N. $S5_q$, just like **S5**, contains the reduction laws that enable us to simplify iterated modalities. Another interesting property of $S5_q$ is that it makes BF provable.

Theorem 20.17 $S5_q \vdash \forall x \Box \alpha \supset \Box \forall x \alpha$

Proof

(1)	$S5_q \vdash \forall x \Box \alpha \supset \Box \alpha$	A4
(2)	$S5_q \vdash \Box (\forall x \Box \alpha \supset \Box \alpha)$	N 1
(3)	$S5_q \vdash \Box (\forall x \Box \alpha \supset \Box \alpha) \supset (\Diamond \forall x \Box \alpha \supset \Diamond \Box \alpha)$	T 20.2
(4)	$S5_q \vdash \Diamond \forall x \Box \alpha \supset \Diamond \Box \alpha$	MP 3,2

---

[11] Kripke [35] outlines a semantics with variable domains. Williamson [67] provides an articulated defence of the fixed domain.

(5) $\mathbf{S5_q} \vdash \Diamond\Box\alpha \supset \alpha$ T 20.8

(6) $\mathbf{S5_q} \vdash \Diamond\forall x\Box\alpha \supset \alpha$ T 9.9 4,5

(7) $\mathbf{S5_q} \vdash \forall x(\Diamond\forall x\Box\alpha \supset \alpha)$ T 14.6 6

(8) $\mathbf{S5_q} \vdash \forall x(\Diamond\forall x\Box\alpha \supset \alpha) \supset (\forall x\Diamond\forall x\Box\alpha \supset \forall x\alpha)$ A6

(9) $\mathbf{S5_q} \vdash \forall x\Diamond\forall x\Box\alpha \supset \forall x\alpha$ MP 8,7

(10) $\mathbf{S5_q} \vdash \Diamond\forall x\Box\alpha \supset \forall x\Diamond\forall x\Box\alpha$ A5

(11) $\mathbf{S5_q} \vdash \Diamond\forall x\Box\alpha \supset \forall x\alpha$ T 9.9 10,9

(12) $\mathbf{S5_q} \vdash \Box\Diamond\forall x\Box\alpha \supset \Box\forall x\alpha$ T 20.1 11

(13) $\mathbf{S5_q} \vdash \forall x\Box\alpha \supset \Box\Diamond\forall x\Box\alpha$ T 20.13

(14) $\mathbf{S5_q} \vdash \forall x\Box\alpha \supset \Box\forall x\alpha$ T 9.9 13,12

$\square$

This property is interesting because BF is not provable in every system of modal predicate logic constructed in the way explained. As it turns out from lines (5) and (13), the proof of BF requires B. So, BF is not provable in $\mathbf{K_q}$, $\mathbf{T_q}$, or $\mathbf{S4_q}$. Here we will restrict consideration to systems that include BF, for BF holds in the semantics defined in Sect. 20.5. So we will use the notation Sq+BF to indicate a system of modal predicate logic obtained by adding BF to Sq.

At the semantic level, the systems of modal predicate logic obtained in this way are closely related to their propositional counterparts. A remarkable fact is that the properties of models considered in Sects. 20.3–20.4 characterize both the systems of modal propositional logic and the correspondent systems of modal predicate logic. If we stipulate that $\mathcal{F}$ is a frame *for* a system when the theorems of the system are valid on $\mathcal{F}$, this fact is expressed by the following two theorems.

Theorem 20.18 *If $\mathcal{F}$ is a frame for S, then $\mathcal{F}$ is a frame for Sq+BF.*

Proof Assume that $\mathcal{F}$ is a frame for S. Then it is provable that the axioms of Sq+BF are valid on $\mathcal{F}$. For any axiom α of Sq+BF, three cases are possible.

Case 1. α is obtained by substitution from a theorem of S, that is, for some theorem β of S, α is the result of replacing the sentence letters $\gamma_1, \ldots, \gamma_n$ that occur in β with formulas $\gamma_1', \ldots \gamma_n'$ of Sq+BF. Suppose that there is a model $\langle W, R, D, I \rangle$ based on $\mathcal{F}$ such that, for some $w \in W$, α is not true in w. Let $\langle W, R, V \rangle$ be a model of the language of S such that, for every γ_i in β, V assigns 1 to γ_i in a world iff in $\langle W, R, D, I \rangle$ the corresponding formula γ_i' in α is true in the same world. Since β is formed from $\gamma_1, \ldots \gamma_n$ by means of the connectives $\sim, \supset, \Box$, which are defined exactly in the same way, in $\langle W, R, V \rangle$ we get that β is false in w. So there is a model based on $\mathcal{F}$ in which β is false in some world. Since this cannot happen, being $\mathcal{F}$ a frame for S, it follows that α is valid on $\mathcal{F}$.

Case 2. α instantiates A4-A7. As it turns out from Sect. 15.1, the formulas of a predicate language that instantiate A4-A7 are valid. Since the language of Sq+BF differs from a predicate language only in that it involves relativization to worlds, we can prove theorems analogous to Theorems 13.4–15.6, showing that the formulas of Sq+BF that instantiate A4-A7 are valid on every frame. It follows that α is valid on $\mathcal{F}$.

Case 3. α instantiates BF. In this case α is valid on $\mathcal{F}$ because it is valid in every model, as noted in Sect. 20.5.

Since the axioms of Sq+BF are valid on $\mathcal{F}$, and the rules MP and N preserve validity—as they preserve satisfaction in a world—the theorems of Sq+BF are valid on $\mathcal{F}$. □

Theorem 20.19 *If $\mathcal{F}$ is a frame for Sq+BF, then $\mathcal{F}$ is a frame for S.*

Proof Assume that $\mathcal{F}$ is not a frame for S, namely, that there is a model $\langle W, R, V \rangle$ based on $\mathcal{F}$ in which a theorem α of S is false in some w. Let $\gamma_1, \ldots \gamma_n$ be the sentence letters that occur in α. Let $\gamma'_1, \ldots \gamma'_n$ be atomic formulas of the language of Sq+BF each of which is formed by a one-place predicate letter and one variable. Let β be the formula obtained by replacing $\gamma_1, \ldots \gamma_n$ with $\gamma'_1, \ldots \gamma'_n$. Since β is obtained by substitution from α, it is a theorem of Sq+BF. Now consider a model $\langle W, R, D, I \rangle$ such that I satisfies the following condition: for every γ'_i in β and every object $o \in D$, o belongs to the extension that the predicate letter in γ'_i has in a world iff γ_i is true in that world in $\langle W, R, V \rangle$. So γ'_i is satisfied by an assignment in a world iff γ_i is true in that world. Since β is formed from $\gamma'_1, \ldots \gamma'_n$ by means of the connectives $\sim, \supset, \square$ in the same way in which α is formed from $\gamma_1, \ldots \gamma_n$, it follows that β is not satisfied by some assignment in w. Therefore, $\mathcal{F}$ is not a frame for Sq+BF. □

20.7 Soundness and Completeness

Let us conclude with a brief survey of the soundness and completeness results that can be proved for the systems outlined in the foregoing sections. Soundness and completeness are defined relative to classes of frames as follows:

Definition 20.12 A system is *sound with respect to a class of frames* C iff all its theorems are C-valid.

Definition 20.13 A system is *complete with respect to a class of frames* C iff all its C-valid formulas are theorems.

The soundness results that concern the systems considered can be obtained by means of the following theorem:

Theorem 20.20 *If Γ is a set of formulas and C is a class of frames such that every formula in Γ is C-valid, then $\mathbf{K} + \Gamma$ is sound with respect to C.*

Proof Every axiom of $\mathbf{K}$ is C-valid because it is valid on every frame. Every formula in Γ is C-valid by hypothesis. Since MP and N preserve validity, it follows that every theorem of $\mathbf{K} + \Gamma$ is C-valid. □

First, from Theorem 20.20, assuming that $\Gamma = \emptyset$ and C is the class of all frames, we get that **K** is sound with respect to the class of all frames. Given Theorem 20.18, the same goes for $\mathbf{K_q}$+BF. Second, from Theorem 20.20, assuming that $\Gamma = \{T\}$ and C is the class of reflexive frames, we get that **T** is sound with respect to the class of reflexive frames. Given Theorem 20.18, the same goes for $\mathbf{T_q}$+BF. Third, from Theorem 20.20, assuming that $\Gamma = \{T, B\}$ and C is the class of reflexive and symmetric frames, we get that **B** is sound with respect to the class of reflexive and symmetric frames. Given Theorem 20.18, the same goes for $\mathbf{B_q}$+BF. Fourth, from Theorem 20.20, assuming that $\Gamma = \{T, S4\}$ and C is the class of reflexive and transitive frames, we get that **S4** is sound with respect to the class of reflexive and transitive frames. Given Theorem 20.18, the same goes for $\mathbf{S4_q}$+BF. Finally, from Theorem 20.20, assuming that $\Gamma = \{T, S5\}$ and C is the class of reflexive, symmetric, and transitive frames, we get that **S5** is sound with respect to the class of reflexive, symmetric, and transitive frames. Given Theorem 20.18, the same goes for $\mathbf{S5_q}$.

The issue of completeness is more complex, as is easy to imagine. A detailed exposition of the completeness proofs for the ten systems outlined would be too demanding. But their overall structure is similar: first it is shown that every consistent set of formulas can be extended into a negation-complete theory, then it is shown that such theory has a canonical model. In the case of modal propositional logic, the canonical model is constructed by defining the set of worlds as a set of sets of atomic formulas of L_m, so that α turns out true in w if and only if $\alpha \in w$. In the case of modal predicate logic, instead, it is constructed by defining the set of worlds as a set of sets of atomic formulas of L_{qm} and the domain as a set of terms of L_{qm}.[12]

Exercises

20.1 Formalize in L_m the following sentences:

(a) If God exists, its existence is necessary
(b) If God does not exist, its non-existence is not necessary
(c) Necessarily, if God exists, then he exists

20.2 In the early Middle Ages, some philosophers discussed the issue of whether God's foreknowledge is compatible with human freedom. In particular, Augustine and Boethius considered the following argument:

> If God has foreknowledge that a man will do x, then it is necessary that he will do x. If it is necessary that a man will do x, then he is not free with respect to doing x. Therefore, if God has foreknowledge that a man will do x, the man is not free with respect to doing x.

---

[12]Hughes and Cresswell [27], pp. 111–124 and 256–265, provide a detailed exposition of these completeness results.

Aquinas suggested that this argument is flawed, in that its first premise hides an ambiguity between *necessitas consequentiae* and *necessitas consequentis*. Spell out Aquinas' point by formalizing the argument in L_m.[13]

20.3 Explain why $\Box\alpha$ is valid if α is a tautology.

20.4 Does the conclusion of this argument logically follow from its premise?

Necessarily, God exists. Therefore, God exists.

20.5 How does the semantics of L_m account for the apparent validity of the argument considered in Exercise 20.4?

20.6 Can the apparent validity of the argument considered in Exercise 20.4 be explained in terms of derivability in **K**?

20.7 Can the apparent validity of the argument considered in Exercise 20.4 be explained in terms of derivability in **T**?

20.8 The sentence 'Bachelors are necessarily unmarried' admits two readings, one *de dicto*, the other *de re*. Provide two formulas of L_{qm} that display these two readings.

20.9 The sentence 'The number of the planets is necessarily odd' admits two readings, one *de dicto*, the other *de re*. Assuming that L_{qm} is enriched by adding the symbol $=$, provide two formulas that display these two readings.

20.10 Does 'Some rich could be poor' admit only two readings?

---

[13] Aquinas, *Summa contra gentiles* I, 67, 10.

Solutions

Chapter 1

1.1 The butler is not the murderer.

1.2 Yes. Just as there are sentences that nobody has ever uttered or thought (because they are useless, or too long, or clearly false), there are sets of sentences that nobody has ever uttered or thought.

1.3

(1)	If I'm innocent, I will appear before the judges
(2)	I will appear before the judges
(3)	I'm innocent

1.4

(1)	If I will appear before the judges, I'm guilty
(2)	I will not appear before the judges
(3)	I'm not guilty

1.5 You didn't come to my aunt's dinner.

1.6 He is not a surfer

1.7

(1)	Either you taught me to persuade anyone of anything or you didn't
(2)	If you did, I don't have to pay
(3)	If you didn't, I don't have to pay
(4)	I don't have to pay

1.8 Yes. The definition of argument does not rule out this possibility.

1.9 There are two arguments.

© The Author(s), under exclusive license to Springer Nature Switzerland AG 2021
A. Iacona, *LOGIC: Lecture Notes for Philosophy, Mathematics, and Computer Science*, Springer Undergraduate Texts in Philosophy,
https://doi.org/10.1007/978-3-030-64811-4

1.10 (a) and (b) are lexically ambiguous because 'end' can be read both as 'goal' and as 'last event'. (a) may true on the first reading, but it is definitely false on the second. (b) is trivially true on the second reading, but false on the first.

Chapter 2

2.1 Yes.

2.2 No.

2.3 Yes.

2.4 Yes.

2.5 Yes. An example is the set whose only element is 'Everything is red and not red'

2.6 (a) entails (b).

2.7 Yes.

2.8 In that case $\emptyset$ entails $\sim\alpha$. Since it is impossible that α is true, given the inconsistency of Δ, it is impossible that $\sim\alpha$ is false.

2.9 Socrates' attack may be phrased as an argument whose first premise is (1) as understood by Thrasymachus: the just is the advantage of the stronger$_1$. In this case Socrates does not commit the fallacy of *ignoratio elenchi*. But since 'strong' is understood as 'physically strong' in (2), the argument equivocates on the meaning of 'strong'.

2.10 *Prima facie*, the argument seems to be the following:

    (1)   The student told me that I am her favourite professor

    (2)   No student would lie to her favourite professor

    (3)   The student told the truth

This argument is invalid, for (1) and (2) may be true even if (3) is false: imagine Jane, the student, telling Smith that she is her favourite professor, when in reality Jane's favourite professor is Jones, to whom she never lies. Why does the professor suggest instead that the principle applies? The answer is that the professor takes for granted an additional premise, which indeed makes the argument valid, that is, 'I am the student's favourite professor'. But since the added premise is the conclusion that the professor wants to draw in the first place, the argument evidently begs the question. So the text hides a *petitio principii*.

Chapter 3

3.1 Exercise 1.3: affirming the consequent; Exercise 1.4: denying the antecedent.

3.2 (b) and (c).

3.3 Yes. The second set does not contain 1. It contains the set that has 1 as its only element.

3.4 Yes. $\emptyset \subseteq \emptyset$.

3.5 No.

3.6 (a) $\{1, 2, 3\}$; (b) $\{1, 2, 3\}$; (c) $\{\{1\}, 1, 2, 3\}$.

3.7 (b).

3.8 None.

3.9 Yes. Assume that A and B are both denumerable. Consider an enumeration $\langle a_1, a_2, a_3, \ldots \rangle$ of A and an enumeration $\langle b_1, b_2, b_3, \ldots \rangle$ of B. We can associate a_1 to 0, a_2 to 2, a_3 to 4, and so on. Similarly, we can associate b_1 to 1, b_2 to 3, b_3 to 5, and so on. Consequently, there is a one-to-one function that maps $A \cup B$ onto $\mathbb{N}$, the function that associates a_1 to 0, b_1 to 1, a_2 to 2, and so on.

3.10 Yes. Assume that A is denumerable and B is countable. If B is denumerable, then $A \cup B$ is denumerable (see Exercise 3.9). If B is finite, hence contains n elements for some n, each of the elements of $A \cup B$ can be associated with one and only one natural number by assigning the first n natural numbers to the elements of B and continuing with the elements of A from $n + 1$ on.

Chapter 4

4.1 Yes.

4.2 (a) $\sim p \vee q$; (b) $\sim(p \vee q)$.

4.3 $\sim(p \wedge q)$

4.4 (a) p; (b) $\sim p \supset p$.

4.5 They realize the same truth function because the value of $\sim p \supset p$ is 1 when p has value 1, and it is 0 when p is 0.

4.6 Yes, given that $\{\sim, \supset, \wedge, \vee\}$ is adequate.

4.7 (a),(b),(c): If it is raining, it is not cold.

4.8 Exercise 4.1: (a) $p \supset q$, (b) $\sim q \supset \sim p$. Exercise 4.7: (a)–(c) $p \supset \sim q$ ($p =$ It is raining, $q =$ It is cold).

4.9 $p \vee \sim p, p \supset \sim q, \sim p \supset \sim q / \sim q$ ($p =$ You taught me to persuade anyone of anything, $q =$ I have to pay).

4.10 $p \supset q, r \supset \sim q / \sim p \vee \sim r$ ($p =$ I have 3 euros, $q =$ I can buy an ice cream, $r =$ The ice cream shop is closed)

Chapter 5

5.1 (a) No; (b) No; (c) Yes.

5.2 None of the operations stated in clauses 2–5 of Definition 5.1 allows the addition of a single bracket, left or right: either brackets are not required, or they are added in matched pairs.

5.3 No. Each formula has a unique tree, because the syntax of L leaves no room for ambiguity.

5.4 $p \vee \sim q$

5.5 $\vee$

5.6 (a) 1; (b) 1; (c) 0.

5.7 (a)

p	$\sim\sim p$
1	1
0	0

(b)

p	q	$\sim q \supset \sim p$
1	1	1
1	0	0
0	1	1
0	0	1

(c)

p	q	$\sim p \vee q$
1	1	1
1	0	0
0	1	1
0	0	1

5.8 Of course: *any* assignment of values to the sentence letters is an interpretation.

5.9 No. For any sentence letter α, there is some interpretation V such that $[\alpha]_V = 0$.

5.10 No. For any interpretation V and any formula α such that V verifies α, there is another formula $\sim\alpha$ such that V falsifies $\sim\alpha$, given that $[\alpha]_V = 1$ iff $[\sim\alpha]_V = 0$.

Chapter 6

6.1 No. Every atomic formula is verified by some interpretation.

6.2 If $\alpha \vDash \beta$, then no interpretation falsifies $\alpha \supset \beta$, which means that $\alpha \supset \beta$ is a tautology. Inversely, if $\alpha \supset \beta$ is a tautology, then $\alpha \vDash \beta$, because there is no interpretation that verifies α but falsifies β.

6.3

p	q	$p \supset q$	q	p
1	1	1	1	1
1	0	0	0	1
0	1	1	1	0
0	0	1	0	0

p	q	$p \supset q$	$\sim p$	$\sim q$
1	1	1	0	0
1	0	0	0	1
0	1	1	1	0
0	0	1	1	1

6.4 Following the formalization provided in Exercise 4.3, the following table shows that $p \vee \sim p, p \supset \sim q, \sim p \supset \sim q \vDash \sim q$.

p	q	$p \vee \sim p$	$p \supset \sim q$	$\sim p \supset \sim q$	$\sim q$
1	1	1	0	1	0
1	0	1	1	1	1
0	1	1	1	0	0
0	0	1	1	1	1

6.5 (a)

p	$p \supset p$
1	1
0	1

(b)

p	$\sim(p \wedge \sim p)$
1	1
0	1

(c)

p	$(p \vee \sim p)$
1	1
0	1

6.6 (a)

p	$p \wedge p$
1	1
0	0

(b)

p	$p \vee p$
1	1
0	0

(c)

p	q	$p \wedge q$	$q \wedge p$
1	1	1	1
1	0	0	0
0	1	0	0
0	0	0	0

(d)

p	q	$p \vee q$	$q \vee p$
1	1	1	1
1	0	1	1
0	1	1	1
0	0	0	0

6.7

p	q	$\sim(p \vee q)$	$\sim p \wedge \sim q$
1	1	0	0
1	0	0	0
0	1	0	0
0	0	1	1

p	q	$\sim(p \wedge q)$	$\sim p \vee \sim q$
1	1	0	0
1	0	1	1
0	1	1	1
0	0	1	.1

p	q	$p \supset q$	$\sim q \supset \sim p$
1	1	1	1
1	0	0	0
0	1	1	1
0	0	1	1

p	q	r	$(p \wedge q) \supset r$	$p \supset (q \supset r)$
1	1	1	1	1
1	1	0	0	0
1	0	1	1	1
1	0	0	1	1
0	1	1	1	1
0	1	0	1	1
0	0	1	1	1
0	0	0	1	1

6.8 This follows from Exercise 6.2 and the meaning of $\equiv$.

6.9 If α and β are contradictory, no interpretation verifies $\alpha \wedge \beta$. So there is no interpretation that falsifies $\sim(\alpha \wedge \beta)$.

6.10 Yes. Transitivity follows from Cut, as explained in Sect. 2.5.

Chapter 7

7.1

1	(1)	p	A
2	(2)	$\sim p$	A
3	(3)	$\sim q$	A
1,2	(4)	$\sim\sim q$	I$\sim$ 3,1,2
1,2	(5)	q	E$\sim$ 4

7.2

1	(1)	$p \supset (p \supset q)$	A
2	(2)	p	A
1,2	(3)	$p \supset q$	E$\supset$ 1,2
1,2	(4)	q	E$\supset$ 3,2
1	(5)	$p \supset q$	I$\supset$ 2,4

7.3

1	(1)	$p \supset q$	A
2	(2)	$p \supset {\sim}q$	A
3	(3)	p	A
1,3	(4)	q	E$\supset$ 1,3
2,3	(5)	${\sim}q$	E$\supset$ 2,3
1,2	(6)	${\sim}p$	I${\sim}$ 3,4,5

7.4

1	(1)	${\sim}p \supset p$	A
2	(2)	${\sim}p$	A
1,2	(3)	p	E$\supset$ 1,2
1	(4)	${\sim}{\sim}p$	I${\sim}$ 2,3,2
1	(5)	p	E${\sim}$ 4

7.5

1	(1)	$p \wedge q$	A
1	(2)	p	E$\wedge$ 1
1	(3)	q	E$\wedge$ 1
1	(4)	$q \wedge p$	I$\wedge$ 3,2

7.6

1	(1)	$p \wedge q$	A
2	(2)	$p \supset {\sim}q$	A
1	(3)	p	E$\wedge$ 1
1,2	(4)	${\sim}q$	E$\supset$ 2,3
1	(5)	q	E$\wedge$ 1
1	(6)	${\sim}(p \supset {\sim}q)$	I${\sim}$ 2,5,4

7.7

1	(1)	$p \vee q$	A
2	(2)	p	A
2	(3)	$q \vee p$	I$\vee$ 2
4	(4)	q	A
4	(5)	$q \vee p$	I$\vee$ 4
1	(6)	$q \vee p$	E$\vee$ 1,2,3,4,5

7.8

1	(1)	$p \vee q$	A
2	(2)	$\sim p$	A
3	(3)	p	A
4	(4)	$\sim q$	A
2,3	(5)	$\sim\sim q$	I$\sim$ 4,3,2
2,3	(6)	q	E$\sim$ 5
7	(7)	q	A
1,2	(8)	q	E$\vee$ 1,3,6,7,7

7.9

1	(1)	$(p \vee r) \supset q$	A
2	(2)	p	A
2	(3)	$p \vee r$	I$\vee$ 2
1,2	(4)	q	E$\supset$ 1,3
1	(5)	$p \supset q$	I$\supset$ 2,4
6	(6)	r	A
6	(7)	$p \vee r$	I$\vee$ 6
1,6	(8)	q	E$\supset$ 1,7
1	(9)	$r \supset q$	I$\supset$ 6,8
1	(10)	$(p \supset q) \wedge (r \supset q)$	I$\wedge$ 5,9

7.10

1	(1)	$(p \supset q) \wedge (r \supset q)$	A
2	(2)	$p \vee r$	A
3	(3)	p	A
1	(4)	$p \supset q$	E$\wedge$ 1
1,3	(5)	q	E$\supset$ 4,3
6	(6)	r	A
1	(7)	$r \supset q$	E$\wedge$ 1
1,6	(8)	q	E$\supset$ 7,6
1,2	(9)	q	E$\vee$ 2,3,5,6,8
1	(10)	$(p \vee r) \supset q$	I$\supset$ 2,9

Chapter 8

8.1

1	(1)	$p \vee \sim p$	A
2	(2)	$p \supset \sim q$	A
3	(3)	$\sim p \supset \sim q$	A
4	(4)	p	A
2,4	(5)	$\sim q$	E$\supset$ 2,4
6	(6)	$\sim p$	A
3,6	(7)	$\sim q$	E$\supset$ 3,6
1,2,3	(8)	$\sim q$	E$\vee$ 1,4,5,6,7

8.2 (a)

1	(1)	$p \wedge \sim p$	A
1	(2)	p	E$\wedge$ 1
1	(3)	$\sim p$	E$\wedge$ 1
	(4)	$\sim(p \wedge \sim p)$	I$\sim$ 1,2,3

(b)

1	(1)	$\sim(p \vee \sim p)$	A
2	(2)	p	A
2	(3)	$p \vee \sim p$	I$\vee$ 2
1	(4)	$\sim p$	I$\sim$ 2,3,1
1	(5)	$p \vee \sim p$	I$\vee$ 4
	(6)	$\sim\sim(p \vee \sim p)$	I$\sim$ 1,5,1
	(7)	$p \vee \sim p$	E$\sim$ 6

8.3 (a) is Exportation, the principle verified in Exercise 6.7. (b) and (c) are verified in Exercise 6.6. For (d) see Exercise 5.7. The truth table for (e) is the following:

p	q	r	$(p \supset q) \wedge (r \supset q)$	$(p \vee r) \supset q$
1	1	1	1	1
1	1	0	1	1
1	0	1	0	0
1	0	0	0	0
0	1	1	1	1
0	1	0	1	1
0	0	1	0	0
0	0	0	1	1

8.4 To derive p from $p \wedge p$ it suffices to use E$\wedge$, and to derive $p \wedge p$ from p it suffices to use I$\wedge$.

8.5

1	(1)	p	A
2	(2)	$\sim p$	A
1	(3)	$\sim p \supset p$	I$\supset$ 2,1
1	(1)	$\sim p \supset p$	A
2	(2)	$\sim p$	A
1,2	(3)	p	E$\supset$ 1,2
1	(4)	$\sim\sim p$	I$\sim$ 2,3,2
1	(5)	p	E$\sim$ 4

8.6 The proof is like that of Theorem 8.5, replacing α with $\sim\alpha$.

8.7 (a)

1	(1)	$p \vee q$	A
2	(2)	$\sim p \wedge \sim q$	A
3	(3)	p	A
2	(4)	$\sim p$	E$\wedge$ 2
3	(5)	$\sim(\sim p \wedge \sim q)$	I$\sim$ 2,3,4
6	(6)	q	A
2	(7)	$\sim q$	E$\wedge$ 2
6	(8)	$\sim(\sim p \wedge \sim q)$	I$\sim$ 2,6,7
1	(9)	$\sim(\sim p \wedge \sim q)$	E$\vee$ 1,3,5,6,8

(b)

1	(1)	$\sim(\sim p \wedge \sim q)$	A
2	(2)	$\sim(p \vee q)$	A
3	(3)	p	A
3	(4)	$p \vee q$	I$\vee$ 3
2	(5)	$\sim p$	I$\sim$ 3,4,2
6	(6)	q	A
6	(7)	$p \vee q$	I$\vee$ 6
2	(8)	$\sim q$	I$\sim$ 6,7,2
2	(9)	$\sim p \wedge \sim q$	I$\wedge$ 5,8
1	(10)	$\sim\sim(p \vee q)$	I$\sim$ 2,9,1
1	(11)	$p \vee q$	E$\sim$ 10

(c)

1	(1)	$p \wedge q$	A
2	(2)	$\sim p \vee \sim q$	A
3	(3)	$\sim p$	A
1	(4)	p	E$\wedge$ 1
1,3	(5)	$\sim(\sim p \vee \sim q)$	I$\sim$ 2,4,3
7	(6)	$\sim q$	A
1	(7)	q	E$\wedge$ 1
1,7	(8)	$\sim(\sim p \vee \sim q)$	I$\sim$ 2,7,6
1,2	(9)	$\sim(\sim p \vee \sim q)$	E$\vee$ 2,3,5,6,8
1	(10)	$\sim(\sim p \vee \sim q)$	I$\sim$ 2,2,9

(d)

1	(1)	$\sim(\sim p \vee \sim q)$	A
2	(2)	$\sim p$	A
2	(3)	$\sim p \vee \sim q$	I$\vee$ 2
1	(4)	$\sim\sim p$	I$\sim$ 2,3,1
1	(5)	p	E$\sim$ 4
6	(6)	$\sim q$	A
6	(7)	$\sim p \vee \sim q$	I$\vee$ 6
1	(8)	$\sim\sim q$	I$\sim$ 6,7,1
1	(9)	q	E$\sim$ 8
1	(10)	$p \wedge q$	I$\wedge$ 5,9

8.8 To derive $\sim(p \vee q)$ from $\sim p \wedge \sim q$ one can use I$\sim$. For assuming $p \vee q$ one gets $\sim(\sim p \wedge \sim q)$, as is shown in Exercise 8.7 (a). To derive $\sim p \wedge \sim q$ from $\sim(p \vee q)$, one can use I$\sim$ and E$\sim$. For assuming $\sim(\sim p \wedge \sim q)$ one gets $p \vee q$, as is shown in Exercise 8.7 (b). By means of similar derivations one can prove $\sim(p \wedge q) \dashv\vdash \sim p \vee \sim q$, taking into account Exercise 8.7 (c) and (d).

8.9 Yes. See Exercise 8.7 (a).

8.10 An inductive definition of the set of formula of L^- is constituted by clauses 1–3 of Definition 5.1.

Chapter 9

9.1 Let d be derivation of γ from α and β and let d' be a derivation of δ from α and γ. If one eliminates from d' the assumptions α and γ and one adds the remaining part of d' to d, one gets a derivation that includes α and β as assumptions and ends with δ.

9.2 A1

1	(1)	α	A
2	(2)	β	A
1	(3)	$\beta \supset \alpha$	I$\supset$ 2,1
	(4)	$\alpha \supset (\beta \supset \alpha)$	I$\supset$ 1,3

A2

1	(1)	$\alpha \supset (\beta \supset \gamma)$	A
2	(2)	$\alpha \supset \beta$	A
3	(3)	α	A
1,3	(4)	$\beta \supset \gamma$	E$\supset$ 1,3
2,3	(5)	β	E$\supset$ 2,3
1,2,3	(6)	γ	E$\supset$ 4,5
1,2	(7)	$\alpha \supset \gamma$	I$\supset$ 3,6
1	(8)	$(\alpha \supset \beta) \supset (\alpha \supset \gamma)$	I$\supset$ 2,7
	(9)	$(\alpha \supset (\beta \supset \gamma)) \supset ((\alpha \supset \beta) \supset (\alpha \supset \gamma))$	I$\supset$ 1,8

A3

1	(1)	$\sim\alpha \supset \sim\beta$	A
2	(2)	β	A
3	(3)	$\sim\alpha$	A
1,3	(4)	$\sim\beta$	E$\supset$ 1,3
1,2	(5)	$\sim\sim\alpha$	I$\sim$ 3,2,4
1,2	(6)	α	E$\sim$ 5
1	(7)	$\beta \supset \alpha$	I$\supset$ 2,6
	(8)	$(\sim\alpha \supset \sim\beta) \supset (\beta \supset \alpha)$	I$\supset$ 1,7

9.3 Yes, because $\mathbf{G}^-$ includes I$\supset$. Given any derivation of β from $\Gamma \cup \{\alpha\}$, to obtain a derivation of $\alpha \supset \beta$ from Γ it suffices to add α as an assumption (in case it is not already there) and derive $\alpha \supset \beta$ by means of I$\supset$.

9.4 Like the proof of theorem 9.22, replacing α with $\sim\alpha$ and using SE.

9.5 The left-to-right direction of the biconditional holds because if $\vdash \alpha \supset \beta$, then β is derivable from α by means of MP. The right-to-left direction is given by the deduction theorem (Theorem 9.8).

9.6 This follows from Exercise 9.5 and the meaning of $\equiv$.

9.7

(1)	$\vdash \sim\alpha \supset (\alpha \supset \beta)$	T 9.10
(2)	$\vdash \sim(\alpha \supset \beta) \supset \sim\sim\alpha$	SE 1
(3)	$\vdash \sim(\alpha \supset \beta) \supset \alpha$	SE 2

(1)	$\vdash \beta \supset (\alpha \supset \beta)$	A1
(2)	$\vdash \sim(\alpha \supset \beta) \supset \sim\beta$	SE 1

9.8 From Theorem 8.5 and Exercise 8.6 we know that the two biconditionals hold for $\mathbf{G}^-$. Since $\mathbf{L}$ is deductively equivalent to $\mathbf{G}^-$, the same biconditionals hold for $\mathbf{L}$.

9.9 A derivation is a finite sequence of formulas. So, if there is a derivation of α from Γ, there is a derivation of α from a finite subset Δ of Γ. The converse conditional holds by Monotonicity.

9.10 Let Γ be a set of formulas, and let Δ be the deductive closure of Γ. Suppose that Δ is inconsistent. Then for some α, both α and $\sim\alpha$ are derivable from Δ. Since Δ is deductively closed, this means that $\alpha \in \Delta$ and $\sim\alpha \in \Delta$. But Δ contains exactly the formulas that are derivable from Γ. So α and $\sim\alpha$ are derivable from Γ, which means that Γ is inconsistent.

Chapter 10

10.1 Suppose that S is consistent. Then any two formulas α and $\sim\alpha$ are such that at least one of them is not provable in S.

10.2 Suppose that S is inconsistent. Then α and $\sim\alpha$ are theorems of S for some α. But from $\{\alpha, \sim\alpha\}$ we can derive any formula, provided that Explosion holds in S.

10.3 Suppose that T is consistent and negation-complete. Then, for any α such that $\alpha \notin T$, we have that $\sim\alpha \in T$. So α cannot consistently be added to T.

10.4 Assume that T is maximally consistent. Then T is consistent by definition. To see that T is negation-complete, suppose that $\alpha \in/ T$ and $\sim\alpha \in/ T$. Then, $T \cup \{\alpha\}$ and $T \cup \{\sim\alpha\}$ are inconsistent. By Theorem 9.29, we get that $T \vdash \sim\alpha$ and $T \vdash \sim\sim\alpha$, which means that T is inconsistent.

10.5 No. For example, neither p nor $\sim p$ is a theorem of **L**.

10.6 Same as above.

10.7 Yes. The set of valid formulas of **L** is decidable for the reason explained in Sect. 6.5, that is, we have the truth tables.

10.8 Yes. Since **L** is sound and complete, the set of theorems of **L** is identical to the set of valid formulas of **L**.

10.9 Yes. Since **L** and **G**$^-$ are deductively equivalent, the set of theorems of **G**$^-$ is identical to the set of theorems of **L**.

10.10 Without assuming the biconditional as induction hypothesis it would be impossible to complete the two cases of the induction step.

Chapter 11

11.1 For every x, if x is demonstrable, x's contrary is contradictory. For every x, if x is distinctly conceivable, x is not contradictory. For every x, if x is conceived as existent, x can be conceived as non-existent. For every x, if x exists, x's non-existence is not contradictory. For every x, if x exists, x's existence is not demonstrable.

11.2 (1) For every x, if x is distinctly conceivable, x is not contradictory
    (2) For every x, if x is conceived as existent, x can be conceived as non-existent
    (3) For every x, if x exists, x's non-existence is not contradictory 1,2
    (4) For every x, if x is demonstrable, x's contrary is contradictory
    (5) For every x, if x exists, x's existence is not demonstrable 3,4

11.3 (a) For every x, if x is a whale, x is a mammal.
    (b) For every x, if x makes silly jokes, x is silly.
    (c) For every x, if x is a cat, x does not like swimming.

11.4 For every x, x is identical to x.

11.5 (a) For every x, if x is a man and x is happy, there is a y such that y is a shirt of x and y suits x.
    (b) There is an x such that x is a dog and, for every y, if y is a cat, x likes y.
    (c) For every x and every y, there is a z such that y loves z, x loves y.

11.6 (a) For every x, if Sophie eats x, x is a vegetable and x is pesticide-free.
    For every x, if Sophie eats x and x is a vegetable, x is pesticide-free.

    (b) For every x such that x is a pw, if Astrid gives 100 euro to x, x is happy.
    For every x such that x is a pw, if Astrid gives 100 euro to x, Astrid is happy.

    (c) For every x, if x is a nn, there is y such that y is a nn and $y > x$.
    There is x such that x is a nn and, for every y, if y is a nn, $x > y$.

11.7 If 'The capital of Italy is charming' is paraphrased in the way explained, it is easy to see how the first argument can be treated as formally valid, given that its premise clearly entails that there is an x such that x is capital of Italy and x is charming. The same does not hold for the second argument.

11.8 (a) There is an x such that x is an abominable snowman, and for every y such that y is an abominable snowman, $y = x$, and x is hairy.
    (b) There is no x such that x is an abominable snowman and, for every y such that y is an abominable snowman, $y = x$.

11.9 The sentence can be understood in two ways. One is: there is an x such that x is king of France, and no y other than x is king of France, and x is not bald. The other is: there is no x such that x is king of France, and no y other than x is king of France, and x is bald.

11.10 It is not a real identity statement because 'the author of *Waverley*' is not really a singular term. What the sentence says is that, for some x, x is author of *Waverley*, and for every y, if y is author of *Waverley*, $y = x$, and x is Scott.

Chapter 12

12.1 (a) Ldo; (b) Lod (L = loves, d = Desdemona, o = Othello).
12.2 No.
12.3 (a) $\forall x \sim Mx$; (b) $\forall x Mx \supset \forall x \sim Sx$; (c) $\sim \forall x Mx \supset \sim \forall x \sim Sx$ (M = material, S = spiritual).
12.4 (a) $\forall x(Px \supset \sim Rx)$; (b) $\sim \forall x(Px \supset Wx)$; (c) $\forall x(Wx \supset Px)$
(P = philosopher, R = rich, W = wise).
12.5 (b) $\forall x Mx \supset \sim \exists x Sx$, (c) $\sim \forall x Mx \supset \exists x Sx$.
12.6 (a) $\sim \exists x(Px \wedge Rx)$; (b) $\exists x(Px \wedge \sim Wx)$.
12.7 (a) $\exists x Kxd$; (b) $\exists x Kox$; (c) Koo (d = Desdemona, o = Othello, K = killed).
12.8

$\exists x(Kx \wedge \forall y(Ky \supset y = x) \wedge \sim Bx)$
$\sim \exists x(Kx \wedge \forall y(Ky \supset y = x) \wedge Bx)$
(K = king of France, B = bald)
12.9 (a) $\forall x((Mx \wedge Hx) \supset \exists y(Syx \wedge Uyx))$
(M = man, H = happy, S = shirt of, U = suits)
(b) $\exists x(Dx \wedge \forall y(Cy \supset Lxy))$
(D = dog, C = cat, L = likes)
(c) $\forall x \forall y(\exists z Lyz \supset Lxy)$
(L = loves)
$\forall x(Esx \supset (Vx \wedge Px))$
12.10 (a) $\forall x((Esx \wedge Vx) \supset Px)$
(E = eats, s = Sophie, V = vegetable, P = pesticide-free)
$\forall x((Px \wedge Gax) \supset Hx)$
(b) $\forall x((Px \wedge Gax) \supset Ha)$
(G = gives 100 euros to, a = Astrid, P = poor woman, H = happy)
$\forall x(Nx \supset \exists y(Ny \wedge Gyx))$
(c) $\exists x(Nx \wedge \forall y(Ny \supset Gxy))$
(N = natural number, G = greater than)

Chapter 13

13.1 Yes. L_q has denumerably many predicate letters, denumerably many individual constants, denumerably many variables, and a finite set of connectives and auxiliary symbols. The union of two denumerable sets is denumerable (see Exercise 3.9), and the union of a denumerable set and a countable set is denumerable (see Exercise 3.10).
13.2 (a) Yes; (b) Yes; (c) Yes.

13.3 Yes. It suffices to apply Definition 13.1 to decide, for any finite sequence of symbols of L_q, whether or not it is a formula of L_q.

13.4 Suppose that α is satisfied by all assignments in $\mathcal{M}$. Then for any σ, α is satisfied by every x-variant of σ. Consequently, $\forall x\alpha$ is satisfied by σ. The converse conditional directly follows from Theorem 13.4.

13.5 By clause 3 of Definition 13.7, any assignment satisfies $Px \supset Px$, no matter whether it satisfies Px. So $\forall x(Px \supset Px)$ is satisfied by all assignments in every model.

13.6 (a) follows from Theorem 13.5. To see that (b) holds, assume that σ satisfies Lab. Then, some z-variant of σ fails to satisfy $\sim Laz$. This entails that σ does not satisfy $\forall z\sim Laz$, hence that σ satisfies $\sim\forall z\sim Laz$. (c) holds because if σ satisfies the first two formulas, then every y-variant of σ satisfies $\sim\forall z\sim Laz \supset Lya$ and $\sim\forall z\sim Laz$, hence Lya by Theorem 13.3. It follows that σ satisfies $\forall y Lya$.

13.7 The argument is formalized as $Ps/\exists x Px$, that is, as $Ps/\sim\forall x\sim Px$. To see that $Ps \vDash \sim\forall x\sim Px$, suppose that σ does not satisfy $\sim\forall x\sim Px$. Then σ satisfies $\forall x\sim Px$. So every x-variant of σ satisfies $\sim Px$, which means that every x-variant of σ does not satisfy Px. This is to say that no assignment satisfies Ps, so that σ does not satisfy Ps.

13.8 It suffices to describe a model whose domains contain four objects, two sailors s_1, s_2 and two girls g_1, g_2, and where R (understood as 'love') holds exclusively between s_1 and g_1 and between s_2 and g_2.

13.9 The two sentences are formalized as $\forall x\exists y Ryx$ and $\exists x\forall y Rxy$, that is, as $\forall x\sim\forall y\sim Ryz$ and $\sim\forall x\sim\forall y Rxy$, where R stands for 'is a cause of'. But we saw that $\forall x\sim\forall y\sim Ryx \nvDash \sim\forall x\sim\forall y Rxy$ (see Exercise 13.8).

13.10 Yes. The form of this argument is $\forall x\forall y(\exists z Lxz \supset Lyx), Lab/\forall y Lyb$, which is equivalent to $\forall x\forall y(\sim\forall z\sim Lxz \supset Lyx), Lab/\forall y Lyb$. From Exercise 13.6 we get what follows:

(a) $\forall x\forall y(\sim\forall z\sim Lxz \supset Lyx) \vDash \forall y(\sim\forall z\sim Laz \supset Lya)$

(b) $Lab \vDash \sim\forall z\sim Laz$

(c) $\forall y(\sim\forall z\sim Laz \supset Lya), \sim\forall z\sim Laz \vDash \forall y Lya$

Therefore, $\forall x\forall y(\sim\forall z\sim Lxz \supset Lyx), Lab \vDash \forall y Lya$. Moreover, $\forall y Lya \vDash Lba$ by Theorem 13.5. Now we can apply the same kind of reasoning, by replacing a with b and b with a in (a)-(c) above. So we get $\forall y Lyb$.

Chapter 14

14.1 (a) α; (b) α. Note that (b) holds only on the assumption that x is substitutable for y in α. For example, if α were $\forall x Py$—so that x were *not* substitutable for y in α—we would get that $(\alpha)_y^x = \forall x Px$, and consequently that $((\alpha)_y^x)_x^y = \forall x Px$.

14.2 $(\alpha)^y_x$. Note that, in $((\alpha)^a_x)^y_a$, the individual constant a occurs the second time as a term to be replaced. This is nothing but a generalization of the notation adopted for A4.

14.3 The proof of theorem 14.18 is as follows. Assume that $\Gamma \cup \{\alpha\} \vdash \beta$ and $\Gamma \cup \{\alpha\} \vdash \sim\beta$ for some β. By the deduction theorem (Theorem 14.7) it follows that $\Gamma \vdash \alpha \supset \beta$ and $\Gamma \vdash \alpha \supset \sim\beta$. By Theorem 14.13 we get that $\vdash (\alpha \supset \beta) \supset ((\alpha \supset \sim\beta) \supset \sim\alpha)$, so $\Gamma \vdash \sim\alpha$. Now assume that $\Gamma \vdash \sim\alpha$. Then $\Gamma \cup \{\alpha\} \vdash \sim\alpha$. But since $\alpha \in \Gamma \cup \{\alpha\}$, we also get that $\Gamma \cup \{\alpha\} \vdash \alpha$. Therefore, $\Gamma \cup \{\alpha\}$ is inconsistent. The proof of theorem 14.19 is similar, but switching α and $\sim\alpha$, and using Theorem 14.14 instead of Theorem 14.13.

14.4 Yes. First, the language of **Q** is decidable (see Exercise 13.4). Second, the set of its axioms is decidable: for every formula of **Q**, we can check mechanically whether it instantiates A1–A7. Third, the set of the derivations in **Q** is decidable: for any finite sequence of formulas of **Q**, we can check mechanically whether it satisfies Definition 14.1.

14.5 The proof is like that of Theorem 9.31.

14.6 Consider any β_i where $1 \leq i \leq n$. If $\beta_i \in \Gamma$, by hypothesis a does not occur in β_i, so $(\beta_i)^x_a = \beta_i$. If β_i is an axiom, $(\beta_i)^x_a$ is an axiom as well, as is easy to verify. Finally, if β_i is obtained by means of MP from two formulas $\beta_k \supset \beta_i$ and β_k, also $(\beta_i)^x_a$ is obtained from two formulas $(\beta_k \supset \beta_i)^x_a$ and $(\beta_k)^x_a$, where $(\beta_k \supset \beta_i)^x_a = (\beta_k)^x_a \supset (\beta_i)^x_a$.

14.7 Suppose that $\beta_1, \ldots, \beta_n$ is a derivation of α from Γ and a does not occur in Γ. From the solution of Exercise 14.6 we get that there is a derivation of $(\beta_n)^x_a$ from Γ. More precisely, there is a derivation of $(\beta_n)^x_a$ from a subset Δ of Γ which contains exactly the formulas of Γ used in $(\beta_1)^x_a, \ldots, (\beta_n)^x_a$. Since x does not occur in Δ, by the generalization theorem (Theorem 14.6) we get that $\Delta \vdash \forall x (\alpha)^x_a$. So there is a derivation of $\forall x (\alpha)^x_a$ from Δ in which a does not occur. The same sequence of formulas is a derivation of $\forall x (\alpha)^x_a$ from Γ.

14.8 The solution of Exercise 14.7 shows that, if $\Gamma \vdash (\alpha)^a_x$, then for some variable y that does not occur in $(\alpha)^a_x$, there is derivation of $\forall y ((\alpha)^a_x)^y_a$ from Γ in which a does not occur. Since a does not occur in α, $((\alpha)^a_x)^y_a = (\alpha)^y_x$ (see Exercise 14.2). Therefore, $\Gamma \vdash \forall y (\alpha)^y_x$. Moreover, $\forall y (\alpha)^y_x \supset \alpha$ is an instance of A4, because $((\alpha)^y_x)^x_y = \alpha$ (see Exercise 14.1 (b)). So, $\forall y (\alpha)^y_x \vdash \alpha$. By the generalization theorem (Theorem 14.6) it follows that $\forall y (\alpha)^y_x \vdash \forall x \alpha$. Since $\Gamma \vdash \forall y (\alpha)^y_x$ and $\forall y (\alpha)^y_x \vdash \forall x \alpha$, $\Gamma \vdash \forall x \alpha$.

14.9 Yes. The proof of theorem 10.10 provided in Sect. 10.4 requires Lindenbaum's lemma (Theorem 10.9) and Theorem 9.29. Since **Q** does not differ from **L** as far as the justification of the lemma is concerned, and Theorem 9.29 can be replaced by Theorem 14.18, Theorem 10.10 holds for **Q** as well.

14.10 (a) No; (b) Yes; (c) No.

Chapter 15

15.1 Suppose that the addition makes Γ inconsistent. Then $\Gamma \vdash \alpha$ and $\Gamma \vdash \sim\alpha$ for some α. A derivation of α from Γ is a finite sequence of formulas $\beta_1, \ldots \beta_n$, so it contains a finite number of new individual constants. Let $a_1, \ldots, a_m$ be these constants. Let $x_1, \ldots, x_m$ be distinct variables that do not occur in the derivation. If $\beta'_1, \ldots, \beta'_n$ is the sequence of formulas obtained from $\beta_1, \ldots, \beta_n$ by replacing $a_1, \ldots, a_m$ with $x_1, \ldots, x_m$, it turns out that $\beta'_1, \ldots, \beta'_n$ is a derivation of β'_n from Γ. For given any β_i such that $1 \leq i \leq n$, either $\beta_i \in \Gamma$, or β_i instantiates A1-A7, or β_i follows from two formulas β_k and $\beta_k \supset \beta_i$. In the first case $\beta'_i = \beta_i$, given that no additional individual constant occurs in Γ. In the second case β'_i is an axiom. In the third case there are two formulas β'_k and $(\beta_k \supset \beta_i)'$ that precede β'_i, where $(\beta_k \supset \beta_i)' = \beta'_k \supset \beta'_i$. So β'_i follows from those formulas. A similar reasoning holds for the derivation of $\sim\alpha$. This contradicts the initial hypothesis that Γ is consistent.

15.2 If α' is an alphabetic variant of α, by Theorem 14.17 $\alpha \dashv\vdash \alpha'$. By the soundness theorem (Theorem 15.11) it follows that $\alpha \dashv\vDash \alpha'$.

15.3 It is necessary because it legitimates the use of the lemma (Theorem 13.2) and A4. From the supposition that σ does not satisfy $\forall x \beta$ one could not conclude directly that $T \nvdash \forall x \beta$, because one would have no assurance that t is substitutable for x in β. Instead, the move from β to β' guarantees that the substitutability requirement is satisfied, as it turns out from Theorem 14.17.

15.4 Yes. It is countable because the set of terms of $\mathsf{L_q}$ is denumerable. $\mathsf{L_q}$ has denumerably many individual constants and denumerably many variables, so the set of terms of $\mathsf{L_q}$ is the union of two denumerable sets (see Exercise 3.9).

15.5 No. For example, neither Fa nor $\sim Fa$ is a theorem of $\mathbf{Q}$.

15.6 No. See the example above: Fa can be added to T without making it inconsistent.

15.7 No. Since $\mathbf{Q}$ is sound and complete, the set of its valid formulas and the set of its theorems are the same set.

15.8 Assume that $\Gamma \vDash \alpha$. Then, by the completeness theorem (Theorem 15.14), $\Gamma \vdash \alpha$. From this and Theorem 14.20 it follows that there is a finite subset Δ of Γ such that $\Delta \vdash \alpha$. By the soundness theorem (Theorem 15.11) we get that $\Delta \vDash \alpha$.

15.9 Assume that Γ is unsatisfiable. Then, $\Gamma \vDash \alpha$ and $\Gamma \vDash \sim\alpha$ for some α. By Theorem 15.16 it follows that there is a finite subset Δ of Γ such that $\Delta \vDash \alpha$ and there is a finite subset Δ' of Γ such that $\Delta' \vDash \sim\alpha$. Consequently, $\Delta \cup \Delta' \vDash \alpha$ and $\Delta \cup \Delta' \vDash \sim\alpha$. Since $\Delta \cup \Delta'$ is a finite subset of Γ, there is a finite subset of Γ which is unsatisfiable.

15.10 Assume Theorem 15.15. If $\Gamma \vDash \alpha$, then $\Gamma \cup \{\sim\alpha\}$ is unsatisfiable. So there is a finite subset Δ of $\Gamma \cup \{\sim\alpha\}$ such that Δ is unsatisfiable. From this we get that $\Delta \cup \{\sim\alpha\}$ is unsatisfiable, so that $\Delta \vDash \alpha$. The other direction of the biconditional is given by Exercise 15.9.

Chapter 16

16.1 Yes, provided that the basic code is appropriately defined and the alphabet of L is finite. Otherwise some numbers would have more than one decomposition.

16.2 Yes. Since the set of valid formulas of L⁻ is decidable, it is also effectively enumerable.

16.3 Yes. Again, this follows from the decidability of the set of valid formulas of L⁻.

16.4 Yes.

16.5 No.

16.6 Yes.

16.7 Yes.

16.8 By Theorem 16.2, the set of theorems of S is effectively enumerable. The negation-completeness of S entails that, for every formula α of S, either α or $\sim\alpha$ will turn up at some point in the enumeration of the theorems of S, so there is an effective method to tell whether α is a theorem of S.

16.9 If S is inconsistent, every formula of S is a theorem of S (see Exercise 10.2). Since the set of formulas of S is decidable, this makes S trivially decidable.

16.10 This directly follows from the solution of the previous exercise, given Church's thesis.

Chapter 17

17.1 (a) $\forall x(Wx \supset x = a)$ (W =win this race, a = Alf)
(b) $\forall x \, x \neq n$ (n = Napoleon)
(c) $\forall x(Lxx \supset \forall y \sim Lxy)$ (L =love)

17.2 Suppose that $\{Mx, \sim My\}$ has a model $\mathcal{M}$. Then $[Mx]_\mathcal{M} = 1$ and $[\sim My]_\mathcal{M} = 1$. It follows that $[\forall x Mx]_\mathcal{M} = 1$ and $[\forall y \sim My]_\mathcal{M} = 1$. But $[\forall x Mx]_\mathcal{M} = 1$ iff $[\forall y My]_\mathcal{M} = 1$ (see Exercise 15.2), so we get that $[\forall y My]_\mathcal{M} = 1$ and $[\forall y \sim My]_\mathcal{M} = 1$, which is absurd.

17.3 Let $\mathcal{M}$ be the intended model of T and assume that all the formulas in Γ are true in $\mathcal{M}$. Since the remaining axioms of S+Γ are true in every interpretation of the language of S+Γ, and MP preserves satisfaction, all the theorems of S+Γ are true in $\mathcal{M}$. Now suppose that $\vdash \alpha$ in S+Γ. Then α is true in $\mathcal{M}$. It follows that $\sim\alpha$ is not true in $\mathcal{M}$. Therefore, $\nvdash \sim\alpha$ in S+Γ. The reasoning is analogous to that employed in the consistency proofs considered so far. The only difference is that we use truth in a model rather than validity.

17.4 The first formula can be proved as follows. From A2 we get that $\vdash (x = y \supset (x = x \supset y = x)) \supset ((x = y \supset x = x) \supset (x = y \supset y = x))$. From A9 we get that $\vdash x = y \supset (x = x \supset y = x)$. So, $\vdash (x = y \supset x = x) \supset (x = y \supset y = x)$. Moreover, $\vdash x = y \supset x = x$, for $\vdash x = x \supset (x = y \supset x = x)$

by A1, and $\vdash x = x$ by A4 and A8. So, $\vdash x = y \supset y = x$. By the generalization theorem (Theorem 14.6), then, $\vdash \forall x \forall y (x = y \supset y = x)$. The second formula can be proved as follows. From A9 we get that $\vdash x = y \supset (y = z \supset x = z)$. By the generalization theorem (Theorem 14.6), then, $\vdash \forall x \forall y \forall z (x = y \supset (y = z \supset x = z))$.

17.5 Yes.

17.6 Yes.

17.7 Yes.

17.8 Yes. This simply follows from Exercises 17.5–17.7.

17.9 Yes. The proper axioms of **PA** are true in the intended model of **PA**. This entails that every theorem of **PA** is true in that model, and so that **PA** is consistent (see Exercise 17.3).

17.10 No. Let $\mathcal{M}$ be a normal model such that $M = \{e_0, \ldots, e_n\}$, where e_0 is denoted by the numeral 0. If PA1 is true in $\mathcal{M}$, then any term formed by adding at least one occurrence of s to 0 denotes an object other than e_0. This means that at most $n - 1$ elements of M can be denoted by such terms. But if PA2 is true in $\mathcal{M}$, then for each element e_i of M, there must be a distinct object denoted by the term formed by adding s to the term that denotes e_i. So PA1 and PA2 can't both be true in $\mathcal{M}$.

Chapter 18

18.1 No. This holds only for finite sets.

18.2 Assume that $|A| < |B|$ for every finite A. If B were finite, we would have that $|B| < |B|$, which is impossible.

18.3 No. By definition, an interpretation of the language of a first-order theory includes a non-empty domain.

18.4 Yes. For example, $\mathbf{Q_i}$ admits models of cardinality 1.

18.5 Yes. One example is **PA** (see Exercise 17.10).

18.6 Any model of T must have a domain with exactly one element.

18.7 Yes. A function h such that $h(\text{Colisseum}) = \text{Rome}$, $h(\text{Mole Antonelliana}) = \text{Turin}$, and $h(\text{Holy Spirit}) = \text{Paris}$ is an isomorphism which maps M onto M'.

18.8 Let $\mathcal{M}$ and $\mathcal{M}'$ be two models of T. Since $\mathcal{M}$ and $\mathcal{M}'$ contain exactly one element, there is a one-to-one correspondence between M and M'. Moreover, since T is maximally consistent, every formula has one and the same value in $\mathcal{M}$ and $\mathcal{M}'$. For example, either $\forall x P x$ belongs to T or it doesn't. If it does, then it is true both in $\mathcal{M}$ and in $\mathcal{M}'$, if it doesn't then it is false both in $\mathcal{M}$ and in $\mathcal{M}'$.

18.9 All its models are isomorphic (see Exercise 18.8).

18.10 Since all its models have cardinality 1 and are isomorphic, it is trivially the case that all its models of cardinality 1 are isomorphic.

Chapter 19

19.1 Yes. Completeness does not entail negation-completeness.

19.2 No. For example, neither Fa nor $\sim Fa$ are provable in $\mathbf{Q_i}$.

19.3 Yes. If $\mathbf{PA} \vDash \alpha$, then $\mathbf{PA} \vdash \alpha$. This follows from the completeness of $\mathbf{Q_i}$.

19.4 As explained in Sect. 19.1, it is plausible to assume that any question that can be framed in the language of a theory of arithmetic has a definite answer. Any formula of $\mathbf{PA}$ expresses a statement about numbers, which intuitively is either true or false. This is to say that, for any formula of $\mathbf{PA}$, either the formula itself or its negation expresses a truth of arithmetic. By contrast, it would be wrong to assume that, for any formula of $\mathbf{Q_i}$, either the formula itself or its negation expresses a truth of first-order logic with identity. For example, neither Fa nor $\sim Fa$ express such a truth. The truths of first order logic with identity are the logical truths expressible in $\mathsf{L_{qi}}$, and these are the only truths that we want to be provable in $\mathbf{Q_i}$.

19.5 $\mathbf{PA}$ is recursively axiomatized.

19.6 Because *Prf* and diagonalization are recursively decidable.

19.7 No. The proof simply requires that *Gdl* is expressible in $\mathsf{L_a}$.

19.8 Yes. In this case it is crucial that *Gdl* is representable in $\mathbf{PA}$.

19.9 Yes. Theorem 19.1 shows that G is true in the intended model of $\mathbf{PA}$. However, G is not true in every model of $\mathbf{PA}$. If it were, then it would provable in $\mathbf{PA}$ by the completeness of $\mathbf{PA}$ (see Exercise 19.3). So there are models of $\mathbf{PA}$ in which G is false.

19.10 If there is a model of $\mathbf{PA}$ in which G is false, it is a non-standard model, given that if it were isomorphic to the intended model of $\mathbf{PA}$, it would make G true by Theorem 18.6.

Chapter 20

20.1 (a) $p \supset \Box p$; (b) $\sim p \supset \sim \Box \sim p$; (c) $\Box(p \supset p)$ ($p =$ God exists).

20.2 Let p stand for 'God has foreknowledge that a man will do x', q stand for 'The man will do x', and r stand for 'The man is not free with respect to doing x'. The argument can be formalized either as $p \supset \Box q, \Box q \supset r / p \supset r$ or as $\Box(p \supset q), \Box q \supset r / p \supset r$. In the first case it is valid. Suppose that $[p \supset r]_{\mathcal{M},w} = 0$, so $[p]_{\mathcal{M},w} = 1$ and $[r]_{\mathcal{M},w} = 0$. Then either $[\Box q]_{\mathcal{M},w} = 1$, so $[\Box q \supset r]_{\mathcal{M},w} = 0$, or $[\Box q]_{\mathcal{M},w} = 0$, so $[p \supset \Box q]_{\mathcal{M},w} = 0$. Instead, in the second case it is invalid. Suppose that there are exactly two worlds w and w', both accessible from w, such that $[p]_{\mathcal{M},w} = 1$, $[q]_{\mathcal{M},w} = 1$, $[r]_{\mathcal{M},w} = 0$, $[p]_{\mathcal{M},w'} = 0$, $[q]_{\mathcal{M},w'} = 0$, $[r]_{\mathcal{M},w'} = 1$. In this case $[\Box(p \supset q)]_{\mathcal{M},w} = 1$, $[\Box q \supset r]_{\mathcal{M},w} = 1$, but $[p \supset r]_{\mathcal{M},w} = 0$. Aquinas' point is that the most plausible reading of the first premise, or the only reading on which the first premise is true, is that on which it has logical form $\Box(p \supset q)$. So either the argument is invalid, or one of its premises is unjustified.

20.3 Since α is true for any assignment of values to the sentence letters it contains, we get that $[\alpha]_{\mathcal{M},w} = 1$ for every w and $\mathcal{M}$. So, for every w and w' such that w' is accessible from w, $[\alpha]_{\mathcal{M},w'} = 1$.

20.4 Well, it depends. If 'logically follow' is understood in terms of **K**, then the answer is no. The argument is formalized in $\mathsf{L_m}$ as $\Box p/p$. As noted in Sect. 20.4, there are non-reflexive models that provide counterexamples to this form.

20.5 The argument is valid according to any interpretation of $\Box$ that accords with **T** and its extensions. For every reflexive model $\mathcal{M}$ and every w, we have that, if $[\Box p]_{\mathcal{M},w} = 1$, then $[p]_{\mathcal{M},w} = 1$.

20.6 No, because p is not derivable from $\Box p$ in **K**.

20.7 Yes, because **T** includes the axiom schema T.

20.8 $\Box \forall x(Bx \supset Ux), \forall x(Bx \supset \Box Ux)$ ($B = $ 'bachelor', $U = $ 'unmarried')

20.9 $\Box \exists x(Nx \wedge \forall y(Ny \supset y = x) \wedge Ox), \exists x(Nx \wedge \forall y(Ny \supset y = x) \wedge \Box Ox)$ ($N = $ 'number of the planets, $O = $ 'odd')

20.10 No. A third reading is $\exists x \Diamond(Rx \wedge Px)$.

Bibliography

1. Anderson, A. R., & Belnap, N. (1975). *Entailment: The Logic of Relevance and Necessity*. Princeton University Press, Princeton.
2. Barcan, R. (1946). A functional calculus of first order based on strict implication. *Journal of Symbolic Logic, 11*, 1–16.
3. Boole, G. (1947). *The Mathematical Analysis of Logic*. Macmillan, Barclay, & Macmillan, Cambridge.
4. Carnap, R. (1947). *Meaning and Necessity*. University of Chicago Press, Chicago.
5. Church, A. (1935). An unsolvable problem of elementary number theory. Preliminary report. *Bulletin of the American Mathematical Society, 41*, 332–333.
6. Church, A. (1936). A note on the Entscheidungsproblem. *Journal of Symbolic Logic, 1*, 40–41.
7. de Swart, H. (2018). *Philosophical and Mathematical Logic*. Springer.
8. Lemmon, E. J., & Scott, D. S. (1977). *The 'Lemmon Notes': An Introduction to Modal Logic*. Basic Blackwell, Oxford.
9. Edgington, D. (2011). Indicative conditionals. In E. Zalta (Ed.), *Stanford Encyclopedia of Philosophy*. https://plato.stanford.edu/archives/fall2020/entries/conditionals/.
10. Etchemendy, J. (1990). *On the Concept of Logical Consequence*. Harvard University Press, Cambridge (Mass).
11. Enderton, H. B. (1972). *A mathematical introduction to logic*. Academic, San Diego.
12. Feys, R. (1937). Les logiques nouvelles des modalités. *Revue Nêoscholastique de Philosophie, 40*, 517–553.
13. Frascolla, P. (2014). *Introduzione alla logica*. Il Mulino, Bologna.
14. Frege, G. (1879). *Begriffsschrift, eine der arithmetischen nachgebildete Formelsprache des reinen Denkens*. Halle a. S. Louis Nebert.
15. Frege, G. (1891). Funktion und Begriff. *Vortrag, gehalten in der Sitzung vom 9, der Jenaischen Gesellschaft für Medizin und Naturwissenschaft*.
16. Frege, G. (1892). Über Sinn und Bedeutung. *Zeitschrift für Philosophie und philosophische Kritik, 100*, 25–50.
17. Boolos, G. S., Burgess, J. P., & Jeffrey, R. (2010). *Computability and Logic*. Cambridge University Press, Cambridge.
18. Gentzen, G. (1934). Untersuchungen über das Logische Schliessen. *Matematische Zeitschrift, 39*, 176–210 and 405–431.
19. Gödel, K. (1930). Die Vollständigkeit der Axiome des logischen Funktionenkalküls. *Monatshefte für Mathematik und Physik, 37*, 349–60.

20. Gödel, K. (1931). Über formal unentscheidbare Sätze der Principia Mathematica und verwandter Systeme I. *Monatshefte für Mathematik und Physik, 38*, 173–198.
21. Grice, P. (1975). Logic and conversation. In P. Cole & J. L. Morgan (Ed.), *Syntax and Semantics – Speech Acts* (pp. 41–58). Academic Press, New York.
22. Henkin, L. (1949). The completeness of the first-order functional calculus. *Journal of Symbolic Logic, 14*, 159–166.
23. Herbrand, J. (1930). Recherches sur la théorie de la démonstration. *Travaux de la Société des Sciences et des Lettres de Varsovie*, 33.
24. Heyting, A. (1930). Die formalen Regeln der intuitionistischen Logik. *Sitzungsberichte der preußischen Akademie der Wissenschaften*, pp. 42–65.
25. Hilbert, D., & Bernays, P. (1939). *Grundlagen der Mathematik II*. Springer, Berlin.
26. Hobbes, T. (1656). *Elements of Philosophy Concerning Body*. Leybourn for Andrew Crooke, London.
27. Hughes, G. E., & Cresswell, M. J. (1996). *A New Introduction to Modal Logic*. Routledge, London.
28. Hume, D. (1779). Dialogues Concerning Natural Religion. London.
29. Hunter, G. (1971). *Metalogic: An introduction to the Metatheory of standard first order logic*. University of California Press, Berkeley.
30. Iacona, A. (2018). *Logical Form: Between Logic and Natural Language*. Springer, Cham.
31. Iacona, A. (2019). Future Contingents. *Internet Encyclopedia of Philosophy*. https://www.iep.utm.edu/fut-cont/.
32. Jaśkowski, S. (1934). On the rules of suppositions in formal logic. *Studia Logica, 1*, 5–32.
33. Kneale, W., & Kneale, M. (1962). *The Development of Logic*. Oxford University Press, Oxford.
34. Kripke, S. (1959). A completeness theorem in modal logic. *Journal of Symbolic Logic, 24*, 1–14.
35. Kripke, S. (1963). Semantical considerations on modal logic. *Acta Philosophica Fennica, 16*, 83–94.
36. Leibniz, G. W. (1875). *Die philosophischen Schriften von G. W. Leibniz*. C. I. Gerhardt, Weidmann, Berlin.
37. Leibniz, G. W. (1903). *Opuscules et fragments inédits de Leibniz*. L. Couturat, Paris.
38. Leibniz, G. W. (1710). *Théodicée*. Amsterdam.
39. Lemmon, E. J. (1993). *Beginning Logic*. Chapman and Hall, London.
40. Lewis, C. I. (1914). The calculus of strict implication. *Mind, 23*, 240–247.
41. Lewis, C. I. (1918). *A Survey of Symbolic Logic*. University of California Press, Berkeley.
42. Lewis, C. I., & Langford, C. H. (1932). *Symbolic Logic*. Dover, New York.
43. Löwenheim, L. (1915). Über Moglichkeiten im Relativkalkül. *Mathematische Annalen, 76*, 447–470.
44. Łukasiewicz, J. (1929). *Elementy logiki matematycznej. Skrypt autoryzowany*. Wydawnictwi Koła Matematyczno-Fizycznego Słuchaczów Uniwersytetu Warszawskiego.
45. Lull, R. (1609). *Raymundi Lullii Opera ea...* Zetzner, Strasbourg.
46. Maltsev, A. I. (1936). Untersuchungen aus dem Gebiete der mathematischen Logik. *Novaya Seriya*, pp. 323–336.
47. Peano, G. (1889). *Arithmetices principia: nova methodo exposita*. Bocca, Turin.
48. Peano, G. (1897). Studii de Logica Matematica. *Atti della Reale Accademia delle scienze di Torino, 32*, 565–583.
49. Peters, S., & Westerståhl, D. (2006). *Quantifiers in Language and Logic*. Oxford University Press, Oxford.
50. Plato. (1991). *The Republic: The Complete and Unabridged Jowett Translation*. Vintage Book, New York.
51. Post, E. (1921). Introduction to a general theory of elementary propositions. *American Journal of Mathematics, 43*, 163–185.
52. Post, E. (1944). Recursively enumerable sets of positive integers and their decision problems. *Bulletin of the American Mathematical Society, 50*, 284–316.

53. Priest, G. (2008). *An Introduction to Non-Classical Logics*. Cambridge University Press, Cambridge.
54. Quine, W. V. O. (1968). Ontological relativity. *Journal of Philosophy, 65*, 185–212.
55. Russell, B. (1905). On denoting. *Mind, 14*, 479–493.
56. Russell, B. (1906). The theory of implication. *American Journal of Mathematics, 28*, 159–202. ˙
57. Russell, B., & Whitehead, A. N. (1910–1913). *Principia Mathematica*. Cambridge University Press, Cambridge.
58. Sainsbury, M. (2001). *Logical Forms*. Blackwell, Oxford.
59. Skolem, T. (1920). Logisch-kombinatorische über die Untersuchungen Erfüllbarkeit oder Beweisbarkeit mathematischer Sätze nebst einem Theoreme über dichte Mengen. *Videnskapsselskapet Sktrifter, I. Matematisk-naturvidenskabelig Klasse, 4*:1–36.
60. Smith, P. (2013). *Introduction to Gödel's Theorems*. Cambridge University Press, Cambridge.
61. Smith, P. (2020). *An Introduction to Formal Logic*. 2nd edn. Cambridge University Press, Cambridge.
62. Tarski, A. (1930). Fundamentale Begriffe der Methodologie der deduktiven Wissenschaften. I. *Monatshefte für Mathematik und Physik, 37*, 361–404.
63. Tarski, A. (1983). On the concept of logical consequence (1936). In *Logic, Semantics, Metamathematics* (pp. 409–420). Hackett, Indianapolis.
64. Tarski, A. (1983). Pojęcie prawdy w językach nauk dedukcyjnych (1933), translated as 'The Concept of Truth in Formalized Languages'. In *Logic, Semantics, Metamathematics* (pp. 152–278). Hackett, Indianapolis.
65. Turing, A. (1936). On computable numbers, with an application to the Entscheidungsproblem. *Proceedings of the London Mathematical Society, 42*, 230–365.
66. Williamson, T. (1994). *Vagueness*. Routledge, London.
67. Williamson, T. (2013). *Modal Logic as Metaphysics*. Oxford University Press, Oxford.
68. Wittgenstein, L. (1992). *Tractatus Logico-Philosophicus*. Routledge, London.

Index

A

Accessibility, 183
Adequate set of connectives, 40
Affirming the consequent, 28
Alphabet, 30
Alphabetic variant, 135
Ambiguity, 7
Argument, 1
Argument (of a function), 32
Arithmetization of syntax, 148
Assignment, 122

B

B, 187
Barcan formula, 192
Biconditional, 39
Bivalence, 8
Bound variable, 119

C

Cardinality, 161
Categoricity, 168
Characteristic function, 57
Church's thesis, 128
Closed formula, 119
Completeness, 92
Completeness theorem (**L**), 93
Completeness theorem (**Q**), 143
Conclusion, 1
Conjunct, 36
Conjunction, 36
Consequent, 25

Consistency (of a set of formulas), 71
Consistency (of a set of sentences), 15
Consistency (of a system), 91
Consistency theorem (**L**), 92
Consistency theorem (**Q**), 140
Context sensitivity, 7
Contradiction (between two formulas), 54
Contradiction (between two sentences), 16
Contraposition, 19
Countable set, 33
∪, 11
Cut, 17

D

⊫, 54
⊣⊢, 72
Decidability (of a set), 58
Decidability (of a system), 147
De dicto/de re, 193
Deduction theorem, 81
Deductive closure, 90
Definite description, 106
Denumerable set, 33
Denying the antecedent, 28
Derivability, 71
Derivation, 61
Derived rule, 75
Diagonalization, 174
Disjunct, 36
Disjunction, 36
Domain (of a model), 122
Domain (of a relation), 12
Double Negation, 15

© The Author(s), under exclusive license to Springer Nature Switzerland AG 2021
A. Iacona, *LOGIC: Lecture Notes for Philosophy, Mathematics, and Computer Science*, Springer Undergraduate Texts in Philosophy,
https://doi.org/10.1007/978-3-030-64811-4

E
Effective computability, 57
Effective enumerability, 147
Effectively axiomatized system, 81
Effectively axiomatized theory, 156
Effective method, 57
Element, 11
Empty set, 11
∅, 11
Entailment, 15
Enumeration, 33
≡, 39
Equivalence (between two sentences), 15
Equivalence relation, 12
Excluded Middle, 8
Existential quantifier, 112
Existential sentence, 100
∃, 112
Extension (of a set of formulas), 94

F
Fallacy, 20
Fallacy of equivocation, 20
Finite set, 33
First-order language, 153
First-order logic, 153
First-order logic with identity, 154
First-order system, 153
First-order theory, 155
∀, 110
Formalization, 30
Formal language, 29
Formal system, 30
Formal validity, 27
Formation rule, 30
Formula, 30
Frame, 183
Free variable, 119
Function, 32

G
G, 61
Generalization theorem, 133
Gödel numbering, 148
Gödel sentence, 175
Gödel's first incompleteness theorem, 175
Gödel's second incompleteness
          theorem, 178

H
Homomorphism, 164

I
Ignoratio elenchi, 21
∈, 11
Individual constant, 109
Induction principle, 81
Inductive definition, 45
Inference rule, 30
Infinite set, 33
Intended model, 156
Intension/extension, 7
Interpretation (of a language), 48
Interpretation function, 122
Isomorphism, 164

K
K, 184
K$_q$, 194

L
L, 79
L, 35
L$_a$, 156
L$_m$, 182
L$_q$, 109
L$_{qi}$, 154
L$_{qm}$, 191
Left-hand side/right-hand side, 39
Lindnbaum's lemma, 94
Logical consequence, 53
Logical constant, 26
Logical equivalence, 54
Logical form, 29
Löwenheim-Skolem theorems, 162

M
Maximal consistency (of a set of formulas), 94
Metalanguage, 31
Model (of a language), 122
Model (of a theory), 156
Modus ponens, 26
Modus tollens, 26
Monotonicity, 17
Multiple generality, 104

N
ℕ, 33
n-tuple, 12
Necessitas consequentiae/necessitas
          consequentis, 184
Necessitation, 185
Negation-completeness, 93

Non-Contradiction, 16
Non-standard model, 168
Normal model, 154
$\notin$, 11
$\nvDash$, 53
$\nvdash$, 71

O
Object language, 31
ω, 176
One-to-one correspondence, 32
Open formula, 119
Operation, 33
Ordered pair, 12

P
PA, 158
Peano Arithmetic, 158
Petitio principii, 22
Predicate letter, 109
Premise, 1
Proof (in a system), 72
Proof by Contradiction, 16
Proof by induction, 81
Pseudo Scotus, 18

Q
Q, 131
$\mathbf{Q_i}$, 154
Quantified sentence, 100

R
$\mathbb{R}$, 33
Range (of a relation), 12
Recursive enumerability (of a set), 151
Recursive function, 128
Recursively adequate theory, 159
Recursively axiomatized system, 151
Recursively decidable property or relation, 151
Recursively decidable system, 151
Reductio ad absurdum, 4
Reflexive relation, 12
Relation, 12

S
S4, 188
$\mathbf{S4_q}$, 194
S5, 189
$\mathbf{S5_q}$, 193
Satisfaction, 121
Satisfiability (of a set of formulas), 54
Scope, 47
Scope ambiguity, 114

Sentence letter, 35
Sentential connective, 36
Sequence, 33
Sequent, 75
Set, 11
$\sim$, 15
Soundness (of an argument), 2
Soundness (of a system), 92
Soundness theorem (**L**), 93
Soundness theorem (**Q**), 140
Standard model, 168
Subset, 11
$\subseteq$, 11
Substitution of Equivalents, 85
Substitutivity, 41
Superset, 11
$\supset$, 26
Symmetric relation, 12
Syntactic tree, 46

T
T, 187
$\mathbf{T_q}$, 194
Tautology, 53
Term, 111
Theorem, 72
Theory, 89
Transfinite number, 161
Transitive relation, 12
Truth conditions, 6
Truth function, 36
Truth-functional connective, 37
Truth table, 49
Truth value, 6
Turing's thesis, 129

U
Union, 11
Universal generalization, 133
Universal Instantiation, 127
Universal quantifier, 110
Universal sentence, 100

V
Validity (of a formula), 53
Validity (of an argument), 14
Valuation, 48
Value (of a function), 32
$\vDash$, 53
$\vee$, 36

W
$\wedge$, 36

CPSIA information can be obtained
at www.ICGtesting.com
Printed in the USA
LVHW060841210621
690744LV00002B/162